WELFARE

OTHER BOOKS BY MARTIN ANDERSON

Conscription: A Select and Annotated Bibliography

The Federal Bulldozer: A Critical Analysis of Urban Renewal, 1949–1962

WELFARE

The Political Economy
of Welfare Reform
in the United States

MARTIN ANDERSON

HOOVER
INSTITUTION

STANFORD
UNIVERSITY

Copyright

Copyright © 1978 by the Board of Trustees of Leland Stanford Junior University.
All rights reserved under International and Pan-American Copyright Conventions.
Published in the United States by the Hoover Institution Press, Stanford, California.

Library of Congress Cataloging in Publication Data

Anderson, Martin
    Welfare : the political economy of welfare reform in the United States.
    Includes bibliographical references and index.
1. Public welfare—United States.   2. United States—social policy.
3. Guaranteed annual income—United States.   I. Title.
HV95.A755   361.6'2'0973   77-20644
ISBN 0-8179-6811-3

Design

Design and Typography by Ted Ligda. The typeface selected for this book is Baskerville,
a facsimile of a Roman letter first used in England, about 1760, by John Baskerville, the
greatest type founder and printer of his era. His types, most of which are based on the
letters of Caslon, are of exceptional beauty, the italic forms in particular being superior
to any created up to that time.

Production

Printed in the United States of America by The National Press, Palo Alto, California.
Bound by Cardoza-James Binding Company, San Francisco.

Permission to Reprint

Acknowledgment is made to the following source for permission to reprint:
M. H. Polanyi, née Duczynska : Excerpt from *The Great Transformation* by Karl Polanyi
(New York, Toronto : Farrar & Rinehart, Inc., 1944). Copyright, 1944, by Karl Polanyi
(later assigned to M. H. Polanyi, née Duczynska).

First edition.

Hoover Institution Press Publication 181

To Arthur F. Burns

1

ACKNOWLEDGMENTS

All studies in political economy owe deep intellectual debts to earlier works by economists and political scientists, from Adam Smith to Milton Friedman. This study is no exception. An equal debt is owed to the men and women who make public policy, who struggle with the maddeningly complex aspects of reality, and who somehow craft the policies—for better or worse—that we examine, criticize, and, sometimes, praise.

For this particular study, I am especially indebted to Arthur F. Burns. As Counsellor to the President in 1969 he had the responsibility of dealing directly with the problem of improving our nation's welfare system. During that time, as his deputy, I learned a great deal about the scope of that problem, and about the immense difficulty of coming up with answers that are equitable, financially sound, and politically possible—all at the same time. Some of Burns's advice to the President was heeded at that time. Too much of it was not. If it had been, some of our current difficulties might have been avoided.

A number of scholars and policy makers read all or part of the manuscript in one or another of its early drafts. Their comments and criticisms improved it, and their words of encouragement made it easier to write the final draft. They include Annelise

Anderson, Dennis Bark, Arthur F. Burns, Richard Burress, Glenn Campbell, Rita Campbell, Barry Chiswick, Robert Carleson, David Dawson, Roger Freeman, Rose Friedman, Alan Greenspan, Paul Hanna, Robert Hessen, Michael Keeley, Everett Ladd, Seymour Martin Lipset, Thomas Moore, Richard Nathan, Alvin Rabushka, Murray Rothbard, Dan Troop Smith, Thomas Sowell, Joan Kennedy Taylor, Darrell Trent, Richard Whalen, and Richard Wirthlin. I am also indebted to a number of people in government who provided me with counsel, analysis, data, and statistics.

My research assistant, Barbara Honegger, was consistently helpful through the manuscript's many stages of development—researching, checking data, and finally typing and editing each draft. Many of her thoughtful editorial comments are incorporated in the writing. Besides myself, she is the only person who has read the book at least a half a dozen times—and shall probably continue to hold that distinction.

Liselotte Hofmann edited the final manuscript and compiled the index with professional skill.

Ted Ligda of A&P Typesetters set the manuscript in hot metal in his typesetting shop in Redwood City, California. One of the most interesting and enjoyable parts of writing the book were the few hours I spent watching him transform edited copy into small, gleaming lead lines of type. He also designed the format, choosing a blend of typeface, spacing, and page size that should add immeasurably to the readability of the book.

Mickey Hamilton, general manager of the Hoover Institution Press, facilitated the production of the book in literally dozens of ways, providing helpful counsel every step of the way—on everything from editing to production, jacket copy design, and distribution.

This book is part of a larger research project on income redistribution in the United States that has been under way at the Hoover Institution for several years. Financial support for the project has been provided by the Smith Richardson Foundation,

Inc., and in large measure its generous support and understanding patience in awaiting the results have made this book possible.

Finally, I am indebted to my colleagues at the Hoover Institution, to its Director, Dr. W. Glenn Campbell, and to many other scholars from various departments at Stanford University for providing a congenial atmosphere of intellectual curiosity and rigor. In fact, there were times when it was a lot of fun.

MARTIN ANDERSON

Palo Alto, California
March 1978

CONTENTS

WELFARE

INTRODUCTION

> Government, as the most conspicuous object in society, is called upon to give signal of what shall be done; and, in many ways, to preside over, further, and command the doing of it. But the government cannot do, by all its signaling and commanding, what the society is radically indisposed to do.
>
> Thomas Carlyle, 1843

Since the middle of the 1960s, welfare reform has been a major issue on the political agenda of the United States, and a swirling controversy has surrounded it. The question has been endlessly discussed in professional journals, books, academic conferences, political campaigns, the press, and in hundreds of hours of congressional testimony. But all attempts to radically reform the welfare system have failed. The problem of welfare reform is still with us—as unresolved and as intractable as ever. The question is, Why?

The purpose of this book is to examine the essentials of that debate, to try to explain the reasons behind the current unrest about our welfare system, and to discuss the major reasons why all attempts to radically change our welfare system have resulted in dismal failure. Most of this book is based on official government publications, their reports and their statistics, on articles in academic journals, and on other books dealing with various aspects of welfare. The rest is based on my personal experience with attempts to reform welfare on a national basis, and on the personal experience of others.

My first exposure to the complexities of welfare reform came in 1968. Earlier that year I had become research director for Richard Nixon's presidential campaign. By then welfare reform had achieved the status of a standard major campaign issue. If you were going to run for President of the United States, you had to have a welfare reform program. Second nature to Democrats, it was a somewhat treacherous issue for a Republican candidate. Nixon knew this and decided to confound his opponents—and the press. Rather than sidestepping the issue, he made it one of his major campaign planks. Like all presidential candidates Nixon didn't have time for thoughtful reflection on all the intricacies of the major issues confronting him. Nor did his staff. None of us fully comprehended the difficulties we would encounter when Nixon made it clear to us that he wanted a comprehensive program to aid the poor, and that he meant to place it high on his policy priority list.

After weeks of frantic work by speechwriters and researchers the program, called *Bridges to Human Dignity*, emerged. It pledged to "improve and streamline" existing welfare programs, to lend a helping hand to the poor "to take them from dependency to human dignity," to "provide incentives for families to stay together," to provide strong incentives to work, to start getting the poor "off the welfare rolls and onto the payrolls." Not remarkable by Democrats' standards, it was pretty bold stuff for a conservative Republican in 1968. The Democrats lost an issue, the press seemed baffled, and Nixon was very pleased with himself.

No one in the 1968 campaign predicted even the possibility that Nixon would, in less than a year, go far beyond his campaign pledges and propose one of the most sweeping social changes in the history of this country. Yet, within weeks after taking office Nixon made it known that he was willing to entertain radical thoughts about welfare reform. He didn't dismiss the recommendations of his campaign task force on welfare, chaired by Richard Nathan of the Brookings Institution, or of Arthur F. Burns, the newly appointed Counsellor to the President for domestic affairs. He simply said he wanted to consider *all* the alternatives. Undoubtedly suspicious of what Nixon "really" had in mind, the advocates of a guaranteed income calmed their qualms and quietly dusted off the welfare reform plans that had been sitting on their shelves for the last few years.

In the mid-1960s a number of fairly high-level bureaucrats in the Department of Health, Education and Welfare and in the Office of Economic Opportunity developed detailed plans for a guaranteed income. When the scheme was presented to President Johnson and his chief assistant for domestic affairs, Joseph A. Califano, it was rejected. Johnson thought it was too radical. But those who had spent years developing the plan did not give up. They carefully filed the guaranteed income blueprints in their green file cabinets. And they waited.

There were dark days at HEW after Nixon squeaked by Humphrey in one of the closest elections in American history. But they brightened soon after Nixon's inauguration. The bureaucrats realized that the guaranteed income was once again alive and well in Washington. Daniel P. Moynihan, an experienced Democrat sympathetic to the idea of a guaranteed income and an old hand at bureaucratic maneuvering, was directing Nixon's Urban Affairs Council. The Urban Affairs Council was, in effect, the domestic cabinet of the Nixon Administration. Robert Finch, totally inexperienced in welfare and with a reputation for being easily persuaded, was the new Secretary of HEW. Finch's deputy, the man who ran the day-to-day affairs of HEW, was a very liberal Republican, John Veneman. The President's staff was almost wholly virgin in the ways of Washington, and they were very busy. And President Nixon was willing to consider any and all proposals to reform welfare. The proponents of some variant of a guaranteed income could hardly believe their good fortune, and they quickly made Moynihan the chief instrument in their drive to enact a guaranteed income into law.

In the early days of Nixon's administration Moynihan realized that while Nixon's advisors were not enthusiastic about radical welfare reform they were generally ignorant of the substance of such a policy and inexperienced in the policymaking process. Moynihan and his staff quickly declared bureaucratic war on the other elements of the White House staff involved in domestic policy and rapidly carved out welfare reform as one of their major responsibilities.

Moynihan came to the struggle with distinct disadvantages. He was a liberal Democrat. He was not an expert on welfare reform. And he was not yet on the same intimate terms with Nixon as those who had campaigned with him in 1968 and earlier. But he also had considerable advantages. He was one of the very few people on the White House staff who had operated in the Washington bureaucracy and understood it. He had an extensive network of contacts throughout HEW and OEO, many of them Democrats shocked at Humphrey's defeat, who flooded him with research data and other information. And he had great persuasive resources. In the sea of dark gray and blue that surrounded Nixon, Moynihan, in his cream-colored suit and red bow tie, gleamed like a playful porpoise. He was a charming Irish rogue, a delightful dinner companion, a fascinating teller of tales. His presence lighted the gloom of national policy deliberations, and even his opponents liked to have him around. The President liked to read his memoranda, sometimes even searching through the pile on his desk to find them.

The chief obstacle in Moynihan's quest to persuade Nixon of the virtues of radical welfare reform was Arthur F. Burns. Burns was a distinguished economist from Columbia University, chairman of President Eisenhower's Council of Economic Advisers, a brilliant and prudent analyst of public policy, and a conservative. I had been appointed Special Assistant to the President and was assigned to be Burns's deputy. On paper our office had responsibility for the overall development of domestic policy. When Nixon decided to make welfare one of the central pieces of his domestic program—partly out of a desire to reform the welfare system for the benefit of the poor and partly out of a desire to confound the Democrats—and gave Moynihan and the Urban Affairs Council the green light to proceed, he also directed Burns to submit welfare reform recommendations to him.

The bright, clear notions some of us had developed during the campaign about how a President and his staff would make national policy soon tarnished and blurred. We had naïvely assumed that we would simply review whatever issue was a problem, identify the major areas of difficulty, consult leading experts, and with their help craft a solution. And while those recommendations were being introduced as legislation to the Congress we would go on to the next problem. After all, we were considered to be fairly bright, some of us had Ph.D.'s, and all of us had had a certain amount of experience in formulating public policy positions.

It didn't quite work out that way, for a number of reasons. First was the magnitude and complexity of the task itself. When President Eisenhower left office in early 1961, there were somewhere around forty major domestic programs. When Nixon took office there were over 400. Arthur Burns, I, and others on our staff soon discovered that while it was difficult to come up with a better program in any one of these areas, it was even more difficult to find out exactly what was going on in the existing programs. For example, if we had spent only one day on each major problem, and worked Sundays and holidays (which we did), it would still have taken us well over a year to work our way through all the programs. But one day is not enough to grasp the full implications of any government program. For some, one month might be enough. Other problems, such as welfare reform and the ending of the draft, required many months and even years before those involved felt any degree of confidence in what they were doing. The domestic side of the federal government had gotten so big that it was literally impossible to grasp it, intellectually, in its entirety.

The result is that you must depend on the bureaucracy that is there when you arrive. The bureaucrats are always more than happy to oblige. When Nixon made clear his intent to push welfare reform, Moynihan was quickly provided with a detailed plan by fellow Democrats in the federal bureaucracy. The welfare reform plan that had been brusquely dismissed by President Johnson was hauled out and dusted off. The plan was rewritten, numbers were updated, and a few new ideas were added. It was then rechristened the Family Security System (later to be changed to the Family Assistance Plan), and presented by Moynihan to Nixon's domestic cabinet in one of the first meetings of the Urban Affairs Council. Nixon was delighted to get a detailed welfare reform plan on such short notice. Burns and his small staff did finally develop an alternative plan. But by then it was late April 1969, and the detailed welfare reform proposal touted by Moynihan and backed up by computer printouts from HEW had become established as the basis for all welfare reform discussion.

It was a classic example of the power of research in the making of national policy. Any newly elected President, his White House staff, and his major Cabinet appointments are so frantically busy during the first year in office that the amount of time they can devote to specific issues, even major ones, is minimal relative to the time that is required to do the job adequately. At the same time, a newly elected President will almost certainly have a number of campaign commitments—made in the heat of political battle when time is even shorter—to fulfill. Once in office there is no time during the first year to develop the kind of comprehensive legislative proposals that are necessary to cope with the complex, detailed issues they purport to deal with. But the public, and especially the media, is not disposed to waiting much beyond 100 days before clamoring for results—for fulfillment of campaign pledges, for comprehensive legislative packages, for answers. In this situation there is only one thing a newly elected administration can do. It must choose "off the shelf" from among the legislative plans that are available.

And that is what Nixon finally did. Frustrated by the increasingly bitter internal staff dispute about the merits of Moynihan's radical welfare reform plan and under strong media pressure to produce a legislative proposal, he sent—just 200 days after taking office—a welfare proposal to the Congress. He ignored the warnings by Burns and others that the legislation was unsound.

Within months it was clear that Burns had been right and Moynihan wrong. The difficulties with the Family Assistance Plan (FAP), which were uncovered during the few short months preceding Nixon's television address on welfare to the nation, were laid bare by the rough questioning of the congressional committees. The rest is history. Nixon's Family Assistance Plan limped along gamely until it finally died early in 1972.

In March 1971, I resigned my White House appointment to become a senior fellow at the Hoover Institution at Stanford University. The prospects for further attempts at radical welfare reform seemed low. The focus of the Nixon Administration was beginning to turn toward thoughts of reelection in 1972, and welfare reform seemed unlikely to become a major campaign weapon against the Democrats.

But the proponents of radical welfare reform were undaunted. During the 1972 presidential campaign George McGovern succumbed to the blandishments of some of his advisors and proposed a variant of welfare reform that would give everyone $1,000 a year. Unfortunately he had not worked out the details before he bought the idea. When pressed by the national press corps as to how much it would cost, he could not even estimate it. Amid ridicule by his opponents and hand-wringing by his supporters he was forced to abandon his proposal before the vote was taken in November.

The Republicans were more cautious. When the party met to renominate Nixon and Agnew at Miami Beach in August of 1972, the humiliating defeat of the Family Assistance Plan was fresh in their memories. As a consultant to the Republican National Committee I was the head writer for the platform committee at the convention. When the agenda moved to welfare reform there was no sentiment at all for further tilts with the windmill of radical reform. The platform committee, and later the convention as a whole, unanimously adopted the following plank: "We flatly oppose programs or policies which embrace the principle of a government-guaranteed income. We reject as unconscionable the idea that all citizens have the right to be supported by the government, regardless of their ability or desire to support themselves and their families."

The reelection of Richard Nixon in 1972 reactivated some half-hearted efforts to resurrect a major welfare reform plan, but the memories of the Family Assistance Plan and the developing Watergate scandal effectively combined to abort them. But when Gerald Ford suddenly assumed office on August 9, 1974, as our first unelected President, the welfare bureaucrats went back to work. Here was an unexpected opportunity—a new President without their having to wait until 1976. Caspar Weinberger, whom Nixon had appointed Secretary of HEW in early 1973, was kept on by President Ford, and was apparently persuaded by the HEW professionals that the potential benefits of radical welfare reform outweighed its intractable difficulties. Late in 1974, Weinberger enthusiastically began to develop a new proposal for Ford, called the Income Supplementation Plan (ISP).

In November 1974 I was contacted by Kenneth Cole, the director of the Domestic Council, and asked to come to Washington to chair an ad hoc White House task force on welfare reform. The purpose of the task force was to review the latest welfare proposal that was moving toward Ford's desk. I agreed. A few days later the small task force, composed of representatives from the White House staff, the Council of Economic Advisers, the Department of Agriculture, the Brookings Institution, HEW, and the Office of Management and Budget, began evaluating the latest attempt at radical welfare reform.

On November 13, 1974, Secretary Weinberger briefed the President and his top domestic advisors in the Roosevelt Room of the White House on the merits of the Income Supplementation Plan. It was like going back in time five years. As if nothing had happened in the meantime, the essentials of the old Family Assistance Plan—using larger numbers—were spelled out once again under new labels. The President was assured that the costs would be minimal, that there would be strong incentives to work, that fraud and abuse would be reduced, and that the simplified administrative structure would ensure a more effective, more fair welfare system. President Ford, who had voted for Nixon's Family Assistance Plan while a congressman from Michigan, was interested but noncommital.

The results of the White House task force were ready within a few weeks. Some of us had hoped that five years of intense study and discussion of the welfare question would have yielded significant improvements. They had not. Over 20 million more Americans would have been eligible for welfare under the Income Supplementation Plan than under the current welfare system. Three estimates of the additional cost were prepared by the task force: a "low" estimate ($8 billion) based on the most optimistic estimates for each element, a "medium" estimate ($19 billion) based on the most likely estimates, and a "high" estimate ($29 billion) based on the most pessimistic estimates. The effective tax rates ISP would have imposed on welfare recipients for working— even without accounting for the tax effect of medicaid and public-housing subsidies—ranged between 70 and 80 percent.

President Ford rejected the plan. For a while thereafter efforts at radical welfare reform were confined to the drawing boards of the academicians. Numerous groups, including Nelson Rockefeller's Commission on Critical Choices for Americans and the Council on Trends and Perspective of the U.S. Chamber of Commerce, tried to solve the puzzle. None succeeded. During the 1976 presidential campaign, welfare reform surfaced once again as a major issue. Both President Ford and Jimmy Carter called for a comprehensive reform of the existing welfare system, and the Democratic Party, meeting in New York City, adopted a welfare reform platform plank calling for "an income floor both for the working poor and [for] the poor not in the labor market."

After Jimmy Carter assumed office on January 20, 1977, the

same forces that had pressed on Nixon eight years before began to press on him. President Carter obviously knew what he wanted in the way of welfare reform insofar as *principle* was concerned. During the campaign he had pledged a major reform of welfare. But he had not worked out the details. As the pressure grew on him to deliver on his campaign pledge of welfare reform, he was inexorably forced to rely on the Washington bureaucracy he had campaigned so effectively against. Within a week after Carter took office his new Secretary of HEW, Joseph A. Califano, announced plans for a major study of welfare to produce recommendations on how President Carter should carry out his campaign pledge. A promise was soon made to have the entire program ready by May 1, 1977.

On May 2, 1977, President Carter announced that the existing welfare system was "worse than we thought," and that "the complexity of the system is almost incomprehensible." But unfazed by this newly acquired wisdom, he further announced that the full details of his program would be ready by the first week in August of 1977. He then set forth twelve goals that would guide the development of his welfare reform plan. The first and most important goal specified by President Carter was that his plan would have "no higher initial cost than the present system."

Less than three weeks after President Carter's confident announcement, Secretary of HEW Califano sent him a memorandum warning him that what he intended to do was *politically impossible*. The memorandum noted, "The politics of welfare reform are treacherous under any circumstances, and they can be impossible at no higher initial cost, because it is likely that so many people who are now receiving benefits will be hurt."[1] Carter acquiesced, reneged on his pledge of no higher initial cost than the present system, and authorized Califano and Secretary of Labor F. Ray Marshall to "develop a program along the outlines *they* set down."[2]

By then Carter had no choice. Like his predecessors, he had become politically committed to a course over which he no longer had effective control. Once he was firmly committed to the overall goal of radical welfare reform, the specifics of the program—the cost, the level of benefits, and the financial incentives to work— went out of his hands and into those of the HEW professionals. When President Carter unveiled the details of his radical welfare reform plan on August 6, 1977, he flew to Plains, Georgia, to do it. By that time his pledge of no additional cost had been abandoned. The new administration "estimate" of the additional cost of the program was now over 6 billion.[3]

The outcome of President Carter's radical welfare reform proposal is still in doubt. But whatever its fate the national debate on welfare reform is sure to continue. If Carter's plan fails to pass the Congress, another will take its place. On the other hand, if his plan should pass, the focus of the debate will shift quickly to the consequences of its implementation.

Fortuitously, Carter's welfare reform plan, if passed, would not go into effect until at least October 1, 1980—thirty-four days before the next presidential election. And hard evidence, based on actual experience, could not form the basis for a national policy debate until the presidential election of 1984.

References for Introduction

1 Austin Scott, "Carter Endorses Tentative Plan on Welfare Reform," *The Washington Post*, May 27, 1977, page 1.

2 Ibid. (Italics added.)

3 Jimmy Carter, "Message to the Congress of the United States," released by Office of the White House Press Secretary, August 6, 1977, page 6.

I

WINNING THE WAR ON POVERTY

The old order changeth, yielding place to new.
Alfred Tennyson, 1869

First Thesis: *The "war on poverty" that began in 1964
has been won. The growth of jobs and income in the
private economy, combined with an explosive increase
in government spending for welfare and income transfer
programs, has virtually eliminated poverty in the United
States. Any Americans who truly cannot care for themselves are now eligible for generous government aid in
the form of cash, medical benefits, food stamps, housing,
and other services.*

In the early 1960s the United States, after eight years of peace
and steadily increasing prosperity, roused itself and threw its
considerable resources into two mighty efforts—bringing freedom
to the people of South Vietnam and prosperity to the poor in
America. At first the efforts on both fronts were tenuous and tentative. Then the tragic death of John Kennedy thrust Lyndon
Johnson into the presidency. With characteristic force and impetu-
osity, and eager to establish himself as one of our great presidents,
Johnson rapidly and dramatically escalated both wars.

In 1964 the troops started pouring into Vietnam and that
same year back home a "war on poverty" was declared. Never
before had the country committed itself simultaneously to two

such major ventures. The economic strain was soon felt, as rising taxes and inflation held down the living standards of Americans. But both wars continued unabated until Johnson, under pressure, chose not to run again, and his successor took office in early 1969.

We are all too familiar with the consequences of the war in in Vietnam. Billions of dollars were spent, thousands of Americans were killed or maimed, and the Vietnamese people now live under a totalitarian regime with fewer freedoms than before. But most of the nation has lost sight of Johnson's other war. Our deep ignorance concerning what happened in the war on poverty is matched only by our acute awareness of all that happened in Vietnam.

As the war on poverty began to gain momentum in 1965, federal, state, and local governments together were spending over $77 billion a year on social welfare programs. Most of this government spending was for social security benefits and education. Just slightly over $6 billion was being spent on direct welfare. The task of eliminating poverty was viewed as extraordinarily difficult, if not impossible. At that time, some 33 million Americans were officially classified as poor. The poverty line was then a little over $3,000 a year for a family of four. Each year it was adjusted upwards to account for inflation. Tens of billions of dollars would have to be given to all those below the official poverty line if they were to catch or surpass that ever upward-moving standard that divided the country into the poor and the nonpoor.

And the money was given. An almost bewildering array of Great Society programs was launched, all with the central purpose of transferring tax dollars from the middle- and high-income classes to the low-income class. Millions of government checks, for tens of billions of dollars, were printed and mailed and cashed. The most ambitious attempt to redistribute income ever undertaken in the United States had begun.

As the efforts to combat poverty accelerated, a peculiar thing occurred. The harsh criticism of government efforts to reduce poverty that were prevalent in the early 1960s did not diminish. In fact, after the federal government officially declared war on poverty, the criticism of welfare seemed to grow in step with the proliferation of anti-poverty programs. Welfare programs were denounced as stingy, unfair, demeaning to recipients, contributing to the breakup of families, and so narrow in their coverage that many poor Americans were destitute, some of them actually starving. Even the specter of hunger in America was raised on the evening television news. The people most knowledgeable about our welfare programs denounced the entire welfare system, calling it a dismal failure, bankrupt, a mess in need of total reform. The more government seemed to do, the worse the situation seemed to become.

The most serious charge of all was that the war on poverty, in spite of the billions being spent, was not achieving its main goal: to raise poor people's incomes above the poverty line. As the monetary costs of waging wars both at home and abroad mounted, inflation began to take its toll. The official poverty line was adjusted upwards each year for inflation. But as the economy grew and welfare programs expanded and poor people's incomes increased, it appeared that the line that they had to cross moved ahead of them at about the same pace.

In a book published in 1975, *Progress against Poverty: A Review of the 1964–1974 Decade*, two experts from the University of Wisconsin's Institute for Research on Poverty ruefully concluded, "Twenty-three million persons still endured extremely low income in 1973. . . . We estimate that the depressed economic environment of 1974–1975 led to a rise in the number of poor persons to 25.1 million . . . in 1974, and 27.1 million . . . in 1975. If these projections are correct, *the nation will have made no progress in eliminating absolute poverty since the mid-1960's.*"[1]

About the same time the Joint Economic Committee of the Congress published the results of its massive three-year study of the nation's welfare programs. The first page of the committee's summary made the same point: "In spite of massive and increasing expenditures, poverty as officially measured is not falling sharply. Twenty-three million people, about 1 in every 9, were poor in 1973; many are growing poorer as inflation erodes their already limited purchasing power."²

The source of these discouraging judgments on progress against poverty in the United States is an annual statistical publication compiled by the Bureau of the Census. In its latest report, published in June 1977, the Bureau of the Census declared that "there were 25.9 million persons below the poverty level in 1975, comprising 12 percent of all persons. Between 1974 and 1975 the number of persons below the low-income level *increased* by 2.5 million. . . . The increase of 2.5 million low-income persons during the 1964–1975 period was the largest single year increase observed since 1959."³

According to the official government statistics there has been virtually no change in the poverty level since 1968. For the entire period from 1968 to 1975 the proportion of Americans in poverty apparently hovered around 12 percent. In fact, the Census Bureau reports that there were 500,000 *more* poor people in 1975 than there were in 1968. Essentially we have been told that while some progress was made in reducing poverty during the early 1960s, little, if any, progress has been made since 1968. Most of us, not having the capability or the desire to conduct our own census, accepted what we were told.

Yet one wonders. The United States is the richest nation in the world. Its citizens are, by and large, uncommonly generous and benevolent. Individuals contribute billions of dollars every year in small, private acts of charitable giving. Private charitable institutions spend billions more. Federal, state, and local governments spend tens of billions of dollars every year on welfare and income transfer programs. The economy has been growing steadily, creating more and more jobs. Is it possible that some 26 million people still live in abject poverty, having "extremely low incomes"; that one-eighth of this great nation is literally poor?

In 1975 a little-noticed study of income redistribution in the United States was published by Edgar Browning, a professor of economics at the University of Virginia. Browning noted that while government spending on social welfare programs had almost tripled from $77 billion in 1965 to $215 billion in 1973, the number of Americans officially defined as poor had dropped by less than a third during the same period. He sought to explain how such a massive redistribution of income could have had such an apparently small effect on poverty.

Using an analytical procedure developed in earlier studies of income redistribution by Benjamin Okner and Robert Lampman, two of the country's most noted authorities on welfare, he was somewhat startled to discover that, because government redistribution of income had grown so rapidly during the eight years preceding 1973, the net transfer of income to the poorest fourth of the population from the other three-fourths was so great that "the total value of the resources consumed by the poor in 1973 was enough to raise every officially poor family 30 percent above its poverty line." Browning concluded, "In view of these figures it appears incredible that there was a single poor person left in the United States in 1973."[4]

In trying to ascertain how so much money could be taken from middle- and high-income workers and given to poor people with such negligible effect on poverty, Browning examined a number of possible explanations. He discarded them one by one, and finally settled on the fact that the official statistics of the Bureau of the Census are wildly inaccurate and grossly overstate the amount of poverty in the United States. Commenting on the usefulness of the federal government's official statistics, he observed, "Because the Census Bureau's statistics on income distribution and the official poverty counts ignore in-kind transfers, they are now largely useless as a basis for rational analysis of questions concerning income distribution."[5]

Unfortunately, these are and have been for some time the only aggregate statistics available. For many years major decisions on welfare policy have been based on official statistics that have been strongly biased in the direction of overstating poverty. In a sense there has been a deliberate "cover-up" of the true extent of poverty in the United States. The Census Bureau has always taken great care to point out—in the depths of the appendices and in the fine print of the footnotes—that its numbers are not perfect. It states, "The results are subject to errors of response including underreporting and nonreporting in addition to sampling variability. In most cases, the information obtained for money income is based not on records kept but on the memory or knowledge of one person, usually the wife of the family head. The memory factor in data derived from field surveys may produce biases."[6]

Indeed, it may produce biases. Consider what would happen if a stranger walked up to the front door of your home unannounced, and asked your spouse how much income your family had last year from wages and salaries, from interest, from dividends, from welfare payments, and from self-employment.

Besides the bias due to capricious memories, ignorance, and deliberate deception, the official income statistics are further distorted for the poor by the Census Bureau's *complete disregard* of any income received in the form of tangible services. People are not even asked if they receive food stamps, live in public housing, or are eligible for medicaid.

The result is a strong, consistent bias in the official statistics understating the amount of income Americans receive, especially those in low-income groups.

What Browning discovered in 1975 others have known about for years. In 1970 Edward Banfield, professor of government at Harvard University, wrote, "Some statisticians believe that most figures used considerably exaggerate both the number of persons whose incomes are low year after year and the lowness of their incomes. The poor (and the nonpoor as well) generally under-report their incomes, perhaps because they do not always know how much they receive or perhaps they are unwilling to tell. Also, every survey catches some people who at that particular time are below their normal incomes. (Thus, in 1960 it was found that in the large cities consumers with incomes under $1,000 were spending $224 for every $100 of income received. . . .) Even if one takes the reported incomes as given, questions of interpretation arise. One economist, using the same figures as the Council of Economic Advisers, cut its estimate of the amount of poverty in half—from 20 percent of the population to 10 percent."[7]

In early 1975, Roger Freeman, senior fellow at the Hoover Institution at Stanford University, wrote, "The annual income surveys of the Bureau of Census materially underreport income and . . . cash (money) income omits income in kind. . . . Low-income persons get food stamps, housing subsidies, medical benefits, etc., none of which are counted as income. . . . This makes income appear lower than it actually is. . . . In other words, an unknown number of persons and families have a money income below the official poverty level in a particular year but may not be poor in any meaningful sense of the word."[8]

The welfare experts have all known this, probably for the last fifteen or twenty years. But few, if any, have had a clear idea of the extent of the understatement of income and how it varied from the rich to the poor. The Census Bureau continued to publish its erroneous statistics, all the while giving itself deniability by pointing out in some obscure part of the text that "the under-reporting and nonreporting" should be taken into account when using its statistics.

But the people who used the statistics, the policymakers in government and the researchers in academia, had no valid way to make corrections in the official government numbers. One man's corrections or adjustments were as good as any other man's. Consequently, they were forced either to ignore the income statistics altogether or to use them, consoling themselves with the knowledge that they were the best available. Inevitably they used them.

Back in 1965, the in-kind income of welfare recipients was relatively small, and even with the acknowledged underreporting of income the degree of overstatement of poverty was perhaps negligible. But as the value of in-kind income grew over the years, and as the level of actual poverty fell, the total amount of in-kind income not counted and income not reported accounted for a larger and larger percentage of what was officially reported as poverty.

Over the years, the discrepancy between what was actually happening to the poor in America and what the statisticians in Washington were telling us grew wider and wider. Finally the "poverty gap" in the official Census Bureau statistics became so apparent that it was almost embarrassing to use the numbers. Almost—for virtually without exception everyone went on using them.

I recall one personal experience. In early 1969, while a Special Assistant in the White House, I was assigned to act as deputy to Arthur Burns, who was then in overall charge of domestic policy for President Nixon. One of our first major tasks was to evaluate the effectiveness of the country's welfare programs and propose alternatives. In our analyses we had no choice but to use the poverty statistics from the Census Bureau. There was no feasible alternative.

There have been sporadic attempts to correct the numbers. Academicians, and even the Census Bureau itself, attacked parts of the problem. In 1972, for example, the bureau reported that it had obtained only "87.0 percent of all wage and salary income, 81.7 percent of all social security benefits, and 65.5 percent of all public assistance benefits."[9] But the results of such studies, though helpful, never gave any clear indication of the order of magnitude by which the official government statistics overstated poverty in the United States.

Some analysts began making educated guesses. In 1976 John Palmer and Joseph Minarik of the Brookings Institution, two acknowledged experts in the field of welfare, speculated that "a definition of household income that both includes the recipients' cash valuation of in-kind benefits and adjusts for underreporting of cash income would probably reflect a current poverty rate close to 5 percent rather than the official level of 12 percent."[10]

But guesses, even by prudent experts, can't be used as a sound basis for policy at the national level. Finally, in frustration, the Congress, using its newly formed research arm, the Congressional Budget Office, decided to answer for itself the question, "How much poverty is there in the United States?"

The results were startling. Using exactly the same poverty line as the venerable Census Bureau, the fledgling Congressional Budget Office reported in June 1977 that its analysis showed less than 14 million Americans in poverty in fiscal 1976—only 6.4 percent of the population.[11]

There are two reasons why these new numbers differ so radically from the traditional Census Bureau numbers. First, the new congressional study counts the value of noncash welfare benefits in determining the yearly income of poor people. Over $40 billion a year is spent by the federal government alone on food stamps, day care, public housing, school lunches, medicaid, and medicare. The Census Bureau statistics ignore the $40 billion in benefits; the Congressional Budget Office statistics do not. Any income statistics that ignore the gigantic sums spent by government on welfare and income transfer programs that provide in-kind benefits are simply not valid. As Alice Rivlin, the director of the Congressional Budget Office, has said, "You can argue whether the line for determining poverty ought to be higher or lower. . . . But you can't argue that because benefits don't come in the form of cash, they're not benefits."[12]

The second reason involves the underreporting of income. The Census Bureau acknowledges it, and has some rough estimates of what it is for various categories of income, but they are not reflected in the final statistics. The Congressional Budget Office, using the estimates of underreporting, makes adjustments that are reflected in its final estimate of poverty.

In a more recent study (October 1977) Morton Paglin, professor of economics and urban studies at Portland State University, refined the poverty corrections even further. In addition to the kind of corrections made in the CBO study, he also corrected for the fact that the Census Bureau neglects to account for households because it unrealistically assumes "that there are no economies of scale and no income sharing unless the persons making up the unit are all related by blood or marriage."[13] The simulation model used by Paglin to estimate the effect of in-kind welfare benefits on the poverty level is similar to the one used by the CBO—with one further refinement. The empirical data base was used to allocate benefits by program and household size, and the simulation was not performed until "the last stage when assumptions about multiple benefits must be made."[14]

Paglin's more refined, more recent estimates of poverty are even more startling than those of the Congressional Budget Office. By his calculations *only 3 percent of Americans were poor in 1975*.[15]

Whereas the official level of poverty reported by the Census Bureau has been essentially constant since 1968, the revised poverty estimates by the Congressional Budget Office and by Professor Paglin both agree that (1) there has, in fact, been a *steady decline* in the poverty level since 1968, and (2) the degree of poverty had shrunk to very low levels by 1975 (the most recent year for which statistics are available).

And this is what one would expect as a result of the massive amount of welfare spending. As Paglin notes, "The [welfare] transfers have been on a sufficiently massive scale to effect a major reduction in the poverty population. It would have been amazing if they had not done so. What is surprising is the lack of recognition of this accomplishment. Social scientists have generally accepted and have given wide currency to the official poverty estimates. It is time for the statistical veil to be lifted so that the poverty problem can be seen in its true dimensions."[16]

For years scholars have been researching and writing about poverty, and policymakers have been passing and implementing laws on welfare. They have all been influenced to some degree by the Census Bureau statistics, *which have consistently overstated the amount of poverty in the United States*. The degree of that overstatement has increased each year as the sharp increase in welfare and income transfer payments by the government failed to be reflected in the official Census Bureau numbers.

According to the Census Bureau, 12.3 percent of all Americans are poor. Revised, more accurate estimates show that if you also take into account the value of the nonmoney income received by poor people, and adjust for the fact that the poor systematically underreport their actual income when asked, the poverty count drops to as low as 3 percent. In effect, the executive branch of the federal government has been telling us that there is four times as much poverty as there really is. And laws have been passed and money has been appropriated and welfare programs have been implemented based on this "evidence."

What makes it truly appalling is that the Census Bureau was fully aware of the work that had been done by the Congressional Budget Office in developing more accurate poverty statistics. The Census Bureau even cites the CBO study in a footnote in its June 1977 report on poverty in the United States.[17] But then, in a classic manifestation of bureaucratic arrogance and interdepartmental jealousy, it neglects to mention the results of the CBO study.

Some welfare experts are beginning to change their minds about the extent of poverty in the United States. Reflecting on the revised CBO statistics, Alice Rivlin commented, "The nation has come a lot closer to eliminating poverty than most people realize."[18] Sar Levitan, a professor of economics at George Washington University who has written extensively on the welfare programs of President Johnson's Great Society, concluded in early 1977 that "if poverty is defined as a lack of basic needs, it's almost been eliminated."[19] And Edgar Browning, without the benefit of the new statistics from the Congressional Budget Office, arrived at a similar conclusion in his 1975 study, which he summed up by stating, "In a meaningful sense poverty had become virtually nonexistent in America by 1973."[20]

The results of the new studies by the Congressional Budget Office and Paglin should not be surprising to anyone familiar with the growth of our economy and the increase in our welfare and income transfer programs over the past thirteen years. Ever since Lyndon Johnson declared a "war on poverty" in 1964, two powerful forces have been pushing more and more Americans out of poverty.

The first, and perhaps most important, force is the strong, sustained economic growth of the private sector. The gross national product of the United States more than doubled from $688 billion in 1965 to $1,710 billion in the third quarter of 1976.[21] This gain of over one trillion dollars in GNP was accompanied by 18 million new jobs. Over 89 million Americans were employed at the end of 1976.[22] The growth in family income was equally dramatic: from about $7,700 in 1965, the average family income in the United States more than doubled to $15,546 in 1975.[23] Even after making allowances for inflation, higher taxes, and a sharp increase in restrictive government regulation, the private economy produced millions of new jobs and significantly higher wages and salaries for workers. Many of these new jobs and higher paychecks undoubtedly went to people classified as poor when the war on poverty began and to others who would have become poor in the meantime.

The second major force removing people from poverty is the vast and growing array of government welfare and income transfer programs. Since the war on poverty began there has been an explosive growth in social welfare spending. Total government spending on all social welfare programs in the United States increased from $77 billion in 1965 to over $286 billion in 1975, close to a fourfold increase in a decade. Spending on direct welfare programs has grown even faster. In 1965 the combined spending of federal, state, and local governments on public welfare was just over $6 billion. By 1975 it was over $40 billion, almost seven times greater.[24]

When President Nixon took office, 48 percent of the fiscal 1969 federal budget was being spent on defense and 30 percent on health, education, and income security. In fiscal 1977, after eight years of Republican administration, the percentages were *exactly reversed*: 30 percent of the federal budget was spent on defense and 48 percent on health, education, and income security.[25]

By the end of 1977 the total amount of money spent cumulatively on public welfare by the federal, state, and local governments since the war on poverty began in 1964 will be roughly $300 billion.[26] The estimated cost of fighting World War II is $288 billion.[27] By the end of 1977 the war on poverty will have cost us more than in World War II.

Today there are some ninety-odd social welfare programs transferring money and services from the producing to the non-producing sectors of our society.[28] Appendix A of this book contains a list and brief descriptions of these programs. Reading the list is an effective way to acquire a feel for the variety and scope of programs in our social welfare system.

The term "social welfare programs" embraces both income transfer programs and welfare programs. The main purpose of *income transfer* programs, such as social security and unemployment compensation, is to provide economic security for workers and their dependents who might suffer a loss of income because of old age, sickness, loss of job, or death. The purpose of *welfare* programs, such as Aid to Families with Dependent Children and medicaid, is to provide cash income and services to poor people who cannot help themselves. Government expenditures for income transfer programs account for the lion's share of social welfare spending. The rest, which is quite substantial, is spent on welfare programs *per se*.

In fiscal 1978 the federal government will spend over $190 billion on its top twelve income transfer and welfare programs. Of this amount, approximately $153 billion will be spent on the six largest income transfer programs. These six major federal income transfer programs[29] are:

Social Security. The aim of this program is "to partially replace income from work that is lost to workers and their dependents because of the worker's retirement in old age, disability severe enough to prevent substantial gainful employment, or death." The budget for social security benefits in fiscal 1978 was $91.8 billion.

Medicare. The objective of the medicare program is to provide "hospital and insurance for social security and railroad retirement beneficiaries who are age 65 and over." It works essentially through intermediaries—such as Blue Cross and other private insurance companies, which determine the amount of payments due and process insurance claims. An expected $26.1 billion will be spent on medicare in fiscal 1978.

Unemployment Compensation. This federal-state program was designed to "provide cash benefits on a regular basis to normally employed workers during limited periods of involuntary unem-ployment." Unemployment benefits of $13.9 billion were expected to be paid during fiscal 1978.

Federal Civil Service Retirement. The civil service retirement system is the basic retirement program for civilian employees of the federal government. It "covers most Federal employees and includes Members of Congress and congressional employees. . . . Benefits (annuities) are paid to qualified employees who retire because of age or disability and to survivors under certain condi-tions. Employees may retire at age 62 after 5 years of service, at age 60 after 20 years of service, or at age 55 with 30 years of service."

One of the curiosities of modern political life is the fact that no federal or congressional employees are required to pay social security taxes. For some reason the senators and congressmen who passed social security for the use of the public, and the social security employees who administer it to the public, apparently thought it wise to exempt themselves.

In fiscal 1978, $11.1 billion was budgeted for retired federal and congressional employees, and for retired congressmen and senators.

Veterans Compensation Pensions. "The military retirement program provides protection against loss of income due to retirement to members of the Armed Forces and their families." There are three major conditions for eligibility: "(1) Disability incurred during active service; (2) age or length of service; and (3) . . . survivors of retired servicemen. . . . Where retirement is based on age and length of service, the general conditions are: 60 years of age (with exceptions for persons in grades above major general, warrant officers, and professors at the service academies); or 20 years of active service." The budget for fiscal 1978 was $9.2 billion.

Temporary Employment Assistance. The purpose of this program is to provide federal grants to states and localities to enable them to create public service jobs. The budget for fiscal 1978 was $1.0 billion.

The major federal welfare programs are:

Medicaid. The legislative objective of medicaid is "to enable each state, at its option, to furnish (1) medical assistance on behalf of needy families with dependent children and needy individuals who are aged, blind, or permanently and totally disabled; and (2) rehabilitation and other services to help such families and individuals attain or retain capability for independence of self care." Federal payments for medicaid were expected to total $11.8 billion in fiscal 1978.

Aid to Families with Dependent Children (AFDC). This program was established to "encourage the care of dependent children in their own homes or in the homes of relatives by enabling each state to furnish financial assistance, rehabilitation, and other services to needy dependent children and the parents or relatives with whom they are living to help maintain and strengthen family life and to help such parents or relatives to attain or retain capability for self-support." The budget for fiscal 1978 was $6.6 billion.

Supplemental Security Income (SSI). In 1974 this federal program replaced welfare assistance to the aged, blind, and disabled. The basic purpose of the program is to provide financial assistance to needy individuals who are aged, blind, or—if age eighteen or older—permanently and totally disabled. The budget for fiscal 1978 was $5.7 billion.

Food Stamps. The purpose of the food stamp program is to "improve the diets of low-income households and to expand the market for domestically produced food by supplementing the food purchasing power of eligible low-income families." The budget for fiscal 1978 was $5.6 billion.

Public Housing. There are a number of housing assistance programs, but the essential purpose of all of them is to help "provide decent, safe, and sanitary low-rent housing and related facilities for low-income families." Approximately $3.7 billion was budgeted for these programs in fiscal 1978.

Child Nutrition. The purpose of this program is to provide adequate school lunches for children by giving special financial assistance to "reimburse all schools for free or reduced-price lunches served to children who are determined by local school officials to be unable to pay the full price for lunches." For fiscal 1978 the estimated cost is $3.3 billion.

In addition to the federal outlays, state and local governments will spend tens of billions of dollars more on social welfare programs of one sort or another. And more billions will be given for social welfare purposes by private individuals, business corporations, and foundations. The total amount of income transfer occurring in the United States is without precedent in the history of mankind.

To be officially poor in 1975 a family of four had to have an income that was less than $5,469 a year. For an individual to be poor, the income dividing line was $2,791 a year for those under 65 years of age, and $2,572 for those over 65.[30] For people who cannot care for themselves, the current array of welfare programs provides a level of support that lifts virtually all of them over the poverty line. There may be some people who, for various reasons, do not apply for the programs—but the programs are there for those who cannot care for themselves and who do apply. In this sense there is little, if any, poverty left in the United States.

There will always be some people who will show up in the "poverty" column of the official statistics for reasons unrelated to real poverty—they may not know their total income, they may deliberately understate it, they may temporarily be living off undeclared assets, they may have private sources of support, and so on. But they are in no sense poor. Whatever small gaps in coverage do exist could be filled by adjustments in current welfare programs and by more efficient, effective administration.

The question of how adequate welfare benefits are is a difficult one to answer with precision, but it is possible to get a reasonably clear idea of the order of magnitude of average benefit payment levels. The difficulty of calculating a more precise distribution of welfare benefit levels stems from a number of causes.

To begin with, welfare rules and regulations and the formulas for determining benefit levels vary significantly from state to state, and often from city to city within a state. The level of welfare benefits tends to be lower than average in the Southern states and in rural areas, and tends to be higher than average in the Northeast, in parts of the West, and in large cities. The resulting benefit structure is so diverse that the acquisition of refined aggregate data is very expensive and time-consuming.

A major problem in assessing the adequacy of welfare payments is the tendency for people to think in terms of the maximum cash payment that one particular welfare program, such as AFDC, provides to a typical family of four that has no income whatsoever, and to compare this level of welfare income with that which can be earned by working. There are three major flaws in this approach: (1) most poor people receiving welfare have numerous other sources of income that should be counted; (2) welfare is now a multiple-program system, with most people on welfare qualifying for two or more programs; and (3) welfare income cannot be compared directly with earned income without making adjustments for taxes and work expenses.[31]

Most poor people on welfare have other sources of income and are not totally dependent on welfare assistance to ensure an adequate level of support. In 1972 approximately half (51 percent) of the total income received by female-headed poor families in the United States came from public assistance payments. A full 28 percent came from private wage and salary income; 12 percent from social security payments; 7 percent from such sources as private pensions and alimony; 1 percent from dividends, interest, and rent; and the remaining 2 percent from sources classified as "other transfer" income. According to the 1974 final report of the Joint Economic Committee's study of public welfare, "In 1972, only 17 percent of the Nation's families who were classified as poor by the Census Bureau had zero money income other than public aid. . . . Only 14 percent of all families, 10 percent of poor white families and 24 percent of poor black families, were totally dependent on cash welfare."[32]

Any attempt to assess the adequacy of welfare payments that does not include all other sources of income to the families or individuals involved is bound to understate the adequacy of welfare. In most cases welfare makes up only a part of the income of poor families and individuals.

In addition, those who are poor generally qualify for benefits from many different welfare programs, some in the form of cash, others in the form of services and goods. For example, a 1973 survey revealed that of all those families receiving AFDC benefits, 99 percent had medicaid health-insurance coverage, 60 percent got food stamps, 14 percent lived in public housing, 9 percent purchased surplus food commodities, 4 percent received social security payments, and 1 percent received veterans' benefits.[33] The multiple, overlapping nature of welfare programs, while being an effective means of ensuring wide coverage of the poor, does compound the difficulty of making accurate estimates of the total value of welfare payments and services that the poor receive.

Finally, most evaluations of the adequacy of welfare neglect the fact that the value of welfare benefits is not comparable to regular earnings. The AFDC program, for example, allows work-related expenses to be deducted from earned income before the amount of the welfare grant is determined. The states have the authority to determine what can be deducted. Consequently, "deductions vary widely, being far below actual work expenses in some states and including items that are not clearly expenses of working (lunch, for example) in others."[34] Typically such deductible work expenses include transportation, day care, and taxes. The essential result of this procedure is that money earned by welfare recipients that can be offset by "work expenses" does not cause any reduction in the recipients' welfare benefits. Working people not on welfare are, of course, not allowed to deduct such expenses in determining the taxes they must pay. As a specific case in point, it "required $619 in gross earnings (after taxes and work expenses of 15 percent of gross earnings) in New York in July 1974 to equal the net of $448 available in food stamps and cash to an AFDC family of four."[35] Thus, every welfare dollar received in this example was worth $1.38 of earned income.

In 1974 a staff study of the Joint Economic Committee found that the national average value of welfare benefits for a family of four on AFDC, who also received food stamps, lived in public housing, and qualified for medicaid coverage, was approximately $5,625 a year, or about $6,400 in terms of equivalent taxable income. This is an average amount. The benefit package is lower in some parts of the country and higher in others. AFDC cash payments alone are relatively low for much of the country, but as the study points out, when "other benefits are added in, and when allowance is made for the tax-free nature of these benefits, the average amount potentially available to the fatherless welfare family begins to compare favorably with what many people earn."[36]

The order of magnitude of these findings was confirmed by a Rand Corporation study of the incidence and level of multiple welfare benefits received by recipients of AFDC in New York City in 1974. The study concluded, "The average AFDC case received $6,088 in total income from welfare and nonwelfare sources during 1974. . . . The average case received nearly $1,900 as a basic AFDC grant; $1,500 in shelter allowances; $500 in food stamps; $1,600 in Medicaid-paid health care; $128 in social services; and $460 in nonwelfare income."[37] The average value of the welfare benefits alone was $5,628 a year, virtually identical to the average national value determined in the Joint Economic Committee staff study.

Since 1974, benefits have continued to increase. Assuming a modest increase of, say, 5 percent a year, the national average value of welfare benefits to an AFDC family of four in 1977 would be over $6,500 a year. For those not living in public housing (and most of them do not) the national average would be in the neighborhood of $6,000 a year. This would be roughly equivalent to $7,000 of earned income before taxes.

The provision of an adequate income may eliminate poverty in the official sense, but it does not guarantee that those who receive welfare will spend that income in a manner that also eliminates the characteristics that many people associate with poverty. A family with an income of $6,000 a year may choose to spend it in ways that will result in their living in poverty. If they personally value nice cars, good liquor, and gambling, they may not have much money left for housing, clothing, and food. An acceptable income from the viewpoint of society does not ensure equally acceptable behavior.

One of the side effects of the massive and rapid effort to abolish poverty is the inevitable waste, inefficiency, fraud, and program overlap that always happen in any "all-out war." Some people are receiving welfare who don't need it, and some are receiving more than they need. Given the strong bias toward underreporting and nonreporting, especially for welfare payments, it is somewhat disconcerting to find the Census Bureau showing in 1975 that some 450,000 families in the United States, all having incomes of over $15,000 a year, also reported receiving an average of $1,342 a year in welfare benefits. In the $15,000 to $20,000 income bracket, 235,000 families received an average welfare payment of $1,655. In the $20,000 to $25,000 income bracket, 102,000 families reported an average welfare payment of $1,794. In the $25,000 to $50,000 income bracket, 101,000 families had average welfare payments of $1,188. And 12,000 families with incomes of over $50,000 a year reported that they also received an average of $1,917 a year in government welfare payments.[38]

There may be some plausible explanation for much of this, but it does seem a bit incongruous to have almost half a million families, all earning over $15,000 a year, also receiving an average of more than $1,300 a year in welfare checks from the government. While we can be sure that those families with high incomes receiving welfare payments merit some further inquiries, we can only wonder about what is not being reported at all.

As the war on poverty was being waged during the last decade, great emphasis was placed on developing welfare programs that would provide adequate levels of support to those who qualified for them. One factor that seems to have been overlooked to a large degree is the cumulative effect of multiple welfare programs on the ultimate beneficiary, the welfare recipient.

Although average levels of welfare benefits have increased significantly, the value of some possible packages of welfare benefits, which can be assembled by the more enterprising poor located in certain states with high welfare benefits, has reached truly unbelievable levels. These are not typical of the welfare system as a whole. But they do exist and they raise serious questions about what the purpose of welfare is in the United States.

In a recent issue of the *Public Interest*, Professor Nathan

Glazer of Harvard University quoted a story that exemplifies the lengths to which our current welfare system can go. It dramatizes how attractive welfare has become as an alternative to work. While an atypical case, it is possible and it does happen. Originally reported in the *Boston Globe*, it goes as follows: "The mother is well-organized. She buys food stamps twice a month, refuses to live in a housing project, is a member of a community women's group at Catholic charities, and is studying for her high school diploma. Her bimonthly cash grant is $466; she gets a flat grant every three months of $142; and her monthly savings from food stamps amount to $86. Her cash income may be given at $599 monthly, or $7,188 a year. If she and her family spent the average amount paid personally for health care in this country (and the mother gets some psychiatric care), this would amount at full costs to an additional $1,750 in health care expenses. Since there are no financial restrictions for this family on the use of health care, and the mother is intelligent and knowledgeable, one may assume that full use of this opportunity is taken. The three older children go free of charge to an alternative school which costs paying pupils $2,000 a year, and another child goes to a day care center whose cost for a paying child would be $1,000 a year. Cash income and free health and educational services to this family thus amount to $16,028. The older children work summers, and I will not cost that out. The family pays no taxes, and need put nothing aside for savings, as the welfare department is committed to meeting its needs. A working head of family would have to earn at least $20,000 to match this standard of living."[39]

About three-fourths of the families in the United States have incomes of less than $20,000 a year.[40]

The number of people remaining in poverty is very small and it grows smaller every day. Virtually all people who cannot truly care for themselves or their families are eligible for a wide variety of cash grants and services that provide a decent and adequate standard of living. The growth of social welfare programs—AFDC, SSI, food stamps, child nutrition, day care, public housing, medicaid and medicare, tuition aid, and social security—has been so comprehensive and diffuse that there is virtually no person in the United States needing help who is not eligible for some form of government aid.

As surprisingly low as the revised estimates of poverty are, the actual figures may be considerably lower. The poverty statistics still contain large numbers of undergraduate and graduate students, some wealthy people living off assets who report no income, recipients of income from illegal activities such as robbery, drug traffic, prostitution, and gambling who obviously aren't eager to report to any government agency, and other people who simply don't like to tell anyone what their true level of income is. Workers who enter or leave the labor force sometime during the year may have substantial earnings that would place them well above the poverty line. Yet they may be counted as officially poor. When the Census count is made early in the year, those questioned are asked how much income the family had during the last calendar year. Someone beginning work on, say, October 1, with an annual salary of $12,000 would only be able to report actual earnings of $3,000 during that calendar year, and thus would be included among the poor. And there are even a few people who deliberately choose not to earn more, even though they are capable of doing so, in order to enjoy a particular life-style that requires a good deal of free time.

As Robert Haveman, fellow of the Institute for Research on Poverty at the University of Wisconsin, wrote in 1977: "The day of income poverty as a major public issue would appear to be past. . . . A minimum level of economic well-being has by and large been assured for all citizens."[41]

The war on poverty has been won, except for perhaps a few mopping-up operations. The combination of strong economic growth and a dramatic increase in government spending on welfare and income transfer programs during the last decade has virtually wiped out poverty in the United States.

There will be isolated instances where a person is unaware

of being eligible, or is unjustly denied aid by a welfare bureaucrat, or simply chooses not to accept the social stigma of being on welfare. But these cases are the exceptions. In fact, just the opposite concern—those getting welfare who have no right to it—is the one that seems to be growing.

When the policymakers were passing and implementing the welfare programs that are currently on the books, their deliberations, it must be remembered, took place in the context of a deep and widely held belief that poverty was widespread and highly intractable to their previous efforts. The welfare and income transfer programs now in place have developed a momentum of growth that is unlikely to slow down in the near future.

We have built up an array of programs and resources to attack a poverty "army" of 25 to 30 million poor people. The "enemy" is no longer there, but the attack goes on unabated. We have built up such a large arsenal of welfare programs, and their momentum of growth is so strong, that we may soon pass into an overkill capability with regard to government measures to combat poverty. Perhaps we already are there.

The "dismal failure" of welfare is a myth. There are many things wrong with our welfare system, but in terms of essentials, in terms of the key goals it was set up to accomplish, it has been a smashing, total success.

The main goal of welfare in the United States, at least as perceived and understood by the vast majority of Americans, is to provide a decent, adequate level of support, composed of both cash and services, to all those who truly cannot care for themselves. The key criteria by which to judge the efficacy of welfare programs are two: the *extent of coverage* and the *adequacy of support*.

Coverage of the eligible welfare population is now virtually universal—if one is sick, or is hungry, or cannot work, or is blind, or has small children to care for, or is physically disabled, or is old—then there are literally dozens of welfare programs whose sole purpose is to provide help.

And the level of help is substantial. The average mother on AFDC with three children qualifies for about $6,000 a year. In some rare cases in high-paying states, this amount can go so high as to be equivalent to an annual before-tax income of over $20,000. Virtually all people who are eligible qualify for government checks and government-provided services that automatically lift them out of the official ranks of poverty.

There may be great inefficiencies in our welfare programs, the level of fraud may be very high, the quality of management may be terrible, the programs may overlap, inequities may abound, and the financial incentive to work may be virtually nonexistent. But if we step back and judge the vast array of welfare programs, on which we spend tens of billions of dollars every year, by two basic criteria—the completeness of coverage for those who really need help, and the adequacy of the amount of help they do receive—the picture changes dramatically. Judged by these standards our welfare system has been a brilliant success.

The war on poverty is over for all practical purposes. We should now begin thinking about how to revise our welfare strategies to deal with the problem of preventing poverty, to make programs more effective and efficient, to eliminate those programs that are not needed, and to focus more on the social problems that widespread welfare dependency will bring.

CITATIONS—CHAPTER I

1   Robert D. Plotnick and Felicity Skidmore, *Progress against Poverty: A Review of the 1964–1974 Decade* (New York: Academic Press, 1975), page 84. (Italics added.)

2   U.S., Congress, Joint Economic Committee, Subcommittee on Fiscal Policy, *Income Security for Americans: Recommendations of the Public Welfare Study* (Washington, D.C., December 5, 1974), page 1.

3   U.S., Bureau of the Census, *Characteristics of the Population below*

the Poverty Level: 1975, Series P-60, No. 106 (Washington, D.C., 1977), pages 1–2. (Italics added.)

4   Edgar K. Browning, *Redistribution and the Welfare System* (Washington, D.C. American Enterprise Institute for Public Policy Research, 1975), pages 14–30.

5   Ibid., pages 29–30.

6   U.S., Bureau of the Census, *Money Income in 1974 of Families and Persons in the United States,* Series P-60, No. 101 (Washington, D.C., 1976), page 169.

7   Edward C. Banfield, *The Unheavenly City: The Nature and Future of Our Urban Crisis* (Boston: Little, Brown and Company, 1970), pages 115–116.

8   Roger A. Freeman, *The Growth of American Government: A Morphology of the Welfare State* (Stanford, California: Hoover Institution Press, 1975), pages 143n–144n.

9   John L. Palmer and Joseph Minarik, "Income Security Policy," in Henry Owen and Charles L. Schultze (editors), *Setting National Priorities: The Next Ten Years* (Washington, D.C.: The Brookings Institution, 1976), page 525.

10 Ibid.

11 U.S., Congress, Congressional Budget Office, "Persons in Poverty Distributed by Various Characteristics and Definitions of Income," revised, unpublished computer printouts (Washington, D.C., 1977), Table 26.

12 Quoted in Mark R. Arnold, "We're Winning the War on Poverty," *The National Observer,* February 19, 1977, page 1.

13 Morton Paglin, "Transfers in Kind: Their Impact on Poverty, 1959–1975" (Paper presented at the Hoover Institution, Conference on Income Redistribution, October 1977), page 14.

14 Ibid., page 32.

15 Ibid., Table 8.

16 Ibid., page 38.

17 U.S., Bureau of the Census, *Characteristics of the Population below the Poverty Level,* page 5n.

18 Quoted in Arnold, "We're Winning the War on Poverty," page 1.

19 Quoted in ibid.

20 Browning, *Redistribution and the Welfare System,* page 2.

21 U.S., Executive Office of the President, Council of Economic Advisers, *Economic Indicators* (Washington, D.C.: December 1976), page 1.

22 U.S., Bureau of Labor Statistics, *Employment and Earnings*, Vol. 23, No. 5 (Washington, D.C., November 1976) page 19, Table A-1.

23 U.S., Bureau of the Census, *Money Income in 1975 of Families and Persons in the United States*, Series P-60, No. 105 (Washington, D.C., 1977), page 2, Table A.

24 U.S., Bureau of the Census, *Statistical Abstract of the United States, 1976* (Washington, D.C., 1976), page 293, Table 459.

25 U.S., Executive Office of the President, Office of Management and Budget, *The Budget of the United States Government, Fiscal Year 1977* (Washington, D.C., 1976), page 57. (Veterans' benefits included as part of defense spending.)

26 U.S., Bureau of the Census, *Statistical Abstract . . . 1976*, page 293, Table 459.

27 Ibid., page 329, Table 519.

28 U.S., Congress, Joint Economic Committee, Subcommittee on Fiscal Policy, *Public Welfare and Work Incentives: Theory and Practice*, prepared by Vee Burke and Alair A. Townsend, Studies in Public Welfare, Paper No. 14 (Washington, D.C., April 15, 1974), pages 45–54.

29 All quotes in the following program descriptions are from U.S. Congress, Joint Economic Committee, Subcommittee on Fiscal Policy, *Handbook of Public Income Transfer Programs*, prepared by Irene Cox, Studies in Public Welfare, Paper No. 2 (Washington, D.C., October 16, 1972); cost estimates are from U.S., Executive Office of the President, Office of Management and Budget, *Budget of the United States Government, Fiscal Year 1978* (Washington, D.C., 1977).

30 U.S., Bureau of the Census, *Characteristics of the Population below the Poverty Level*, page 199, Table A-3.

31 U.S., Congress, Joint Economic Committee, Subcommittee on Fiscal Policy, *Income Security for Americans*, pages 60–61.

32 Ibid., page 65, and page 68, Table 15.

33 Ibid.

34 Irene Lurie (editor), *Integrating Income Maintenance Programs* (New York: Academic Press, 1975), page 30.

35   U.S., Congress, Joint Economic Committee, Subcommittee on Fiscal Policy, *Income Security for Americans*, page 61.

36   U.S., Congress, Joint Economic Committee, Subcommittee on Fiscal Policy, *Welfare in the 70's: A National Study of Benefits Available in 100 Local Areas*, prepared by James R. Storey, Studies in Public Welfare, Paper No. 15 (Washington, D.C., July 22, 1974), page 4.

37   David W. Lyon, Philip A. Armstrong, James R. Hosek, and John J. McCall, *Multiple Welfare Benefits in New York City* (Santa Monica, California: The Rand Corporation, 1976), page vii.

38   U.S., Bureau of the Census, *Money Income in 1975*, pages 40–41, Table 7.

39   Nathan Glazer, "Reform Work, Not Welfare," *The Public Interest*, No. 40 (Summer 1975), page 4.

40   U.S., Bureau of the Census, *Money Income in 1975*, page 40, Table 7.

41   Robert H. Haveman, "Poverty and Social Policy in the 1960's and 1970's—An Overview and Some Speculations," in Robert H. Haveman (editor), *A Decade of Federal Antipoverty Programs: Achievements, Failures, and Lessons* (New York: Academic Press, 1977), page 18.

II

THE POVERTY WALL

As for charity, it is a matter, in which the imme-
diate effect on the persons directly concerned, and
the ultimate consequence to the general good, are
apt to be at complete war with one another.

John Stuart Mill, 1869

*Second Thesis: The virtual elimination of poverty has
had costly social side effects. The proliferation of welfare
programs has created very high effective marginal tax
rates for the poor. There is, in effect, a "poverty wall"
that destroys the financial incentive to work for millions
of Americans. Free from basic wants, but heavily dependent on the State, with little hope of breaking free, they
are a new caste, the "Dependent Americans."*

The virtual elimination of poverty in the United States during
the last decade has not been accomplished without costly social
side effects. The most important and potentially troublesome
effect is the almost complete destruction of work incentives for the
poor on welfare. The nature of our new welfare programs and the
massive increases in welfare payments have combined to sharply
reduce, and in some cases eliminate altogether, any financial
incentive for welfare recipients either to get a job or to attempt
to increase their current low earnings. The welfare system has so
distorted incentives to work that people on welfare now face

higher effective marginal tax rates on earned income than even those making $100,000 a year or more.*

This destruction of work incentives is a direct and necessary consequence of the drive to eliminate poverty. All of our major welfare programs are "income-tested," meaning that the amount of welfare received in cash or in services is dependent on the amount of money the welfare recipient earns. When someone on welfare begins to earn money, or increases his or her earnings, it is assumed that the need for welfare declines, and the amount of welfare payments or services is reduced according to a formula appropriate to the welfare programs providing benefits.

The degree of welfare reduction varies from program to program. It ranges from 25 percent of added earnings for those living in public housing, to 30 percent for food stamps, to just under 67 percent for AFDC, and a full 100 percent for income from assets received by SSI recipients. Under some circumstances the rate can exceed 100 percent of added earnings. For example, medicaid health benefits are terminated entirely when a specified income level is reached, and the value of the benefits lost can easily exceed the added amount of earned income that brought about the loss.

Income-tested welfare programs base their benefit reduction formulas on the amount of income received. If a welfare recipient is receiving money and services from two or more programs, the

---

*The *marginal tax rate* is the tax rate that applies to additional (marginal) earnings above a given base. If, for example, a tax of $100, or 10 percent, is paid on the first $1,000 earned, the marginal tax rate would be 10 percent.

If we now assume that the tax rate on a second $1,000 earned increases from 10 to 15 percent then taxes of $100 will be paid on the first $1,000 earned (at a 10 percent marginal tax rate), and taxes of $150 (at a 15 percent marginal tax rate) will be paid on the second $1,000 earned. Total taxes paid on the full $2,000 of earnings will thus be $250.

Whereas the *average* tax rate for the total $2,000 of earnings in this case will be 12.5 percent ($250 ÷ $2,000), the *marginal* tax rate, which applies only to additional increments of earnings, will be 10 percent on the first $1,000 and 15 percent on the second $1,000.

earning of additional income has a multiplier effect on net take-home "pay." If a person is receiving benefits from three different programs, there will be three separate benefit reductions as soon as the new income is reported.

Most of our welfare programs were designed and developed to take care of the needs of a particular poor segment of the society, and often little or no thought seems to have been given to the effect of their interaction with other welfare or public assistance programs. The result is a cumulative negative effect on a poor person's incentive to work that is devastating.

For example: "In New Jersey an unemployed man with a wife and two children receiving public assistance and food stamps would add only $110 to this net monthly income if he took a full-time job paying $500 a month. In addition, he would lose eligibility for medicaid, which pays an average of $52 a month for the medical bills of an AFDC family in New Jersey. A Tennessee father who is eligible for food stamps and the unemployment insurance maximum gains only $4 a week by taking a part-time job paying $75 a week. A New Jersey mother of three receiving benefits from medicaid, aid to families with dependent children, food stamps, and public housing would gain only about 20 percent of the total income derived from taking a full-time job paying as much as $700 or even $1,000 a month."[1]

A reduction in the amount of one's welfare check has the same effect on one's net pay as the payment of taxes. The amount of the welfare reduction, when expressed as a percentage of new or additional earnings, is equivalent to a marginal tax rate on earned income. Perhaps it should be called a "welfare tax." In the first example cited above, the effective marginal tax rate is 88 percent; in the second it is 95 percent; and in the third, 80 percent.

In 1972 the Joint Economic Committee of the Congress conducted a comprehensive review of welfare programs in the United States. Martha Griffiths, the chairman of the Subcommittee on Fiscal Policy that conducted the study, made this comment on the results of some of its studies: "Current government programs can discourage work effort and result in intolerably little improvement in the income of the beneficiaries. . . . These are the equivalent of *confiscatory tax rates*."[2]

The cumulative effect of our welfare programs on a poor individual's effective marginal tax rate is almost totally unknown to most people, and only dimly perceived by most policymakers. But welfare experts have known about it, and worried about it, for a long time.

In the summer of 1972 about thirty of this country's leading experts in the field of welfare, including scholars from universities and staff members of the Subcommittee on Fiscal Policy of the Joint Economic Committee of the Congress, met for a conference on welfare reform at the University of Wisconsin in Madison. They met to discuss and analyze a new set of welfare studies conducted by the Joint Economic Committee, studies far more detailed and complete than anything of their kind that had ever been done before. Writing about the results of that conference, its organizer, Irene Lurie of the Institute for Research on Poverty at the University of Wisconsin, concluded, "Perhaps the most serious single problem created by a multiplicity of programs is the reduction in the financial rewards from work effort which results from the high tax rate on earnings."[3]

In one of the major findings of its comprehensive public welfare study, the Subcommittee on Fiscal Policy of the Joint Economic Committee reported in late 1974: "Work disincentives are increased when a recipient participates in more than one benefit program, as most do. . . . The cumulative take-back rate [marginal welfare tax rate] could climb to 85 percent. It does not seem reasonable to expect persons to work for a net gain of only 15 cents per extra dollar, especially at possibly unpleasant work. . . . This study found that even though AFDC income exemptions are relatively generous and the food stamp benefit-loss rate low, recipients of combined benefits generally cannot expect to net much from going to work, or from increasing work."[4]

The incredibly high tax rates paid by those on welfare are a serious and direct disincentive to work. Why should someone work forty hours a week, fifty weeks a year for, say, $8,000 when it would be possible not to work at all for, say, $6,000? People on welfare may be poor, but they are not fools. Any rational calculation of the net returns from working by someone on welfare would discourage any but the most doggedly determined.

Some social scientists have suggested that very high rates of taxation, say 40 or 50 percent, are not a serious disincentive to work for the poor, but the weight of the research evidence, and a little common sense, does not bear this out. In a number of recent studies, "several economists [Cain, Watts, Christensen, Green, and Tella] have tried to determine how sensitive low-income families are to high tax rates. Their studies agree that a large transfer of cash causes some to either work fewer hours or withdraw from the labor force altogether, and that higher tax rates also tend to reduce work effort."[5]

There is additional evidence to support the view that the financial disincentives to work are real, that people recognize them, analyze them rationally, and act accordingly. For example, people receiving social security have their benefits reduced if their earnings exceed a certain amount. However, after the age of 72, full benefits are paid regardless of how much the social security recipient earns. One study, by Professor Bowen of Princeton University and Professor Finegan of Vanderbilt University, showed that when men became eligible for social security at age 65 they "dropped out of the labor force at a precipitous rate. Their labor force participation rates declined steadily thereafter until age 72, at which age there was no penalty for work. Then the work rates increased. . . . There being no other compelling reasons for increased work at age 72, the study concluded that the elimination of the 'tax' on earnings caused more people to work."[6]

The evidence also shows that unemployment insurance has had essentially the same effect on work effort. "Both types of work disincentives—receipt of income without work and loss of benefits caused by work—have been studied in unemployment insurance. ... The [unemployment insurance] program illustrates that benefit levels and benefit-reduction rates can affect work adversely."[7] One study of the work behavior of people receiving unemployment benefits in Wisconsin found that "many workers maneuvered their earnings to maximize their total income. . . . These unemployment insurance claimants could have worked more, but were reluctant to have additional earnings serve only to offset their unemployment insurance benefits dollar for dollar."[8]

The effect of very high rates of taxation is apt to be more serious for poor people than for those in middle- or upper-income classes. In his well-known book, *The Unheavenly City*, Edward Banfield observes that "upper- and upper-middle-class people often find intrinsic satisfaction[s] in their work. . . . For the lower-working class they amount to very little: in this subculture, one works only because one has to. . . . The evidence (such as it is) seems to confirm these expectations. . . . Some low-income earners seem to be very sensitive to disincentives. That they will not work when welfare payments are as much or more than they could earn is to be expected, of course."[9]

To further compound the problem, poor people are subject to regular federal, state, and city income taxes when their earnings move over the poverty level. They must pay 5.85 percent of their earnings in social security taxes. When the typical family of four has earnings of over $6,900 a year it must begin to pay federal income taxes. Many states have income taxes that start at fairly low levels of income. And then, of course, there are a number of cities with income taxes, especially those with high welfare populations like New York City. These tax rates are combined with the tax rates resulting from welfare reduction, and they all apply at the critical range of income where a person is just beginning to feel self-sufficient. The tax rates are not directly additive, because welfare programs such as AFDC and food stamps compute benefits due on net earnings after income taxes have been deducted.

There is little that can be done about the problem. The elimination of all federal, state, and local taxes up to, say, $10,000 of annual income would be prohibitively expensive in terms of lost tax revenues, for—to be fair—taxes for everyone earning income within that range, including those not on welfare, would have to be eliminated.

There are only two ways to eliminate the high tax rates implicit in our current array of welfare programs. One is to sharply reduce the basic welfare payment; the other is to hold the basic payment where it is and simply lower the rate at which welfare benefits are reduced as income rises. There are serious problems with both alternatives. The first, lowering welfare payments, is politically impossible today. The second, lowering the welfare reduction rate, would increase the cost of welfare to taxpayers by such phenomenal sums—tens of billions of dollars a year—that it has no better chance of becoming a political reality than the first.

For better or worse, high marginal tax rates are a necessary and enduring part of our current welfare system. The policymakers had no other choice. As the extent and level of welfare escalated rapidly during the last decade, they were required to keep the marginal rate of taxation on welfare and public assistance very high in order to avoid massive increases in the number of Americans eligible for welfare and the spectacular cost that would have followed.

But the acceptance of these high, incentive-destroying tax rates has had an unforeseen cost. With scarcely anyone noticing it, the poor people in this country have been deeply entangled in a welfare system that is rapidly strangling any incentive they may have had to help themselves and their families by working to increase their incomes.

Few deny the depressant effect high marginal tax rates have on the incentive to work and earn more money. Partly in recognition of this fact, the top federal tax rate on earned personal service income was recently lowered from 70 to 50 percent. But as tax disincentives were being reduced for the nonpoor, our welfare programs moved in the opposite direction. In the headlong rush to help poor people, we have created a situation where the poor of America are subjected to significantly higher rates of taxation than the nonpoor.

We have, in ironic consequence of our massive effort to eradicate poverty from the land, virtually destroyed any financial incentive that the poor may have had to improve their economic condition. We have, in effect, created a *poverty wall* with our tax and welfare system that, while assuring poor people a substantial subsistence level of income, also destroys their incentive to work and sentences them to a life of dependency on the government dole. It may not be too long before those on welfare become a truly separate, dependent caste of people in our society, if they have not become so already.

The gross disparity between the tax disincentives faced by welfare recipients and by working people not on welfare is shown graphically in Figure 1.

The working head of a typical family of four pays three major taxes on earned income—social security tax, state income tax, and federal income tax. The social security tax in 1976 was 5.85 percent on all earned income up to $16,500 a year. State income taxes vary widely across the country. Taking California as an example, the state income tax, after allowing for deductions and credits, begins at $10,000 and gradually increases until it peaks at its maximum rate of 11 percent at $33,000.[10] There are also local income taxes in many cities across the country, but they have been disregarded in this example. The last and most important tax is the federal tax on income. After accounting for deductions, exemptions, and normal credits, the federal marginal income tax rate begins at 14 percent for earnings over $6,100 and mounts steadily until it reaches its maximum of 50 percent at $49,800.

The heavy solid line in Figure 1 represents the total marginal tax rate that a typical family of four pays on wages and salaries

FIGURE 1

MARGINAL TAX RATES FOR WELFARE RECIPIENTS
AND FOR WAGE EARNERS

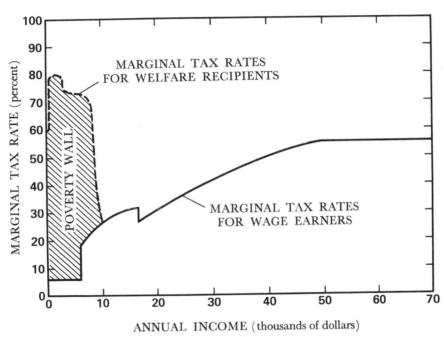

ANNUAL INCOME (thousands of dollars)

as a result of all three of these taxes—social security tax, state income tax, and federal income tax. The total marginal tax rate attributable to the combination of these three taxes in 1976 begins at a little below 6 percent, increases to over 19 percent at $6,100 of income, then climbs steadily to almost 32 percent at $16,500. At this point it drops by 5.85 percent because of the income limitation on the social security tax. Then it begins to climb once again until it peaks at 61 percent for $49,800 of annual income. For any additional income earned over and above $49,800, the marginal rate remains constant at 61 percent.

Thus, the line in Figure 1 labeled "marginal tax rates for wage earners" traces out the course of the total effective marginal tax rate paid on earned income. The distribution of the number of people paying these various rates is highly skewed toward the low end of the income scale. Of all the people who worked and paid federal income taxes in 1973, less than half (46 percent) had marginal tax rates on the highest part of their income that were over 20 percent. Only one-half of one percent had marginal tax rates that exceeded 50 percent. Of course, there are other kinds of income than personal service income on which federal income tax rates of up to 70 percent are paid. However, less than one-tenth of one percent of all taxpayers paid the maximum rate of 70 percent in 1973.[11]

The tax burden facing the poor person on welfare is dramatically different. There is a poverty wall confronting the poor of America that effectively prevents many from ever leaving that status. Perhaps even sadder, it may even take away the hope of doing so.

The nature of the poverty wall that confronts any particular welfare family is determined largely by where the family lives and the number of welfare programs it benefits from. The various combinations possible are almost endless, but a typical case can effectively illustrate the order of magnitude of the marginal income tax rates these families are subject to when welfare benefits are reduced because of increased family income. One such example was recently constructed by Henry Aaron of the Brookings Institution to show the nature of the tax rates faced by an AFDC family of four, who also received medicaid benefits, food stamps, and housing assistance.[12]

As Aaron points out, "The marginal tax rates are high and capricious. On all earnings from $576 to $8,390 per year, the family eligible solely for AFDC and medicaid faces a tax rate of 67 percent. Eligibility for food stamps and housing assistance raises the tax rate as high as 80 percent, and brings it to 73 percent over the income range from $4,000 to $8,300. When earnings reach $8,390, the family is removed from the welfare rolls and at that instant loses $1,000 medicaid benefits and, if eligible, a $288 food stamp bonus."[13]

The dotted line in Figure 1 traces out the course of the

effective marginal tax rates that face a typical welfare family thinking either about going to work or about trying to increase its earnings. While the nature of the marginal tax rates will vary widely from family to family, depending on the welfare programs they receive benefits from, the relative order of magnitude of the tax rates they face compared to nonwelfare workers is clearly shown. Up to earnings of approximately $8,400 a year, welfare recipients typically face effective marginal tax rates that are far, far higher than those faced by the typical working family, in that same range, not receiving welfare. In fact, the tax rates are substantially higher than for all workers not on welfare, regardless of income. It is only when the earned income of welfare recipients reaches about $10,000 a year that they achieve the same tax status as other working Americans.

Today in the United States anyone on welfare trying to move up the income ladder must first surmount a tax rate obstacle that far surpasses anything that workers not on welfare have to contend with. It is hard to disagree with the recent observation of Alair Townsend and James Storey: "It seems to us to be socially destructive to apply a 100 percent or nearly 100 percent tax rate to the very bottom of the income distribution. Such a policy in effect says that the work efforts of recipients are meaningless."[14]

There is one additional tax rate complication that should be noted here. In 1975 an *earned income credit* was added to the federal income tax code. Its basic purpose was to increase the financial incentive to work for the heads of low-income families by giving them money as a reward for working. Past changes in the deductions, exemptions, and credits of the federal income tax have given massive financial relief to poor families by eliminating all federal taxes on incomes of less than $6,100 a year. This new, special "credit" eliminated federal taxes on all incomes up to $6,900 and added a new twist.

The earned income credit applies only to earnings up to $8,000 a year. A family with no income receives no "credit." But, beginning with the first dollar earned, a family gets an earned income credit equal to 10 percent of all earnings up to $4,000 a year. If earnings are $1,000, the "credit" is $100; the maximum "credit" is $400 for earnings of $4,000. Because there are no federal income taxes to be paid within that income range, the "credit" is translated into a federal payment. If the family earnings are $1,000, and they file a federal tax return, the federal government will mail them a check for $100. If their earnings are $4,000, the check will be for $400. For earnings between $4,000 and $8,000 the amount of the earned income credit declines. For earnings of $5,000 the "credit" is reduced to $300; for earnings of $6,000 it is $200; for earnings of $7,000 it is $100; and at $8,000 the "credit" is phased out completely.

The earned income credit is, in effect, a separate welfare program run through the Internal Revenue Service. The federal government now pays low-income workers a bonus of 10 percent on all earnings up to $4,000, and then decreases the size of the bonus by 10 percent as earnings increase to $8,000. In 1976, "$1.3 billion was transferred to 6.3 million low-income tax units" through this so-called tax credit.[15]

The effect of the earned income credit on the total marginal tax rates portrayed in Figure 1 is twofold. The marginal rates shown there are *decreased* by 10 percentage points—for both welfare recipients and wage earners—over the range of income from zero to $4,000. But at the same time the marginal tax rates are *increased* by 10 percentage points—again for both welfare recipients and wage earners—over the range of income from $4,000 to $8,000. The net result is that marginal tax rates are reduced for all those earning less than $4,000 and increased for those earning between $4,000 and $8,000, whether they are on welfare or not. The difference between the marginal tax rates facing welfare recipients and those facing those not on welfare remains the same, so that a person on welfare still faces a much larger marginal tax rate on earnings than someone who is not on welfare.

One notable result of the earned income credit is a *negative* total marginal income tax rate of 4.15 percent on all earned income of less than $4,000 a year. But once the family passes the magic $4,000 level, the marginal tax rate leaps dramatically by 20 percent to just under a "positive" 16 percent. The abrupt 20 percent increase at the $4,000 income level arises from the switch in the character of the earned income credit at $4,000. Up to $4,000 of income the federal government *adds* $100 for every additional $1,000 earned, but between $4,000 and $8,000 it *subtracts* $100 for every $1,000 earned, and this causes the sudden 20 percentage point increase. At $6,100 of income the normal federal income tax comes into play, and the result is an additional sharp increase—between $6,000 and $7,000 the total marginal income tax rate is 29.2 percent, between $7,000 and $8,000 it is 31.8 percent.[16]

The earnings range from $4,000 to $8,000 is a very critical one in terms of work incentives. For many people it is here that the struggle to escape from poverty and welfare will take place. Unfortunately, the earned income credit has instituted a potentially destructive barrier that low-income workers must now deal with. Over a $2,000 span of income, the marginal income tax rate facing them increases over 33 percentage points—from a negative 4.15 percent to a positive 29.2 percent. Instead of facing the kind of gradually rising marginal tax rate shown in Figure 1, many low-income workers, because of the earned income credit, must now cope with an abruptly steep "tax wall" that is similar to the one facing their more unfortunate brothers and sisters on welfare.

The earned income credit will probably not become a permanent part of the federal income tax, but until it is removed it will severely distort the financial incentive effects of the federal income tax. When the effects of the earned income credit are combined with the effects of social security taxes and state income taxes, the path of the total marginal tax rate facing a taxpayer is wondrous to behold, resembling the profile of a roller coaster far more than a sober financial chart. Appendix B of this book contains a more detailed discussion of the marginal income tax rates facing a typical American family.

The exact number of people on welfare facing high effective marginal tax rates is not precisely known because we do not have statistics that reflect program overlaps in the welfare system. It has been estimated that the true size of the welfare rolls is somewhere between 25 and 30 million.[17] This estimate was made in 1972, so the actual number may now be closer to the high end of the estimate, 30 million. If we assume that 30 million people receive some form of income-tested welfare, perhaps as many as two-thirds, or 20 million, of them are subject to the incentive-destroying tax rates shown in Figure 1.

Thus, while poverty was being virtually eliminated during the last decade, a *poverty wall* of high taxation was erected in front of millions of Americans. As more and more reliance was placed on using financial incentives to work to induce people to leave the welfare rolls, government welfare policies themselves raised an effective psychological barrier to their gainful employment. As one staff study prepared for the Joint Economic Committee's study of welfare commented, "In contrast to the rhetoric of Government officials exhorting recipients to work for their income, the Government itself imposes the largest barrier to work."[18]

In effect we have created a new caste of Americans—perhaps as much as one-tenth of this nation—a caste of people free from basic wants but almost totally dependent on the State, with little hope or prospects of breaking free. Perhaps we should call them the Dependent Americans.

CITATIONS—CHAPTER II

1 U.S., Congress, Joint Economic Committee, Subcommittee on Fiscal Policy, press release, Washington, D.C., December 22, 1972.

2 Ibid. (Italics added.)

3 Irene Lurie (editor), *Integrating Income Maintenance Programs* (New York Academic Press, 1975), page 7.

4 U.S., Congress, Joint Economic Committee, Subcommittee on Fiscal Policy, *Income Security for Americans: Recommendations of the Public Welfare Study* (Washington, D.C., December 5, 1974), page 77.

5 Henry J. Aaron, "Alternative Ways to Increase Work Effort under Income Maintenance Systems," in Lurie, *Integrating Income Maintenance Programs*, pages 161–162.

6 U.S., Congress, Joint Economic Committee, Subcommittee on Fiscal Policy, *Public Welfare and Work Incentives: Theory and Practice*, prepared by Vee Burke and Alair A. Townsend, Studies in Public Welfare, Paper No. 14 (Washington, D.C., April 15, 1974), page 31.

7 Ibid., page 32.

8 Ibid.

9 Edward C. Banfield, *The Unheavenly City: The Nature and Future of Our Urban Crisis* (Boston: Little, Brown and Company, 1970), page 122.

10 U.S., Department of the Treasury, Internal Revenue Service, 1976 Federal Income Tax Forms, page 29, schedule Y; State of California, 1976 Individual Tax [forms], page 4.

11 U.S., Department of the Treasury, Internal Revenue Service, "Individual Income Tax Returns," in *Statistics of Income—1973* (Washington, D.C., 1976), page 111, Table 3.14.

12 Henry J. Aaron, *Why Is Welfare So Hard to Reform?* (Washington, D.C.: The Brookings Institution, 1973), pages 32–35.

13 Ibid., pages 33–34.

14 Alair A. Townsend and James R. Storey, "Comments," in Joseph A. Pechman and P. Michael Timpane (editors), *Work Incentives and Income Guarantees: The New Jersey Negative Income Tax Experi-*

ment (Washington, D.C.: The Brookings Institution, 1975), page 202.

15   U.S., Congress, Congressional Budget Office, *Welfare Reform: Issues, Objectives, and Approaches* (Washington, D.C., July 1977), page 15.

16   Martin Anderson, "The Roller-Coaster Income Tax," *The Public Interest*, Number 50 (Winter 1978), pages 17–28.

17   U.S., Congress, Joint Economic Committee, Subcommittee on Fiscal Policy, *Public Income Transfer Programs: The Incidence of Multiple Benefits and the Issues Raised by Their Receipt*, prepared by James R. Storey, Studies in Public Welfare, Paper No. 1 (Washington, D.C., April 19, 1972), page 4.

18   U.S., Congress, Joint Economic Committee, Subcommittee on Fiscal Policy, *Income Transfer Programs: How They Tax the Poor*, prepared by Robert I. Lerman, Studies in Public Welfare, Paper No. 4 (Washington, D.C., December 22, 1972), page vi.

III

THE PUBLIC'S OPINION OF WELFARE

> As force is always on the side of the governed, the
> governors have nothing to support them but opinion.
> It is, therefore, on opinion only that government is
> founded; and this maxim extends to the most des-
> potic and most military governments, as well as to
> the most free and the most popular.
>
> David Hume, 1741

*Third Thesis: The overwhelming majority of Ameri-
cans favor government welfare programs for those who
cannot care for themselves, while at the same time favoring large cuts in welfare spending because of their strong
belief that many welfare recipients are cheating. A guaranteed income is flatly opposed by a two-to-one margin.
Although welfare is generally seen to be a serious problem, it holds very low priority with the public relative to
other problems facing the country.*

The attitude of the American people toward welfare for the poor
is of major importance in the formulation of any national welfare
policy. It is highly unlikely that any significant welfare program
changes can be accomplished if a major part of the American
electorate is strongly opposed. Conversely, it is highly likely that
proposed changes in our welfare system that are compatible with
the beliefs of the public can be made with relative ease. The
American political system, though surely not perfect, is a highly

efficient instrument for implementing the will of the public. From time to time, local and state governments, and the federal government, may institute policies that run counter to deeply held public beliefs. In the short run they may succeed, but over a period of time the public will is inescapable. Either public opinion will change, or the public will change their elected representatives and the policies they support.

Unfortunately, there is no comprehensive, systematic body of information on American attitudes toward poverty and the welfare programs that deal with it. But there have been a number of country-wide, in-depth polls taken during the last decade or so that tell us a considerable amount. Looked at individually, the polls sometimes appear to give ambivalent results. When viewed together, a reasonably comprehensive picture of how the American public feels—both about the problem of poverty and about how to handle it—begins to emerge with a surprising degree of clarity.

The overwhelming majority of Americans have a benevolent and generous attitude toward poor people. In a national Harris survey taken in 1976, fully 94 percent of the public agreed with the view that "it is not right to let people who need welfare go hungry." Only 4 percent disagreed. Seventy-four percent of the people interviewed in the same survey also agreed that "many women whose husbands have left them with several children have no choice but to go on welfare."[1] In an earlier national survey in 1969, the public agreed, 45 percent to 43 percent, that "one of the main troubles with welfare is that it doesn't give people enough money to get along on."[2] The American people have a long record of generosity toward the unfortunate, a generosity that has been demonstrated concretely over the years through private charities, government welfare programs, and foreign aid programs throughout the world.

A number of recent polls also reveal what at first glance appears to be a curious contradiction. By substantial margins these polls show the American public in favor of cutting government spending on welfare programs. In 1974 a national poll conducted by the National Opinion Research Center revealed that 42 percent of the public thought we were spending too much on welfare; 32 percent said it "was about right," and only 22 percent thought we weren't spending enough.[3] That same year a statewide poll in Texas showed people a list of government programs and services and asked, "What programs or services, if any, on this list do you think should be reduced or eliminated from the federal budget?" Welfare was picked by 41 percent of the Texans.[4]

A national Roper poll taken in 1973 showed that 48 percent of Americans thought we were spending too much money on welfare. The same question was repeated in 1974 and 49 percent agreed; only 19 percent thought we were spending too little. There were just two other program areas that were higher on the public's shopping list of government programs to reduce spending on—space exploration and foreign aid.[5] A 1976 statewide poll in Missouri presented a list of government programs and asked, "In which of the following areas, if any, would you be willing to see federal spending cut?" Welfare was the program area most frequently mentioned, with 54 percent of Missourians in favor of cutting welfare spending.[6]

The most recent national poll of the public's attitude toward government spending on welfare, conducted by Harris in 1976, asked the following question: "How serious a loss do you feel it would be if the federal government cut back its programs in welfare by one third of what it is today—a very serious loss, a moderate loss, or hardly a loss at all?" A surprising 58 percent replied that they felt it would be only a "moderate loss" or "hardly a loss at all," while only 38 percent considered it a "very serious loss."[7]

A reduction in federal welfare expenditures by one-third can only be described as a savage cut, and when 58 percent of the public is not seriously bothered by such a prospect it raises some serious questions. How can the great majority of Americans favor the idea of a reasonably high level of welfare support for poor people while simultaneously approving of massive cuts in welfare spending? Are they that cynical? Are they that ignorant of the connection between welfare benefits and federal expenditures? Both, of course, are possible and may account to some extent for the apparent discrepancy; but there is another hypothesis that is more likely and, if true, provides a logical explanation for the apparent ambivalence.

Let us assume those polled approve government welfare spending for people they feel deserve it, those who cannot adequately care for themselves, but they do not approve welfare for those who they feel can take care of themselves if they make an effort. If they also believe that there are many of the latter on the welfare rolls today, it would be logically consistent to support the general idea of government welfare for people who need help and at the same time to call for an overall reduction in welfare spending, which would necessarily imply eliminating the non-needy from the welfare rolls.

Three nationwide opinion polls, one taken in late 1964, one in 1969, and one in 1976, produced results consistent with this explanation. In 1964 the national Gallup poll asked the following question about welfare: "What proportion of persons do you think are on relief for *dishonest* reasons—most, some, hardly any, or none?" Seven percent answered "most," while 61 percent more said "some." By 1969 the number of people in the United States who felt that many on welfare were abusing the system had grown spectacularly. In a 1969 nationwide poll investigating American attitudes toward poverty and the poor, fully 84 percent of the public agreed with the statement that "there are too many people receiving welfare money who should be working." Seventy-one percent agreed that "many people getting welfare are not honest about their need." And in 1976 the national Harris survey found that the public's suspicions of welfare cheating had climbed even higher. Eighty-nine percent agreed that "too many people on welfare cheat by getting money they are not entitled to"; and 64 percent said that the "criteria for getting on welfare are not tough enough."[8]

Summarizing the results of a 1976 Harris poll, *Current Opinion* commented, "Fundamentally, people are ambivalent about welfare. They have compassion for the less privileged, but they are also disturbed by the operation of the welfare system."[9] The seemingly ambivalent attitude of Americans toward welfare is understandable if we keep two things clearly separate. First, the overwhelming majority of Americans, perhaps well over 90 percent, have no basic quarrel with government welfare programs for poor people. Second, well over 85 percent of Americans also believe that *many* people now receiving welfare are cheating, getting money or services they are not entitled to, and could be working.

The public favors help for people who cannot help themselves, but not for those who can. Americans apparently feel that government could both increase aid to the truly poor *and* cut overall welfare spending—if welfare program administrators would get rid of dishonest welfare recipients. This seems to be what they have in mind when they think of welfare "reform."

The public also has decided views about proposed radical changes in our welfare system. A number of national and state polls taken since 1965 show Americans consistently and overwhelmingly rejecting the idea of guaranteeing everyone an income. A national Gallup poll taken in 1965 showed that 67 percent of the country was opposed to a guaranteed income. In two later national Gallup polls taken in 1968, the percentage of those opposed was 58 percent and 62 percent. In a national Opinion Research poll in 1969, 61 percent were opposed; a follow-up survey on this poll in 1972 showed 50 percent opposed. A 1976 statewide poll in Iowa disclosed that 63 percent of Iowans were against a guaranteed income. Since 1965, on average, the polls show that approximately 60 percent of Americans oppose a guaranteed income, 30 percent favor it, and 10 percent have no opinion.

Public opinion on the question of a guaranteed income varies significantly by income and race. In the 1968 Gallup poll 72 percent of those with incomes of $10,000 and over opposed the guaranteed income; for those with incomes between $7,000 and $9,999 the figure was 63 percent; between $5,000 and $6,999 it was 62 percent; between $3,000 and $4,999 it was 54 percent; and even those with incomes under $3,000 opposed a guaranteed income—with 44 percent opposed and 43 percent in favor. Whites opposed a guaranteed income by a more than two-to-one margin—65 percent to 29 percent. In dramatic contrast, non-whites favored a guaranteed income by more than a four-to-one margin—72 percent to 18 percent.

The polls showing that the American public rejects the idea of a guaranteed income by a two-to-one margin are not surprising in light of other polls that underscore the strong value Americans place on work and self-reliance. In 1974 a national poll of young people between the ages of fourteen and twenty-five showed that 74 percent of them agreed that "each individual should be responsible for his own financial well-being."[10] In 1975 a national Harris poll presented a list of factors that some people thought made America great and asked, for each factor, whether or not the public agreed; 87 percent agreed that "hard-working people" were a major factor in making America great.[11] As Alex Inkeles, professor of education and sociology at Stanford University and a senior fellow of the Hoover Institution, recently pointed out in a talk on America's third century, "Instead of God or luck, the great majority of Americans still believe that it is a person's own efforts which account for success or failure in life."[12]

How strongly Americans hold these attitudes on poverty and welfare is difficult to assess. When asked directly in a national Harris survey in 1976 whether they felt "the problem of welfare in this country is very serious, only somewhat serious, or hardly serious at all," 80 percent replied the problem was "very serious." There is no way to tell precisely what they meant by that answer. Some may have been indicating a concern with welfare abuse; others may have been indicating a desire for higher welfare payments, or for radical change, such as the institution of a guaranteed income. However, in view of the public's attitude toward welfare spending, welfare cheating, and a guaranteed income, it seems reasonable to assume that far more were concerned with welfare abuse than with welfare payments that are too low or the absence of a guaranteed income.

When the public was asked the more general, open-ended question "What do you think is the most important problem facing this country today?" poverty received very low priority as compared with other problems of concern to the general public. In the early 1970s the Gallup poll, which periodically asked this question, indicated that 4 or 5 percent of the public felt that poverty and welfare were, in their judgment, the most important problems facing this country, some of them indicating a concern for poor people, others a concern for welfare abuse. By 1974 the perception of poverty and welfare as major national problems had faded to the point where they were dropped from Gallup's summary list of important problems named by the public.

In late 1976 the Gallup poll showed that Americans thought the most important problems then facing the country were the high cost of living (47%), unemployment (31%), dissatisfaction with government (6%), crime (6%), foreign affairs (5%), excessive government spending on social programs (4%), and moral decline (3%).[13]

Welfare and poverty were not on the list.

CITATIONS—CHAPTER III

1   The Harris Survey, February 1976.
2   Opinion Research Corporation poll, Spring 1969; Joe R. Feagin, "Poverty," *Psychology Today*, November 1972, page 107.
3   National Opinion Research Center, University of Chicago, March 1974.
4   The Texas Poll, September 1974.

5 The Roper Organization, Inc., December 1973; December 1974.

6 Navaro Opinion Research, The Missouri Poll, October 1975.

7 The Harris Survey, 1976.

8 The Gallup Poll, November 1964; Opinion Research Corporation Poll, Spring 1969; Feagin, "Poverty," page 107; The Harris Survey, February 1976.

9 *Current Opinion* (Roper Public Opinion Research Center), Volume IV (July 1976), page 65.

10 Gilbert Youth Research poll, March 1974.

11 The Harris Survey, October 1975.

12 Alex Inkeles, "Continuity and Change in the American National Character" (Lecture sponsored by the Hoover Institution, Stanford University, April 12, 1977).

13 The Gallup Poll, October 1976.

IV

THE CLAMOR FOR REFORM

> With most men reform is a trade—with
> others an honest yet lucrative trade—
> with some a swindling trade. Reform
> for its own sake seldom thrives.
>
> John Quincy Adams, 1837

Fourth Thesis: *The clamor for radical welfare reform comes essentially from a small group of committed ideologues who want to institute a guaranteed income under the guise of welfare reform.*

As the number of welfare programs multiplied and the number of people receiving welfare checks and benefits grew, as the amount of the welfare payments increased, as the number of people living in poverty dropped precipitously, one might have reasonably expected to hear a round of cheers for this unprecedented attack on poverty. But this did not happen. The voices of praise were silent. Instead the welfare system was denounced by virtually all those who cared enough about what was going on to comment and write about it. The more money that was transferred from the taxpayers to those without incomes, the more the criticism grew.

Books were written about welfare reform. President Johnson made the war on poverty his major domestic thrust. President Nixon proposed a "Family Assistance Plan" as his domestic policy centerpiece. George McGovern tried to get his campaign moving in 1972 by proposing $1,000 a year for everyone. Hundreds of academic studies poured forth. President Ford tried to develop a plan in 1974, and President Carter, on taking office in 1977, quickly made welfare reform one of his first domestic priorities.

Yet in spite of the powerful pressures for welfare reform, the wonderfully detailed plans that were put forth, and the support of the media, little was accomplished in the way of major, substantial change. The welfare system grew and prospered along traditional lines, almost immune to the mounting chorus of criticism. It is surprising that no radical change took place and that so little credit was given to the system for what it was accomplishing. Perhaps the answer to this anomaly lies in the nature of the several philosophical approaches to welfare that exist in this country, and in the relative power of the groups that hold these views.

There are essentially three philosophical approaches to welfare in the United States. The first is the **private charity** approach. Holders of this view maintain that the State has no business appropriating other people's money to give to those deemed poor. They believe that private charitable organizations and acts of private giving could do the job effectively and with a greater sense of personal caring than the government, and that these private efforts would increase to the extent that government diminished its role in welfare. In today's society the private charity view is held seriously by only a small percentage of the population,* and, except for the very important supplemental role of private charity, has little effect on government policy.

A second philosophical view, the **needy-only** approach, holds that persons who, through no fault of their own, are unable to care for themselves or their families should receive help from the government. The role of government is seen as a limited one.

---

* A national Gallup poll in 1965 asked the public what their "over-all feelings about welfare and relief programs" were. Forty-three percent replied "favorable," 45 percent had "mixed feelings," 6 percent had no opinion; and only 6 percent said they would "do away with the programs."

Welfare payments should go only to needy people, and the amount of that payment should be in proportion to their need. If someone is able to work, welfare should be denied. People on the welfare rolls should be helped and encouraged to become self-sufficient by whatever reasonable means are available and effective. Being on welfare is viewed as a state of dependency, an acknowledgment that one is not able to take care of oneself without help from others.

The needy-only approach to welfare is taken by the over-whelming majority of Americans. It has been the traditional approach to welfare in this country for many years, and support for it is widespread and deep.

The third philosophical approach is a relative newcomer to the United States. Only within the last fifteen years or so has it been discussed seriously and gained support. Its premises are that everyone has a right to a basic level of income, that the govern-ment should guarantee to every citizen a level of cash income high enough for him or her to live in moderate comfort, and that no restrictions whatsoever should be placed on the use of the money. This is the **guaranteed income** approach to welfare. Some holders of this view seem to believe that people basically like to work, that they will do so whenever they are sufficiently rewarded, and that even mild incentives will encourage them to leave the welfare rolls and improve their standard of living.

At the heart of the guaranteed income approach is the prem-ise that people have a *right* to a certain level of income completely independent of their ability to earn. Under a guaranteed income there is no attempt to differentiate between those who cannot help themselves and those who can. The system automatically provides benefits to everyone. It is assumed that no stigma can be attached to those who cannot take care of themselves, as everyone would have the same minimum level of income by right. In special cases of extreme need, the basic income guarantee can be augmented. What distinguishes this philosophical view from the traditional view of welfare in the United States is its assumption of starting with a base income guarantee for everyone, and then building up and out from that base.

While these three approaches to welfare exist side by side, only two of them—the needy-only approach and the guaranteed income approach—are serious contenders for the hearts and minds of welfare policymakers. Private charity is almost universally approved, but few support this approach as the total answer to poverty. One can make a logical, theoretical case for the private charity approach, but it is not politically viable at this time. Almost all Americans today believe that there is a clear role for the government to play in providing cash and services to the poor.

The clamor for welfare reform and the controversy surrounding it stem largely from a deep conflict in the philosophical views of the two remaining groups. The first group—supporting the needy-only approach to welfare—contains the large majority of the American people. They believe there is a clear role for government to play in providing cash benefits and services to the poor, especially to the blind, the disabled, and the aged, but they reject the concept of a guaranteed income by large margins in poll after poll. Their views on welfare, however, are passive. They don't demonstrate; they don't study the welfare system; they don't write or speak about it. Their power lies in their votes, at the polls. They will tolerate and even enthusiastically support a political candidate who pledges to improve welfare—who pledges to see that the really needy get adequate help and to end the welfare abuse and fraud they suspect permeates the entire welfare system.

But they will turn on the candidate who proposes to guarantee an annual income, with their money, to someone who is capable of working and doesn't feel like it. They have a realistic, traditional view of life. They believe there are many people, perhaps even themselves, who, if guaranteed an income, would simply cease working and loaf. And they do not understand, and probably never will understand, why they should work to support someone who prefers not to work.

The advocates of a guaranteed income are different. The

number of advocates and supporters of this philosophical approach is small, but as a group they are very influential. They come from the universities, the welfare agencies that administer the programs, the media, and the government. Some of them are welfare recipients. What they lack in the raw political power of votes, they make up for with the effectiveness and persistence of their advocacy. They study the welfare system, they develop the programs and draft the legislation, they administer the programs and then they criticize them. They write and speak and make their views known, both to the media and to policymakers. On occasion they have been known to demonstrate.

Those who believe in a guaranteed income have been gaining in numbers and in influence over the last fifteen years. They are active and dedicated, and tenaciously pursue the cause they espouse. As an example of the kind of effort that can be mounted, "some 1,300 economists at almost 150 institutions signed a petition to the Congress in 1968 urging adoption of 'a national system of income guarantees and supplements.' "[1]

Almost without exception, the calls for sweeping "welfare reform" over the past fifteen years have come from the supporters of some form of a guaranteed income. What they consider to be reform, however, differs markedly from what the holders of the needy-only approach consider to be reform. The advocates of a guaranteed income want to radically change the current welfare system from welfare for the needy only to a guaranteed income for all. On the other hand, almost everyone else sees welfare reform as something that will ensure that those who need help get help, as something that will remove from the welfare rolls those who are defrauding the system, and will make the programs more efficient and less costly to the taxpayers.

So far the calls for radical welfare reform have been unsuccessful. What appears to be a welfare reform stalemate results primarily from the conflict between what an elite group of welfare intellectuals wants and what the general public wants. The welfare intellectuals have shrewdly highlighted the weak parts of the current welfare system, largely ignoring the vast increase in coverage and in the level of welfare payments. They have proposed reform plans to correct the unveiled abuses and inequities, plans that have as their primary purpose the institution of the principle of a guaranteed income.

The key to the establishment of a guaranteed income in this country is the elimination of any work requirement from our welfare programs. All welfare in the United States is conditioned by the requirement that if people can work, they should work; that they must demonstrate a need for welfare by establishing that they cannot take care of themselves.

This enrages the supporters of a guaranteed income and sometimes leads to irrational polemics on their part. As Henry Aaron once observed, "Critics allege that a work requirement would create a pool of workers forced by the threat of starvation to take any job, however repulsive, at any wage, however low . . . that a work requirement will enslave the poor by requiring that they do the bidding of the authorities to get food for their children."[2]

In view of the government's welfare record over the last decade, this kind of extreme statement probably should not be taken too seriously. But those who want a guaranteed income do understand very clearly the significance of a work requirement, as Aaron explains further: "Many critics oppose a work requirement, also, from a belief that the government of a country as wealthy as the United States is morally obliged to prevent starvation or gross poverty and that cash assistance should be available to the poor as a matter of right."[3]

Perhaps the father of the guaranteed income concept in the United States is Robert Theobald, who made a pellucidly explicit case for it in 1965 in his book *The Guaranteed Income*. In summing up his position he asserts, *"We will need to adopt the concept of an absolute constitutional right to an income. This would guarantee to every citizen of the United States, and to every person who has resided within the United States for a period of five con-*

secutive years, the right to an income from the federal govern-
ment sufficient to enable him to live with dignity. No government
agency, judicial body, or other organization whatsoever should
have the power to suspend or limit any payment assured by these
guarantees."[4]

A guaranteed income was at the heart of President Nixon's unsuccessful Family Assistance Plan. Daniel Patrick Moynihan, the man most responsible for Nixon's adoption of the plan, has, with the candor so typical of him, made it clear what the purpose of his advocacy was: "The main thrust of the legislation was to establish a guaranteed income for the working poor. To concentrate on the welfare aspects of the proposal could only divert attention from its most significant feature."[5]

There are several rationales behind radical welfare reform plans that embody the principle of a guaranteed income. To some guaranteed income advocates the very idea of being dependent is repugnant. The main thrusts of their critiques of welfare seldom charge that the system does not provide enough money, or that some classes of poor people unable to care for themselves are ineligible to receive it. What they object to are the conditions that our society places on those who receive welfare benefits.

Of course, anyone who receives welfare from the government is, by that fact, dependent upon the government for all or part of his subsistence. But this welfare dependency is considered by some to be an unjust stigma to impose on the poor. They seem to feel inordinately guilty about a welfare system that requires someone to acknowledge dependency by receiving benefits from the State.

Moynihan opens his book on President Nixon's radical welfare reform plan with a discussion of welfare dependency: "The issue of welfare is the issue of dependency. It is different from poverty. . . . Being poor is often associated with considerable personal qualities; being dependent rarely so. This is not to say that dependent people are not brave, resourceful, admirable, but simply that their situation is never enviable, and rarely admired. It is an incomplete state in life: normal in the child, abnormal in the adult. . . . Concern for the poor, however, does not necessarily or even commonly extend to those who are dependent, that is to say those who own nothing and earn nothing and depend on society for their livelihood. When such persons are very young or very old, allowances are made. But when they are of the age when other persons work to earn their way and, further, if they are dependent during periods when work is to be had, dependency becomes a stigma."[6] Later, commenting on the attitudes of others in the Nixon Administration who were influential in pushing radical welfare reform, he explains, "Finch, Shultz, Veneman, Nathan, myself—all those principally involved, and first of all the President—looked on welfare dependency as a woeful condition which society must minimize."*[7]

It is true that the issue of dependency can be masked by a guaranteed income. For if we abolished dependency as a condition for receiving welfare payments and services, and everyone received them, there would no longer by any need to distinguish between those who need help and those who do not. Someone fully capable of earning a decent living could decide to stop working and still receive a guaranteed annual income.

But the fact of dependency would remain. Indeed, it would spread, for all who received the guarantee would be dependent upon the government. And it just might be that the stigma of taking one's "guarantee" would soon far exceed the stigma of being on welfare.

To others the guaranteed income is the answer to a lifelong dream of a society in which all have equal incomes. The distribution of income in the United States is a source of great fascination to many welfare intellectuals, and to many other intellectuals as

---

* At the time Robert Finch was Secretary of HEW, George Shultz was Secretary of Labor, John Veneman was Undersecretary of HEW, Richard Nathan was Assistant Director of the Bureau of the Budget for human resource programs, and Daniel Patrick Moynihan was Assistant to the President for Urban Affairs.

well. Any movement toward greater equalization is generally seen as good, any income disparity among individuals as bad. Some would go so far as to suggest that our society would be better off even if all incomes had to be lowered to achieve a greater equality of income.

Alice Rivlin, in the Richard T. Ely lecture at the annual meeting of the American Economic Association in December 1974, addressed the role that economists could play in the growing public debate over income redistribution policy. After predicting an increase in "public awareness and political concern with inequality," she focused on her central theme: "The pay-dirt question, of course, is what policies might change the distribution of income—presumably in the direction of greater equality, since no one is likely to advocate less equality as an explicit objective. . . . If the new eclecticism among economists means, among other things, a new willingness to work hard on the details and possible limitations of policy proposals, it may presage . . . some real, albeit incremental, movement in the direction of a more equal income distribution."[8]

To others the ideals of a guaranteed income seems to have an almost wistful, childlike appeal—the desire to be free from the constraints of reality, to soar off into a dream land of unlimited plenty where all one's basic needs are taken care of by someone else. It is a powerful yearning that runs deep in many, to somehow ensure that all people will have enough money for plenty of food, good clothes, a nice place to live, and the leisure time and resources to do what they wish.

These three desires—the end of dependency, equality of income, and freedom from the responsibility of self-support—seem to haunt and drive the welfare intellectuals. Some have confidently predicted the coming of a cybernetic revolution after which machines would do all the work of men at their bidding. But the machines have so far been somewhat recalcitrant. A touch of neo-romanticism seems to permeate the musings of the guaranteed income ideologues as they struggle to escape the reality of the world as it is, and as it is likely to remain for all of us who are here now—a world where people need help from others and by this very fact are dependent, a world of unequal income, wealth, and power, of unequal talent and beauty, a world where people will always be basically responsible for their own survival and well-being.

The greatest difficulty faced by the proponents of a guaranteed income is the fact that the vast majority of the American people don't accept the idea. Most Americans cannot understand why they should work and support others who, though capable, are not working. They feel it is morally wrong. As Henry Hazlitt once stated, "If you claim a 'right' to an income sufficient to live in dignity, whether you are willing to work or not, what you are really claiming is a right to part of somebody else's earned income. What you are asserting is that this other person has a duty to earn more than he needs or wants to live on, so that the surplus may be seized from him and turned over to you to live on. This is an absolutely immoral proposition."[9]

Any proposal that includes a right to an income necessarily implies that someone is to provide that income, and the rights of the person who is to supply that income are almost always quietly ignored. In his memoirs Arthur Krock deftly identified the basic ethical issue: "In the concept held by self-asserted political liberals of a guaranteed annual income—regardless of the conduct and personal character of its beneficiaries or their will to participate to the full measure of their capacity in the peaceful products of a democratic society—the basic rights have been denied of those who must foot the bills to set the standards by which they are contracted."[10]

As far as the American public is concerned, the idea of a guaranteed income has been crisply rejected in every known public opinion poll that has dealt with the issue. There is little popular support for the principle of a guaranteed income and a decided lack of interest in the subject. As Aaron Wildavsky and William Cavala stated in 1970, "Policies that provide unearned income run counter to widely held and deeply felt American values, such as achievement, work, and equality of opportunity. The large tax increase or drastic reallocation of public funds required to guarantee income has few supporters."[11]

While most of the support for radical welfare reform comes from the political left, a handful of prominent conservatives have also endorsed the idea. The most prominent of these is Milton Friedman, who, together with George Stigler of the University of Chicago, developed the idea of a "negative income tax" in the early 1940s. It was to be the reverse of the regular federal income tax. Instead of taking money from a worker when his earnings exceeded a certain amount of exempt income, the negative income tax would pay him when his earnings fell below this "break-even" level of income. If nothing was earned, he would receive the full amount of the guaranteed income. As his earnings increased, the guarantee would be reduced and phased out completely at the "break-even" level, after which he would have to begin to pay taxes.

Friedman originally saw his plan not so much as a full-fledged guaranteed income of the Theobald variety, but more as a plan that would alleviate poverty directly and efficiently, and that would operate "through the market, not distort the market or impede its functioning."[12] The negative income tax was spelled out in some detail in *Capitalism and Freedom* in 1962, which, fortuitously, just happened to be the time when liberal intellectuals were searching for new ways to combat poverty. Delighted with Friedman's implicit endorsement of the guaranteed income principle in the negative income tax, the political left gave a lot of attention to making maximum use of a conservative's endorsement of a guaranteed income to rebut and confound the criticism that was mounting against the idea.

The negative income tax, like so many other radical welfare reform plans that followed it, had a simplistic beauty that seduced many. But the negative income tax proposal was flawed, not in the logic of its development, but in the validity of its assumptions.

It was assumed that it would replace all other welfare programs, including social welfare programs such as social security. This was politically impossible at the time, and still is. It was assumed that the effective marginal tax rate—the rate at which the income guarantee was reduced as earnings increased—would be 50 percent. The tax rate could not be kept this low, however, without sharply increased federal spending on welfare or a general overall reduction in welfare benefits for those unable to work. Neither was politically possible, and if the tax rate were to rise well over 50 percent, as it would have had to, any financial incentive to work would be virtually destroyed for those receiving benefits.

Perhaps more important, it was apparently assumed that people would not mind endorsing a guaranteed income in principle if it was, in fact, occurring in practice. There is considerable question as to whether or not we have had a de facto guaranteed income. The law has always been clear on the point that welfare is intended only for the needy, and that if one can work, one should work. True, maladministration and fraud often led to situations where people who could work were getting welfare, but the law did not condone such cases in principle. And, even if it were true that there was a de facto guaranteed income, the American people obviously did not want to sanction it morally by incorporating it into the law.

While Friedman's negative income tax never became a reality, it did become the catalyst for many of the reform plans which followed. Friedman, who won the 1976 Nobel Prize in economics, is an eminent scholar who has made many important contributions to the field of economics and is, in addition, an adroit debater. His imprimatur on the basics of radical welfare reform and his deft arguments in favor of the concept blunted fledgling critiques and convinced many of its validity. Had it not been for Friedman's endorsement of the basic principles underlying Nixon's Family Assistance Plan (FAP) and the influence his earlier writings had on George Shultz and others in the Nixon Administration, it is unlikely that FAP would ever have left the White House. Later, when the details of FAP were spelled out, Friedman withdrew his support. But many of those he had previously convinced continued to fight on for the plan.

Support from political conservatives for radical welfare reform has come largely from a few well-known scholars and politicians, such as Milton Friedman, George Shultz, Melvin Laird, and Caspar Weinberger. It was Weinberger who, as Secretary of HEW in 1974, developed an enlarged version of FAP, called the Income Supplementation Plan, at the direction of President Ford. As far as the general conservative public is concerned, there has been little support for radical welfare reform.

The support for radical welfare reform that does exist among some conservatives seems to stem from a number of concerns that differ from those of the liberals. First, many conservatives are strongly attracted to proposals that promise to reduce direct government interference in the lives of the poor as well as the nonpoor. The vision of a single welfare plan, dispensing cash to the truly needy, without any strings attached as to how that money can be spent, is often irresistible. Second, many are convinced that until the welfare system is simplified and all its costs clearly identified it will be impossible to control, let alone reduce, our spiraling welfare expenditures. Third, there is the powerful desire that almost all people seem to have to be "for" something. Conservatives have been attacked so often for so long for being against new government programs that the prospect of being for a new program could, for some, be emotionally satisfying. And finally, conservatives feel as strongly about their fellow men as do liberals. In fact, some believe they feel more strongly. There is great appeal to the idea that they could devise a government program that would help poor people more effectively than the programs devised by their liberal political opponents.

Summing up, there are only a handful of conservatives who favor some form of a guaranteed income, usually of the more pure negative income tax variety, and they favor it not out of any deep belief that people have a right to a guaranteed income from the State, but rather out of the conviction that only such a plan can bring efficiency and equity to the disorganized welfare system they perceive, and thus aid the truly poor more effectively. The vast bulk of support for the principle of a guaranteed income, by whatever name it happens to be going by, comes from the liberals. And their support comes not so much from considerations of efficiency and effectiveness as it does from strong beliefs about economic dependency, equality of income, and the work ethic. They are often deeply committed to the ideas that incomes should be more equal, if not completely equal; that a person should not have to ask for help from government, but should be able to demand it as his right; and that a person should be able to choose whether or not to work rather than face the necessity of working.

The zeal of those who want radical welfare reform can be intense. One of them recently put it categorically, "I believe passionately that poverty . . . can and should be completely eliminated in the United States, *no matter what the cost or the obstacles.* . . . The only way to eradicate poverty is to give money to the people who need it—on no other basis and for no other reason than that they need it. . . . I believe that poverty should be eliminated simply because it should not exist."[13]

The existence of a small, though highly influential, group of people committed to radical welfare reform—sometimes called a guaranteed income, sometimes a negative income tax—has been well known in certain circles for many years. According to an HEW official cited by Professor Kenneth Bowler in his book *The Nixon Guaranteed Income Proposal*, "You have to understand that there has been a conspiracy among lower level bureaucrats in favor of a negative income tax since 1965. They are Democratic appointed officials—most of them economists—who have been pushing for a negative tax program since 1965. They organized the hearings on NIT proposals before the Joint Economic Committee in 1968. Every time there was a review of welfare during the Johnson Administration these guys would propose some form of a negative income tax program, but they could never get Johnson or Wilbur Cohen [Secretary of HEW] to go for it. What happened was that some of these guys, Bateman, Lyday, and Mahoney, stayed on for a while under Nixon and got involved in the welfare debate through Veneman."[14]

For those who are deeply committed, the goal of a guaranteed income sometimes appears to justify means that border on the disingenuous. For example, as the public's distaste for a guaranteed income became more obvious, the term was gradually dropped, until only the most zealous referred to it by name. During the time when the Family Assistance Plan was being developed and debated within the Nixon Administration, the use of the term "guaranteed income" was scrupulously avoided by supporters of the plan. Never once did that term appear in any of the working papers or analyses prepared by HEW or the staff of President Nixon's Urban Affairs Council.

When the first full draft of FAP was presented to the Urban Affairs Council on March 24, 1969, few in the room realized they were being asked to approve a full-scale guaranteed income disguised as a variant of the negative income tax. As Pat Moynihan so candidly reported later in his book, "If liberals outside the Administration could never quite come to see the dimensions and the implications of the Family Assistance Plan, conservatives within did so instantly. The March 24 meeting had scarcely begun when Martin Anderson, representing Arthur Burns, declared that the committee was being presented with a negative income tax. 'Let us call a spade a spade,' he said. 'Let us remember Oscar Wilde's conclusions,' said I, that 'anyone who would call a spade a spade should be compelled to use one.' The general impression in the room was that of two academics fussing about. FAP, as was instantly obvious to anyone familiar with the dynamics of the negative income tax equation, would provide cash income supplements for an enormous population. It could not but have profound consequences."[15]

The principle of a guaranteed income, buried in the original FAP proposal, soon became the crucial point of contention between the advocates of FAP, led by Moynihan, and the opponents of FAP, led by the Counsellor to the President, Arthur Burns. In an April 21, 1969, personal memorandum to President Nixon entitled "Investing in Human Dignity: A Study of the Welfare Problem," Burns identified the plan (which was then tentatively called the Family Security System) as a guaranteed income proposal: "The so-called Family Security System is a plan for guaranteeing incomes of people. In its technical form, it is simply a specific application of the negative income tax, as formulated by Milton Friedman. . . . We have been moving away from the concept of welfare based on disability-related deprivation and need to the concept of welfare as a matter of right."

The battle in the White House in 1969 over the principle of a guaranteed income took the form of whether or not there should be a work requirement. With a strong, clear work requirement the Family Assistance Plan would sharply expand welfare, extending payments to millions of the "working poor" who were not eligible at the time, but it would not morally sanction the idea of "something for nothing." The lack of a work requirement would put the full moral force of the administration (fairly high at that time) behind the principle of a guaranteed income.

For weeks an intense ideological struggle took place in the White House. Memoranda on welfare reform—both pro and con—piled up so high on Nixon's desk that they were claiming an inordinate amount of the President's time. Finally the controversy over a work requirement was settled. In a meeting of the Urban Affairs Council on June 13, 1969, to discuss welfare reform, President Nixon leaned across the long, wooden table in the Cabinet Room and declared, "If we move on Family Security, I feel—we all agree—that we need a strong work requirement."[16]

When Nixon later unveiled his Family Assistance Plan in a nationwide television address on August 8, 1969, he very carefully and pointedly stated, "This national floor under incomes for working or dependent families is not a 'guaranteed income.' Under the guaranteed income proposal, everyone would be assured a minimum income, regardless of how much he was capable of earning, regardless of what his need was, regardless of whether or not he was willing to work. During the Presidential campaign last year, I opposed such a plan. I oppose it now and I will continue to oppose it, and this is the reason: A guaranteed income would undermine the incentive to work; the family assistance plan that I have proposed increases the incentive to work. A guaranteed income establishes a right without any responsibilities; family assistance recognizes a need and establishes a responsibility. It provides help to those in need and, in turn, requires that those who receive help work to the extent of their capabilities. There is no reason why one person should be taxed so that another can choose to live idly."

Nixon's statement clearly reflected his long-held views on a guaranteed income—what he had said during his 1968 campaign, and what he had reaffirmed since becoming President. He was convinced that he had not proposed a guaranteed income, and after watching him on television, so was the rest of the country. That is, almost all of the rest of the country.

The advocates of the guaranteed income in the White House and at HEW blithely ignored the President's announced policy and proceeded to draft the details of FAP so that, while not a guaranteed income plan in name, it would be one in fact. And this was done in apparent disregard of the President's instructions and of what the country expected.

Moynihan, in his 1973 book, *The Politics of a Guaranteed Income*, tries to disengage himself and others from this responsibility by implying that Richard Nixon was simply being devious— which after Watergate was all too easy to believe. He asserts, "The President knew what he was doing, and by most standards would be judged to have been within his rights to guard against an irrational response based on the negative symbolism of ideas such as a 'guaranteed income.' If, as he judged, the American people were willing to support the dependent poor altogether, and to give a hand to the working poor, it was hardly his responsibility to endanger this likelihood by insisting that doing so would involve embracing the principle of a guaranteed income, which he had every reason to think the public would not be willing to do."[17]

To lock in the notion that it was Nixon who was being devious, and not the supporters of the guaranteed income, Moynihan continues, "On August 6, William Safire, in response to a mild demur about the guaranteed-income paragraph in the draft speech, explained, 'You miss Richard Nixon's main point, which is to make a radical proposal seem conservative.' "[18] Moynihan's "mild demur" was part of an intense effort to prevent Nixon from denying the principle of a guaranteed income in his television address to the nation.

I was familiar with the guaranteed income paragraphs. A few days earlier I had drafted them and they had been personally edited by Nixon and cleared by him for inclusion in the television speech. Safire knew this and in all likelihood was so busy that he simply didn't have time to argue with Moynihan. Frustrated there, Moynihan went directly to the President and reports that on the next day, August 7, Nixon told him, "I don't care a damn about the work requirement. This is the price of getting the $1,600."[19] The statement was probably the price of getting Moynihan to stop lobbying him.

The work requirement paragraph stayed in Nixon's speech.

After the television address, Nixon's welfare reform proposal —stated in broad principle——was sent to HEW to be drafted into detailed legislation. And here it experienced a somewhat subtle transformation into the de facto guaranteed income proposal Moynihan describes so eloquently in his book, and which was so decisively defeated in the United States Senate. But by that time Nixon was so publicly committed to his plan, and the working out of the legislative details was so far removed from his effective control, there was little he could do but watch. Perhaps it was a later realization that he may have been hoodwinked that caused his formerly ardent support of welfare reform to turn lukewarm.

It is somewhat ironic that the policy victory Arthur Burns thought he had won in the Cabinet Room in the White House had to await its fulfillment until Congress rejected the President's domestic policy centerpiece—just as Burns and others had expected it would.

While verifiable facts are always more pleasant to deal with, it is important to recognize and understand the motivations that always lie behind public policy recommendations. This is particularly true when a lobbying group is trying to advance legislation that is very much out of favor with the general public. To announce clearly the intent and consequences of the legislation would doom it quickly, leaving only the alternative of presenting rationalizations that may not prove to be sufficiently convincing. As Aaron Wildavsky and William Cavala wrote in 1970, "[Guaranteed] income policies are not serious subjects for discussion in Congress. Those who do care about them are trying to find ways to put them on the agenda of those issues which are safe to discuss."[20]

A radical welfare reform plan may often appear to be illogical and ineffective, when thought of as a plan to reform the existing welfare system. But it may prove to be logical, highly effective, and even brilliant when viewed as a plan to eliminate economic dependency, equalize incomes, and end the necessity of working for a living.

CITATIONS—CHAPTER IV

1   Joseph A. Kershaw, *Government against Poverty* (Washington, D.C.: The Brookings Institution, 1970), page 111n.

2   Henry J. Aaron, *Why Is Welfare So Hard to Reform?* (Washington, D.C.: The Brookings Institution, 1973), page 49.

3   Ibid.

4   Robert Theobald (editor), *The Guaranteed Income: Next Step in*

Economic Evolution? (Garden City, New York: Doubleday and Company, 1965), page 229.

5 Daniel P. Moynihan, *The Politics of a Guaranteed Income: The Nixon Administration and the Family Assistance Plan* (New York: Random House, 1973), page 460.

6 Ibid., pages 17–18.

7 Ibid., p. 462.

8 Alice M. Rivlin, "Income Distribution—Can Economists Help?," Papers and Proceedings of the 87th Annual Meeting of the American Economic Association, *The American Economic Review*, Volume LXV (May 1975), pages 1–15.

9 Chamber of Commerce of the United States, *Proceedings of the National Symposium on Guaranteed Income* (Washington, D.C., December 9, 1966), page 13.

10 Arthur Krock, *Memoirs: Sixty Years on the Firing Line* (New York: Funk and Wagnalls Company, 1968), page 408.

11 Aaron Wildavsky and William Cavala, "The Political Feasibility of Income by Right," *Public Policy*, Volume XVIII (Spring 1970), page 321.

12 Milton Friedman and Rose D. Friedman, *Capitalism and Freedom* (Chicago: University of Chicago Press, 1962), page 191.

13 Davis Macarov, *Incentives to Work* (San Francisco: Jossey-Bass, 1970), page 4. (Italics added.)

14 Kenneth M. Bowler, *The Nixon Guaranteed Income Proposal: Substance and Process in Policy Change* (Cambridge, Massachusetts: Ballinger Publishing Company, 1974), page 45.

15 Moynihan, *Politics of a Guaranteed Income*, page 144.

16 President's Council for Urban Affairs, minutes of the thirteenth meeting, June 13, 1969, page 9.

17 Moynihan, *Politics of a Guaranteed Income*, page 218.

18 Ibid.

19 Ibid., pages 218–219.

20 Wildavsky and Cavala, "Political Feasibility of Income by Right," page 321.

V

THE EFFECT OF WELFARE ON WORK

Work keeps at bay three great evils:
boredom, vice, and need.

Voltaire, 1759

Fifth Thesis: The institution of a guaranteed income will cause a substantial reduction—perhaps as much as 50 percent—in the work effort of low-income workers. As long feared by the public, and recently confirmed by independent research studies, such a massive withdrawal from the work force would have the most profound and far-reaching social and economic consequences for our society.

One of the most important questions that should be asked about any radical welfare reform plan that promises to guarantee incomes is: What effect will it have on the work effort of the poor? Most Americans still believe very strongly in the work ethic. If millions of low-income Americans "retired" from the labor force to live on their income guarantees, there is little question that intense political controversy would follow. Those receiving the guarantee could become a powerful political force, demanding and getting ever-increasing benefits. There would certainly be some negative effect on the economy if large numbers of people stopped working or reduced the number of hours they worked.

A major reduction in the work effort of the low-income population would have endless ramifications—socially, economically, and politically—and the speculation on what the consequences of these ramifications might be is also endless. There seems to be little disagreement with the proposition that any substantial reduction in the work effort of the low-income population would pose the danger of profound, far-reaching social and economic consequences. There is, however, a great deal of uncertainty about whether guaranteeing incomes would really cause the recipients to stop working en masse. And speculation on the possible consequences is idle unless we have sufficient reason to suspect that it might, in fact, happen.

Most people have what, to them, seems a common-sense view of a guaranteed income. If someone has the option of working or not working to obtain the same or virtually the same amount of income, all other things being equal, he will choose not to work. In some cases, of course, social factors such as the work ethic, pride, and what his neighbors might think will induce him to keep on working. But what if a guaranteed income plan should become so widespread that large numbers of his fellow workers in the same income bracket choose not to work, and the social pressure directed against him becomes a pressure not to work? In recent years we have seen such a change in our existing welfare system. Partly because of the sharp increase in the number of people on welfare, and partly because of the efforts of "welfare rights" groups, the stigma of being on welfare seems to have been substantially attenuated. Many on welfare today feel no compunction whatsoever about receiving it, often asserting that they have a right to it. Some workers, who gain great psychological satisfaction from their work, may choose to continue what they are doing in spite of the guarantee. But how many low-income jobs provide that kind of psychological satisfaction? Without actually trying a nationwide guaranteed income, and relying on what we know (or what we think we know) of human nature, it seems reasonable to assume that the fears of large numbers of people quitting work to live off the dole are not unfounded, and that such a possibility is fraught with dangers for our society. As Arthur F. Burns has observed in regard to a guaranteed income, "It seems inescapable that more and more people would make the purely rational decision to remain idle rather than work. [There's a great risk] of a corrosive effect on moral values and attitudes, not only in the case of recipient adults but on their children as well."[1]

This fear is not new. Centuries ago there was concern that giving money to the poor might encourage idleness. As Irwin Garfinkel noted in a paper prepared for the use of the Subcommittee on Fiscal Policy of the Joint Economic Committee in 1974, "The very first parliamentary act which dealt with poverty, the Statute of Laborers in 1349, actually forbade *private* alms-giving to the able-bodied poor. The rationale was that such aid encouraged idleness and other supposedly related moral vices."[2] Over six centuries have passed and many things about welfare have changed, but the basic concern about man's inclination to work when given the alternative of a substantial income guarantee is still with us.

We know that if we increase the effective tax rate closer and closer to 100 percent, a person's incentive to work is diminished. At 100 percent he gets nothing but whatever psychological pleasure there is in the work. Conceivably, under certain circumstances he might continue to work as the rate surpassed 100 percent. But this would be an unusual case.

What happens when a person is guaranteed the same amount of income, or some amount close to it, whether he works or not? *A priori*, we would expect that as the amount he received moved closer and closer to the amount he would receive if he worked, he would work less and less. If the amount of guaranteed income surpassed the amount he could earn by working, the disinclination to work would be even greater. The higher the guarantee relative to the amount he could earn by working, the less inclined the person would be to work—except, of course, for the psychological benefits involved.

The effect of increased income on a person's work effort has been studied intensely by economists for many years, and among them there is almost unanimous theoretical agreement that a guaranteed income would cause significant numbers of people to cease working or reduce the number of hours worked. "Economists assume that, other things being equal, an individual would rather use his time for a nonmarket activity such as leisure than for market work. . . . Increases in income will lead to decreases in market work. Thus, guarantees in income transfer programs lead to reductions in labor supply. Moreover, the larger the guarantee, the greater the capacity of the individual to afford to work less, and hence, the greater the reduction in market work."[3]

But this, of course, is theory. And no matter how convinced we may be in our own minds that many people would gladly swap the cacophony of an alarm clock at 7 o'clock every morning and the necessity of doing what someone else wants them to do forty hours a week, fifty weeks a year, for a leisurely rising time and the freedom to pursue their personal interests, we are still not completely sure what would happen if a real guaranteed income should come to the United States.

Advocates of a guaranteed income themselves have few qualms about the possible adverse affects on our society. Commenting on the psychological aspects of a guaranteed income, psychologist Erich Fromm, an ardent advocate of such a plan, acknowledges that "the most obvious question is whether a guaranteed income would not reduce the incentive to work," but then quickly lays this concern to rest as he continues, "Man, by nature, is not lazy, but on the contrary, suffers from the results of inactivity. People might prefer not to work for one or two months, but the vast majority would *beg to work*. . . . Misuse of the guarantee would disappear after a short time, just as people would not overeat on sweets after a couple of weeks, assuming they would not have to pay for them."[4]

In spite of such enthusiastic professional opinion, a few nagging doubts do remain. Have the economists been wrong in their theory all these years? Are the common-sense instincts of the average American in error? Will a large segment of our society, perhaps as many as 30 or 40 million people, now on welfare or earning relatively low incomes proceed much as they did before they discovered that a reasonably high level of income is guaranteed, whether they work or not? Or will they stop working in significant numbers?

As with all social policy there is no sure answer. There is no foolproof way to know what the social and economic consequences of a new, radical social welfare plan will be until many years after we implement it. When the military draft was ended by President Nixon in 1971, many people feared that our military strength would be sharply reduced as both the number and the quality of recruits dropped. They also predicted an all-black army, an army composed of the children of the poor, or one made up of the misfits of our society. Fortunately, their predictions were wrong. When a national urban renewal program began back in 1949, many scholars, politicians, and social commentators confidently predicted the rebirth of our nation's cities. But no one predicted that urban renewal would scarcely renew a city block, let alone a city, that it would worsen housing conditions for the very people it set out to help, that it would destroy four homes, most of them occupied by blacks, for every home it built—most of them to be occupied by middle- and upper-income whites.[5]

In the case of the guaranteed income, we are more fortunate. During the last decade or so an impressive body of data has been painstakingly accumulated by scholars and governments analysts that allows us to predict what will happen as a consequence of a guaranteed income with far more confidence than we have been able to predict the results of other social policies in the past. These studies concern the behavior of people, in particular welfare recipients and low-income workers, under conditions that simulate to some degree the conditions that would exist under a guaranteed income. Individually, their results are rather tentative and inconclusive. Taken together, their findings are inescapably clear—and alarming.

If we look far enough back in the dusty history books, there is one classic example of what did happen when an industrialized society tried a guaranteed income. To be sure, the experience is not totally transferable as it took place in England during the early nineteenth century, and many aspects of the English economy were quite different from that of the United States in the twentieth century. But it did happen, and it is the only example of such a policy being applied in an English-speaking, industrialized country similar to our own. The history lesson is disquieting.

The following excerpt on the history of the Speenhamland Law, which was in effect in England from 1795 to 1834, is taken from Karl Polanyi's well-known historical work, *The Great Transformation*.

. . . The justices of Berkshire, meeting at the Pelikan Inn, in Speenhamland, near Newbury, on May 6, 1795, in time of great distress, decided that subsidies in aid of wages should be granted in accordance with a scale dependent upon the price of bread, so that a minimum income should be assured to the poor *irrespective of their earnings.*

The magistrates' famous recommendation ran: When the gallon loaf of bread of definite quality "shall cost 1 shilling, then every poor and industrious person shall have for his support 3 shillings weekly, either procured by his own or his family's labor, *or an allowance from the poor rates*, and for the support of his wife and every other of his family, 1 shilling, 6 pence; when the gallon loaf shall cost 1/6, then 4 shillings weekly, plus 1/10; on every pence which the bread prices raises above 1 shilling he shall have 3 pence for himself and 1 pence for the others." The figures varied somewhat in various counties, but in most cases the Speenhamland *scale* was adopted. This was meant as an emergency measure, and was informally introduced. Although commonly called a law, *the scale itself was never enacted.*

Yet very soon it became the law of the land over most of the countryside, and later even in a number of manufacturing districts; actually it introduced no less a social and economic innovation than the "right to live," and until abolished in 1834, it effectively prevented the establishment of a competitive labor market. Two years earlier, in 1832, the middle class had forced its way to power, partly in order to remove this obstacle to the new capitalistic economy. Indeed, nothing could be more obvious than that the wage system imperatively demanded the withdrawal of the "right to live" as proclaimed in Speenhamland—under the new regime of the economic man, nobody would work for a wage if he could make a living by doing nothing.

Another feature of the reversal of the Speenhamland method was less obvious to most nineteenth century writers, namely, that the wage system had to be made universal in the interest also of the wage earners themselves, even though this meant depriving them of their legal claim to subsistence. The "right to live" had proved a deathtrap.

The paradox was merely apparent. Allegedly, Speenhamland meant that the Poor Law was to be administered liberally—actually, it was turned into the opposite of its original intent. Under Elizabethan Law the poor were forced to work at whatever wages they could get and only those who could obtain no work were entitled to relief; relief *in aid of wages* was neither intended nor given. Under the Speenhamland Law a man was relieved even if he was in employment, as long as his wages amounted to less than the family income granted him by the scale.

Hence, no laborer had any material interest in satisfying his employer, his income being the same whatever wages he earned; this was different only in the case standard wages, *i.e.*, the wages actually paid, exceeded the scale, an occurrence which was not the rule in the countryside since the employer could obtain labor at almost any wages; however little he paid, the subsidy from the rates brought the workers' income up to scale.

Within a few years the productivity of labor began to sink to that of pauper labor, thus providing an added reason for employers not to raise wages above the scale. For, once the intensity of labor, the care and efficiency with which it was performed, dropped below a definite level, it became indistinguishable from "boondoggling" or the semblance of work maintained for the sake of appearances. Though in principle work was still enforced, in practice outdoor relief became general and even when relief was administered in the poorhouse the enforced occupation of the inmates now hardly deserved the name of work. This amounted to the abandonment of Tudor legislation not for the sake of less but of more paternalism. The extension of outdoor relief, the introduction of aid-in-wages supplemented by separate allowances for wife and children, each item rising and falling with the bread price, meant a dramatic re-entry in regard to labor of that same regulative principle that was being rapidly eliminated in regard to industrial life as a whole.

No measure was ever more universally popular. Parents were free of the care of their children, and children were no more dependent upon parents; employers could reduce wages at will and laborers were safe from hunger whether they were busy or slack; humanitarians applauded the measure as an act of mercy even though not of justice and the selfish gladly consoled themselves with the thought that though it was merciful at least it was not liberal; and even ratepayers [taxpayers] were slow to realize what would happen to the rates under a system which proclaimed the "right to live" whether a man earned a living wage or not.

In the long run the result was ghastly. Although it took some time till the self-respect of the common man sank to the low point where he preferred poor relief to wages, his wages which were subsidized from public funds were bound eventually to be bottomless, and to force him upon the rates.

Little by little the people of the countryside were pauperized; the adage, "once upon the rates, always on the rates" was a true saying. But for the protracted effects of the allowance system, it would be impossible to explain the human and social degradation of early capitalism.

The Speenhamland episode revealed to the people of the leading country of the century the true nature of the social adventure on which they were embarking. Neither the rulers nor the ruled ever forgot the lessons of that fool's paradise; if the Reform Bill of 1832 and the Poor Law Amendment of 1834 were commonly regarded as the starting point of modern capitalism, it was because they put an end to the rule of the benevolent landlord and his allowance system. The attempt to create a capitalistic order without a labor market had failed disastrously. The laws governing such an order had asserted themselves and manifested their radical antagonism to the principle of paternalism. The rigor of these laws had become apparent and their violation had been cruelly visited upon those who had disobeyed them.

Under Speenhamland society was rent by two opposing influences, the one emanating from paternalism and protecting labor from the dangers of the market system; the other organizing the elements of production, including land, under a market system, and thus divesting the common people of their former status, compelling them to gain a living by offering their labor for sale, while at the same time depriving their labor of its market value. A new class of employers was being created, but no corresponding class of employees could constitute itself. A new gigantic wave of enclosures was mobilizing the land and producing a rural proletariat, while the "maladministration of the Poor Law" precluded them from gaining a living by their labor.

No wonder that the contemporaries were appalled at the seeming contradiction of an almost miraculous increase in production accompanied by a near starvation of the masses. By 1834, there was a general conviction—with many thinking people a passionately held conviction—that anything was preferable to the continuance of Speenhamland. Either machines had to be demolished, as the Luddites had tried to do, or a regular labor market had to be created. Thus was mankind forced into the paths of a utopian experiment.

. . . On the face of it the "right to live" should have stopped wage labor altogether. Standard wages should have gradually dropped to zero, thus putting the actual wage bill wholly on the parish, a procedure which would have made the absurdity of the arrangement manifest. But this was an essentially precapitalistic age, when the common people were still traditionally minded, and far from being directed in their behavior by monetary motives alone. The great majority of the countryfolk were occupier-owners or lifeholders, who preferred any kind of existence to the status of a pauper, even if it was not deliberately burdened by irksome or ignominious disabilities, as subsequently happened. If laborers had been free to combine for the furtherance of their interests, the allowance system might, of course, have had a contrary effect on standard wages: for trade union action would have been greatly helped by the relief of the unemployed implied in so liberal an administration of the Poor Law. That was presumably one of the reasons for the unjust Anti-Combination Laws of 1799–1800, which would be otherwise hardly explicable since the Berkshire magistrates and members of Parliament were both, on the whole, concerned about the economic condition of the poor, and after 1797 unrest had subsided. Indeed, it might be argued that the paternalistic intervention of Speenhamland called forth the Anti-Combination Laws, a further intervention, but for which Speenhamland might have had the effect of raising wages instead of depressing them as it actually did. In conjunction with the Anti-Combination Laws, which were not revoked for another quarter century, Speenhamland led to the ironical result that the financially implemented "right to live" eventually ruined the people whom it was ostensibly designed to succor.

To later generations nothing could have been more patent than the mutual incompatibility of institutions like the wage system and the "right to live," or, in other words, than the impossibility of a functioning capitalistic order as long as wages were subsidized from public funds. But the contemporaries did not comprehend the order for which they were preparing the way. Only when a grave deterioration of the productive capacity of the masses resulted—a veritable national calamity which was obstructing the progress of machine civilization—did the necessity of abolishing the unconditional right of the poor to relief impose itself upon the consciousness of the community. The complicated economics of Speenhamland transcended the comprehension of even the most expert observers of the time; but the conclusion appeared only the more compelling that aid-in-wages must be inherently vicious, since it miraculously injured even those who received it.

The pitfalls of the market system were not readily apparent. To realize this clearly we must distinguish between the various vicissitudes to which the laboring people were exposed in England since the coming of the machine; first, those of the Speenhamland period, 1795 to 1834; second, the hardships caused by the Poor Law Reform, in the decade following 1834; third, the deleterious effects of a competitive labor market after 1834, until in the 1870's the recognition of the trade unions offered sufficient protection. Chronologically, Speenhamland antedated market economy; the decade of the Poor Law Reform Act was a transition to that economy. The last period—overlapping the former—was that of market economy proper. The three periods differed sharply.

Speenhamland was designed to prevent the proletarianization of the common people, or at least to slow it down. The outcome was merely the pauperization of the masses, who almost lost their human shape in the process.[6]

In more recent times there have been three major types of research studies that attempt to estimate the effect of radical welfare reform plans on the work effort of the poor and the near-poor. The first type is based on an analysis of existing welfare programs, of how people now welfare have changed, or not changed, their attitude toward work. The second type, called the "cross-section" study, is essentially an economic and statistical analysis of large quantities of survey data showing how people tend to behave when faced with cash transfer payments and increasingly high marginal tax rates. The third type is composed of a series of direct experiments in which selected families were "given" a form of a guaranteed income and their actions were closely observed and analyzed. All three types of studies have the same goal: to judge the effect of guaranteed welfare payments on the work effort of those who would receive them.

The first group of studies focused on the work effort of mothers in the AFDC program. In the late 1960s Leonard Hausman, a professor of economics and social policy at Brandeis University, analyzed a survey of 50,000 AFDC families taken in late 1967. A goldmine of economic and social data, it included information on the earned income, welfare payments, and hours of work for AFDC mothers in all fifty states. Choosing three states—Alabama, Kentucky, and Mississippi—that "guaranteed different levels of income in the absence of non-welfare income," Hausman developed an economic model that would allow him to make "estimates of the impact of alternative implicit tax rate and guarantee levels embodied in a new income maintenance program on the work effort of female-heads of poor families."[7]

Hausman's findings are clear. He found that an increase in the monthly AFDC payment from $82 to $162 caused a decline of over 36 percent in the market work effort of these female-headed welfare families. In his conclusions he comments that, "if they [AFDC mothers] can reach income targets with less work effort, they will reduce that effort—something that is not implausible for mothers of young children."[8] In a 1974 paper for the Joint Economic Committee, Irwin Garfinkel of the Institute for Research on Poverty at the University of Wisconsin commented further on the implications of Hausman's research results: "If extrapolated, his estimates suggest that a $1,000 increase in the guarantee would lead to a 40-percent decrease in employment rates, while a 10-percent increase in the benefit-loss rate [welfare tax rate] would lead to a 4-percent decrease in employment rates."[9]

A second study of the effect of welfare on the work effort of AFDC mothers was conducted by Larry Orr and Irwin Garfinkel. Their results were similar, though not as alarmingly high. They found that "on average the employment rates of AFDC mothers decreased by about 4.5 percent as the annual guarantee increased by $1,000 . . . [and] that a $1,000 increase in the guarantee had a larger effect the smaller the initial guarantee. An increase from a $500 guarantee to a $1,500 guarantee, for example, led to a decrease in employment rates of about 14 percent."[10]

There is no question about the results of welfare programs on the market work effort of welfare mothers. The higher the welfare payment is relative to what welfare mothers could earn by working outside the home, the less likely they are to work. And the higher the welfare tax imposed on those earnings, the less likely they are to work. In these welfare studies, "the empirical evidence uniformly suggests that the labor supply of female heads of households, like that of wives, is highly responsive both to the amounts of income that they get from sources other than employment and to the net monetary rewards that they can get from working."[11] In other words, female heads of households will substantially reduce the amount of market work they do if they are guaranteed an income in the range envisaged by any of the radical welfare reform plans now being discussed. This effect will be exacerbated if the plan also imposes a high welfare tax on any earned income.

Of even greater interest than the work response of welfare mothers is the question of what would happen to the work effort of millions of low-income male workers, most of them not now on welfare, if they became eligible for some form of a guaranteed income. The second group of studies, those based on the economic and statistical analysis of survey data, focused on possible changes in the work effort of such men. In recent years there have been at least a dozen such studies, including eight major ones by distinguished economists from leading universities and research institutions and from the federal government.

Since all economic studies of this kind are based on aggregate statistical data and are concerned with trying to predict the economic behavior of man, they are inherently imprecise. Nevertheless, the unanimity and consistency of the research findings of these eight studies allow us to place a great deal of confidence in their conclusions—not for making precise quantitative predictions, but rather for estimating the direction and order of magnitude of changes in the work effort of low-income men that are likely to take place if they become eligible for a guaranteed income.

Each of these studies produced evidence that husbands with family responsibilities would substantially reduce their work effort if they were to participate in a radical welfare reform plan that would guarantee them a basic income. The higher the guaranteed income, the more the men would reduce their work effort. The higher the welfare tax rate on earned income, the more they would reduce their work effort. While the estimated degree by which they would reduce their work effort—either by quitting their jobs or by reducing the number of hours worked—varied from study to study, every study concluded that the reduction would be significant.* [12]

---

* The average total-income elasticity calculated for the eight studies is approximately −0.30 with a standard deviation of 0.18. The average substitution elasticity is +0.27 with a standard deviation of 0.29.

In one of the studies, Greenberg and Kosters simulated what would happen if a radical welfare reform program similar to President Nixon's Family Assistance Plan were implemented. They concluded that married male heads of participating families would substantially reduce their work effort. Even though they used a relatively low income guarantee of only $3,500 for a family of four, and a welfare tax rate of 75 percent, it was still estimated that working men with family responsibilities would reduce the number of hours they worked by 29 percent[13]—or, looking at it another way, take the equivalent of fifteen additional weeks of vacation every year. A higher income guarantee of $5,000 or $6,000 a year, which would probably be necessary to make a guaranteed income politically feasible, would imply a substantially greater reduction in work effort.

In a later, unpublished study, "Labor Supply and the Negative Income Tax," Kalachek and Raines used the statistical results of their earlier study to develop an economic model that would simulate the effects of a guaranteed income with a $2,400 annual guarantee for a family of four and a welfare tax rate of 50 percent. Even using these unrealistically low levels of income guarantees and tax rates, they predicted that the implementation of such a plan "would produce a 46-percent reduction in the labor supply of the eligible population. (Male family members would reduce their labor supply by 37 percent.)"[14]

The findings of these analytical studies with regard to the effect that a guaranteed income would probably have on the work effort of men with family responsibilities are disturbing—especially the economic simulations that suggest massive reductions in work effort when only very low levels of guarantees are implemented. There is little doubt that male heads of families will reduce their work effort if a guaranteed income is introduced. The only remaining question is how much. If the reduction in work effort even begins to approach the levels suggested by the analyses developed by Greenberg and Kosters and by Kalachek and Raines, the potential for social disaster is large.

The last group of studies involves direct social experimentation with actual people. The basic idea is to identify a relatively large group of people (large enough for the results to be "statistically significant") whose members share many of the same economic and social characteristics—such as age, income, education, and size and type of family. The selected group is then divided into two parts: the "control" group and the "experimental" group. The members of the control group are theoretically allowed to continue what they were doing before the experiment started, whereas those in the experimental group live under a set of deliberately varied conditions. In the case of the *guaranteed income experiments*, as they came to be known, members of the experimental group were guaranteed a certain amount of income for a fixed period of time, whether they worked or not. To simulate the diverse conditions that might exist under a real guaranteed income plan, the amount of the income guarantee was varied, as was the size of the welfare tax rate that applied to any earnings members of the experimental group might have.

The most highly publicized guaranteed income experiment was the New Jersey Income Maintenance Experiment. Started in August, 1969, and lasting for approximately three years, it was the first large-scale social experiment conducted in the United States. The total cost of the experiment was $7.8 million. Of this amount, 30 percent went to the recipients and 70 percent went to Mathematica and the University of Wisconsin, the two organizations that administered the study and conducted the research.[15] Participating in the project were 1,357 households—725 in the experimental group and 632 in the control group. The participants came from five cities—four in New Jersey and one in Pennsylvania. The families selected had to have at least one male between the ages of eighteen and fifty-eight who could work and the families' income had to be less than 150 percent of the poverty level at the beginning of the experiment. The maximum income guarantee ranged from 50 percent to 125 percent of the poverty level, and the experimental welfare tax rates ranged from 30 to

70 percent.[16] There was no requirement to work in order to qualify for the benefits, although it was necessary to fill out numerous reports.

The New Jersey guaranteed income experiment quickly became controversial. From the beginning the entire project had been somewhat suspect as being a vehicle by which some OEO and HEW bureaucrats could develop "evidence" for the radical welfare reform plans they had been trying to sell to President Johnson since 1965. According to David Kershaw, who was the field director of the New Jersey experiment, "OEO had advocated a national negative-income-tax program in 1965, had been unable to persuade the President to introduce the legislation, and, therefore, had decided to fund a project *designed to produce hard evidence as to its feasibility.* This evidence, it was assumed, could then *be used to persuade politicians and the American public* that a negative income tax would be good social policy."[17] And when it became clear that the experiment would be "sponsored, designed, and even administered by 'believers' in"[18] a guaranteed income, the skepticism grew.

The conviction that the experiment was designed to come up with a predetermined conclusion that would develop political support for a guaranteed income became widespread. As Henry Aaron has noted in a rather devastating critique of the validity of the experiment: "The experiment originated because advocates of large-scale income support for poor intact families realized that propects for such aid were meager unless it could be shown that the recipients would not stop working en masse. The primary motivation for the experiment, therefore, was political, and it was for political purposes that the Office of Economic Opportunity agreed to spend $8 million."[19]

An unlucky thing happened to the experiment during its second year: it was overtaken by a roiling national debate on Nixon's Family Assistance Plan. The proponents of FAP badly needed some solid evidence to support their claim that the radical welfare reform plan they were proposing would not seriously hinder the work effort of the poor, if at all. The experiment going on just a few miles north of them was too seductive to resist. As Moynihan later related it in his book *The Politics of a Guaranteed Income*, "Inevitably there arose a conflict between the methodological demands of social science and the political needs of Congress and the Administration, and, perhaps just as inevitably, the latter won out. In the course of the FAP debate, the persons conducting the New Jersey experiment 'broke into' their data at the request of the OEO." Not too surprisingly the "preliminary data" revealed that "there is *no evidence* that work effort declined among those receiving income support payments. On the contrary, there is an indication that the work effort of participants receiving payments *increased* relative to the work effort of those not receiving payments."[20]

Inevitably there were charges in the press of "rigging" the experiment. The General Accounting Office audited the findings and declared them to be "premature," while the Senate Finance Committee pressed to ascertain whether it had been presented with a political report or valid experimental data. Those connected with the experiment were naturally sensitive to the charges of "rigging" and denied them. According to Moynihan, "The charge was a lie, but probably believed."[21] Whatever the case, the fact that the final results of the New Jersey experiment showed that "the number employed per family was 9.5 percent less for experimental families than for controls" did not help allay the suspicions that had been sown earlier.[22]

The intense publicity that surrounded the controversial New Jersey experiment has apparently led many people to believe that it was the only experiment of its kind. In fact, it was one of *six* major guaranteed income experiments started at about the same time. The New Jersey experiment focused on the work effort of husbands and wives—black, white, and Spanish-speaking—living in an Eastern urban environment. Two other guaranteed income experiments were set up expressly to measure the work behavior of poor families, including dependents, living in rural areas. Collectively called the "Rural Income Maintenance Experiment," they were carried out in two locations, Iowa and North Carolina. A fourth experiment, the "Gary Income Maintenance Experiment," centered on black families, including female-headed families previously on welfare, in the urban environment of Gary, Indiana. The fifth and sixth experiments took place in Seattle, Washington, and in Denver, Colorado. Called the "Seattle and Denver Income Maintenance Experiments," they focused on the work effort of husbands, wives, and female-headed families.

Before reviewing the findings of the six major guaranteed income experiments it is important to step back and carefully examine the validity of the experiments themselves. The experiments suffered a number of methodological difficulties that seriously biased them in the direction of underestimating the reduction in work effort that would take place under a real, nationwide guaranteed income program.

The first of these is the **Hawthorne Effect**. This phenomenon is characteristic of socioeconomic experiments, and was first clearly identified in 1927 during an experiment at Western Electric Company's Hawthorne Works in Cicero, Illinois: "A group of female workers over a period of almost a year were subjected to measured changes in their hours, wages, rest periods . . . in order to determine the effects of the several factors on their performance or work output. The major deduction was that social and psychological influences gave more marked results than changes in wages and hours, which had long been the chief concern of most managers and economists who had assumed that labour was simply a commodity to be bought and sold. . . . *Merely by asking their cooperation in the test, the investigators had stimulated a new attitude among the employees, who now felt themselves part of an important group.*"[23]

All six of the guaranteed income experiments were classic examples of the Hawthorne Effect. All the participants were subjected to what was, for them, an unusual and extensive amount of personal attention. For example, in the New Jersey experiment each family had a minimum of twenty-two personal interviews over the three-year course of the experiment—two preliminary "screening" interviews, twelve quarterly interviews, and eight special interviews.[24] The interviews were long and detailed and asked an incredible variety of personal and economic questions in over fifty subject areas. They included questions on income, hours worked, net worth, property owned, cost of housing, food expenditures, clothing expenditures, child support costs, marital history, family planning, fertility, educational background, children's homework and chores, division of financial responsibility, religion, hobbies, use of leisure time, medical history, family background, political awareness, number of close friends, frequency of visits by relatives, self-esteem, degree of "conservatism" or "liberalism," attitudes toward work, psychological instability, and even anomie.[25]

A careful reading of the list of questions can easily lead one to wonder what the main purpose of the experiments was—to measure the effect of a guaranteed income on work effort or to amass a new body of sociological data on the working poor. In any event, every family that agreed to participate in the experiments had to "sing for their supper" at least twenty-two times in addition to ad hoc interviews or phone calls that arose for other reasons over the course of the experiment. By the time the New Jersey experiment was over, some 20 percent of the original participants had dropped out. They gave many reasons, such as, "Don't want to be bothered by interviewers. . . . Invasion of privacy."[28]

For the families who stayed with the experiment from beginning to end it was surely an intense experience, and this, unfortunately, is just the sort of thing that biases the results of such experiments. The participants quickly learn what the investigators would like, and then may try to please them by acting accordingly. As Mordecai Kurz, professor of economics at Stanford University, and Robert Spiegelman of the Stanford Research Institute have pointed out, "Hawthorne Effects have become well known. . . . If, for example, families on the income maintenance experiment develop a sense of 'experimental responsibility' they may behave quite differently than a control group without such a sense of responsibility."[27]

It would not be unreasonable to assume that some, and perhaps many, of the participants in the guaranteed income experiment developed such feelings of responsibility. As one wrote to those who had run the New Jersey experiment, "I will miss our little get-togethers once a month by mail. I trust our reports will help somehow in the future of our government. . . . I am writing to let you know how much we really appreciated being a member of the experiment. It was just three wonderful years. . . . We sure wish it could have lasted forever. With the great help of these checks we bought a mobile home."[28]

In some cases the Hawthorne Effect generated by the guaranteed income experiments may have been one of fear, rather than one of trying to please. Many participants in the experiments somehow got the idea that their subsidies would be reduced if they quit or lost their jobs. According to Jacob Mincer, professor of economics at Columbia University, "It is my understanding that after about a year in the rural experiment—and I recall a similar progress report on the urban experiment—25 percent of the families thought that their subsidies would be reduced if they quit or lost a job. I am not sure whether this response represented ignorance of the rules of the game on the part of participants or a conviction prevailing despite the overt rules that proper response to the experimental payments must be in the socially appropriate direction that the experiment set out to demonstrate. Whatever the interpretation, ignorance or attitude, the effects were to diminish the observed disincentive effects."[29] If one-fourth of the participants in the experiment were effectively deterred from any serious consideration of reducing their work effort by this factor alone, it would mean that the amount of work reduction that would take place in the absence of such pressure would be one-third greater than that actually measured.

A second serious bias intrinsic to the guaranteed income experiments stems from the small size of the sample. Let us call it the **Small-Scale Effect**. This effect makes it difficult to project what might happen if a guaranteed income were instituted on a nationwide basis. An isolated family, participating in a short-term experiment, is apt to behave very differently than it might if it were only one of thousands of similar families in the same neighborhood, all of whom were aware that millions more like them were participating across the country. In the latter case, the tendency to reduce one's work effort, either by quitting or by working fewer hours, would likely be much greater. As Henry Aaron has observed, "It is quite possible that an organization of negative income tax recipients, similar to the National Welfare Rights Organization, would spring up that might alter attitudes and behavior."[30] A national group encouraging people to apply for the guarantee, and showing them how to maximize their benefits, could have a dramatic effect in lowering the work effort of the low-income population.

Such potentially powerful negative effects on the work effort of the poor would not show up in a short-term, small-scale guaranteed income experiment. As Michael Boskin, professor of economics at Stanford University, has pointed out, "Any peer group or neighborhood effects wherein the individual labor supply disincentives are reinforced by the decreased labor supply of other low-income workers are unlikely to show up in an experiment that is confined to three years, spread over several sites, and limited to a small percentage of the low-income labor force in each locale. We simply do not know how important these effects would be in response to a generous permanent negative income tax."[31] This view is shared by other experts. For example, Irwin Garfinkel has concluded that "because the experiment was temporary and affected only a proportion of the potentially eligible population, the experimental results do not reflect any labor market or community changes in economic variables or in tastes for income vis-à-vis leisure that might result from a real, permanent program."[32] And Richard Nathan of the Brookings Institution has warned, "Is it not possible that adoption of a so-called 'guaranteed-income' program would be interpreted by the eligible population as a congressional sanction for leisure?"[33]

There seems to be little disagreement with the proposition that a full-scale guaranteed income would induce significant social changes that would result in a greater amount of work reduction than would show up in the experimental results. But no one has a clear idea what the magnitude of this effect might be. And the guaranteed income experiments have not furthered our knowledge in this area because, as Henry Aaron succinctly puts it, "the thinness of the sample and the brevity of the experiment make it impossible to observe the impact of a negative income tax on the mores of entire groups."[34] All we do know is that we can expect, with confidence, to find that a full-scale guaranteed income will result in a substantially greater reduction in the work effort of the low-income population than one would anticipate from perusing the results of small-scale experiments.

The third and most serious negative bias that is inherent in the guaranteed income experiments—the **Windfall Effect**—results from the temporary nature and duration of the experiments (three years in most cases). The families who agreed to participate faced a situation in which they were assured a basic annual income for three years, but knew that at the end of the experiment they would once again be on their own in earning a living. If they quit their jobs or reduced their work effort enough to get fired, they were taking a chance of being in a potentially serious situation when the experiment was over and the researchers from Mathematica had gone home. It is usually not easy for a low-income worker to find a job. The prospect of having to start all over at the end of the experiment must have given many of the participants cause to think very carefully about leaving their jobs.

In a fundamental sense the income guarantee of the experiments was viewed as a windfall, an unexpected piece of good fortune that would not last for long. This characteristic of the income guarantee was clearly perceived by the participants.[35] What the experimenters are measuring is, as Jacob Mincer recently characterized it, "the *short-run* response of a particular *part* of the population to a *temporary* flow of cash grants."[36] This is very different from the situation that the same family would face under a full-scale, nationwide guaranteed income program. Under those conditions you would get a *long-run* response of the *entire* low-income population to a *permanent* flow of cash grants. The full faith and credit of the federal government would stand behind an implicit, or explicit, promise to pay the income guarantee on the same steady basis as social security and government employee pensions. A low-income worker could count on receiving his monthly check from Washington, whether he worked or not, for as long into the future as he could imagine. Qualifying for an income guarantee would be very much like winning a sweepstakes ticket that guaranteed a certain amount of annual income for life. In one significant way, however, the income guarantee would probably be superior. Given the potential size of the voting bloc that those on a guarantee would represent, the size of the guarantee would inexorably increase by at least as much as the cost-of-living increased, and perhaps more. It would not seem unduly rash to presume that the low-income population would react very differently to that situation than they have reacted to the short-term experiments, and that the likelihood of their quitting work outright, or reducing the number of hours worked, would be greatly increased.

Some scholars involved in planning the experiments were well aware of the limitations inherent in them and carefully warned of the dangers of taking the results at face value. In developing the design of the Seattle and Denver Income Maintenance Experiments, Mordecai Kurz and Robert Spiegelman emphasized, "In terms of work response, it may be anticipated that an increase in transitory nonwork income will have less of an effect on an individual's work effort than a similar increase in permanent income because of the expectation that, when payments cease, the individual will have to return to work. The risks associated with leaving a job in terms of ability to return, loss of seniority, and loss of efficiency will all influence his decision. . . . The major issue is that *significant experimental errors in this area could have drastic policy implications. If families treated a significant portion of the support as transitory income, then the predictions of our studies could all be biased. The social cost of such an error would be very high.*"[37]

Everyone who has studied the guaranteed income experiments seems to be aware of the potentially high negative bias caused by the relatively short life of the experiments, a bias that causes a substantial underestimate of the amount of work reduction that would take place under a real guaranteed income program. As Henry Aaron has observed, "Nearly everyone agrees that if all other analytical problems are correctly resolved, the brief duration of the experiment is likely to lead to estimates of the sensitivity of labor supply to guarantee levels that are too low."[38]

The real difficulty lies in estimating the size of the Windfall Effect bias. Again, there is fairly unanimous agreement that the size of this bias is substantial, that it is of a different order of magnitude than the other experimental biases. According to Professor Boskin, "The net effect of a permanent negative income tax plan on lifetime wealth is of a *totally different order of magnitude* for low-income families than the corresponding effect for a three-year program. If one adopts the view that low-wage males have an investment in training or in a reputation as a stable worker, they are much less likely to reduce labor supply under a temporary negative income tax than a permanent one."[39]

In recent years some efforts have been made to estimate the size of the Windfall Effect bias. In 1973, three economists—Belton Fleisher and Donald Parsons of Ohio State University, and Richard Porter with the Board of Governors of the Federal Reserve System—developed an economic model that estimated the difference between the amount of work reduction that would take place under a temporary three-year experiment and the estimated amount that would occur under a permanent, guaranteed income program.[40]

Their research focused on the work behavior of a category of workers with relatively strong attachments to the labor force—men between the ages of forty-five and fifty-nine from families with annual incomes below $10,000. They predicted that the expected work reduction of these male family heads would be approximately *four times greater* under a permanent guaranteed income than the amount that would show up in a three-year guaranteed income experiment, and that the full extent of this work reduction would not show up until the sixth or seventh year. They concluded that "in the first year of the [guaranteed income] program, hours supplied would fall 20 percent from the preplan level; a 50 percent decline would not be felt until the sixth or seventh year."[41] It was estimated that the amount of work reduction that would occur under a guaranteed income experiment of three to five years' duration would be a little over 12 percent, an estimate that was remarkably close to what was actually measured. The estimate of the amount of work reduction that would occur under a permanent guaranteed income program was 36 percent after the second year, 44 percent after the third year, and continued to rise until it reached slightly over 50 percent after the seventh year. In one of the classic understatements of academic literature they summarized by saying, "One must conclude that inferences drawn from experimental short-term programs are likely to underestimate the impact of labor supply."[42]

Charles Metcalf, in a theoretical article in the *American Economic Review* in 1973, reached similar conclusions as to the relative size of the Windfall Effect bias: "If the household faces a real annual interest rate of 10 percent . . . and a time horizon of 30 years . . . the bias in the income effect alone would be 2.8 times the measured experimental effect."[43] This means that the total effect is estimated to be 3.8 times as large as the measured experimental effect, a result that closely corresponds to the estimates of 12 percent and 50 percent developed by Fleisher, Parsons, and Porter—that is, 4.2 times as large.

A fourth negative bias introduced into the experiments was the

Welfare Effect. This particular bias primarily affected female heads of families, although the AFDC–UP program—a variant of the AFDC program in some states where the presence of an unemployed father does not disqualify the family from receiving welfare benefits—was important in the New Jersey experiment. The bias was caused by the presence and availability of normal welfare programs in the same localities where the guaranteed income experiments were taking place. For example, the Gary experiment indicated that the amount of work reduction shown for AFDC mothers was relatively small (5 percent), but it was noted that "switching from AFDC to a more adequate income support program may not lead to large reductions in work effort because many female heads may have *already reduced* their hours of work under AFDC."[44] Before joining the guaranteed income experiments the AFDC mothers were, on average, working only slightly over six hours a week.[45]

The change in work effort measured by the guaranteed income experiments is not an absolute change, but rather the change *relative* to a control group. If a substantial drop in the work effort of those on the experiment were matched by a similar drop in the work effort of the control group, the experiment would record no change as a consequence of the guaranteed income. The presence of welfare programs, some of which males were eligible for, induced some members of the control groups to reduce their work effort, thus partially masking the actual reduction in work effort shown by the experimental group. As Garfinkel points out with regard to the New Jersey experiment: "A . . . problem is that during this period New Jersey and Pennsylvania had relatively generous welfare programs for which low income families with an able-bodied male head were eligible: Because *control group* families were already potentially eligible for a welfare program, the differences between the work efforts of the experimental and control groups for all eight plans are smaller than would be anticipated had the experiment been conducted in a State with a less generous welfare program."[46]

Some attempts have been made to measure the size of the Welfare Effect bias. Referring to studies by Garfinkel and Rees, Aaron has noted that "the difference between the labor supply of control and experimental families is smaller in the presence of welfare than in its absence,"[47] and that according to Garfinkel's calculations "the reduction in hours worked would have been less than 13 percent even if welfare had not been present, in comparison with an average reduction of 7.9 percent actually observed."[48] In the New Jersey experiment, then, the amount of work reduction reported was biased downward by over five percentage points because of the Welfare Effect alone.

A fifth bias inherent in the experiments is called the **Truncation Effect**, and derives from having a cut-off limitation on the amount of income a family can have in order to qualify for enrollment in a guaranteed income experiment. Only families with pre-experimental incomes below some specified limit, such as 150 percent of the poverty level, are included in the experiments. One problem with this procedure is that the people selected are more likely to have temporarily lower incomes than the national group they are supposed to represent, and people with temporarily low incomes relative to their normal level of income are more apt to show increases in income in the future than those with normally low incomes. Consequently, the experimental results will tend to mute the amount of work reduction that would occur in a national plan.

Boskin, commenting on the Truncation Effect, has made the following points: "A series of problems makes extrapolation to the entire population hazardous. The truncation of eligibility for the experiment—by preenrollment income— screens the sample on the basis of the dependent variable upon which the experiment concentrates attention, labor supply. Families with wives working substantial amounts of time thus were systematically excluded from the analysis. Hence, the results are not very useful in examining the impact of a negative income tax on the labor supply of wives or female family heads, the labor force groups likely to be most sensitive to wage and income effects on labor supply."[49]

A sixth bias, which we will call the **Non-random Effect**, deals with the manner in which the families selected for the experiments were assigned to the various plans in the experiment. Within each experiment there were a variety of plans, each having a unique combination of income guarantee and tax rate. Unfortunately, the families were not randomly assigned to these various plans. Instead, families with low incomes at the time of enrollment in the experiment were assigned to plans with low-income guarantees; those with the highest incomes were assigned to the plans with the highest income guarantees. This correlation between the families' income at the time of enrollment and the size of the income guarantee insured a smaller measured change in work effort than would have been the case otherwise. By minimizing the treatment effect—the size of the income guarantee relative to the amount of income the family had when the experiment started—the amount of work reduction measured was biased downward.

In summing up the bias effects created by the manner in which the experimental sample was selected and assigned to the various guarantee plans, Aaron has stated, "It seems likely that a combination of factors—truncation of the sample, correlation between income at preenrollment and experimental plan, and the method of estimating normal income and wages—has produced estimates of normal income and wages that may well include the experimental effects they are meant to exclude. This outcome, together with the misspecification of experimental stimulus . . . would seem to *understate* estimates of response to the negative income tax treatments."[50]

A seventh factor not accounted for in the experiments is the effect that the availability of part-time jobs may have on the measured results. Let us call this the **Part-Time Job Effect**. It is likely that most people who decided to reduce their work effort under a guaranteed income program would not quit working altogether, but rather would try to reduce the number of hours they worked. The facility with which this can be accomplished is a function of the availability of part-time jobs. If such jobs are scarce, a person who would like to reduce the number of hours he is working, but who is faced with working either full-time or not at all, will probably choose to work full-time. Under a national guaranteed income program, the increased demand by workers for part-time jobs would probably stimulate the business sector to provide them. As the supply of part-time jobs increased, it would become increasingly easier for someone to reduce his work effort without quitting work entirely. In discussing this issue, Boskin has pointed out that "if indeed there is a labor supply response to a permanent negative income tax, it is likely that it would manifest itself at least partly as an increased demand by workers for part-time jobs. It might then become profitable for firms to increase the supply of such jobs in quantity and variety. This long-run response would *reinforce the initial work disincentive* on the other side of the market."[51]

An eighth bias in the experiments, which we will call the **Early Retirement Effect**, stems from the fact that people may be encouraged to retire early by the existence of a guarantee. As Boskin has also noted, "It may well be that the negative income tax plans do have a *substantial labor supply disincentive* in terms of planned future work effort—for example, earlier retirement."[52] The Early Retirement Effect may cause a substantial reduction in the work effort of older people, say, five to ten years short of retirement. The existence of a permanent guarantee, even though the amount may be significantly lower than what they currently earn, may be enough to persuade some workers who have accumulated substantial capital assets, such as a house owned free and clear, to accelerate their retirement time schedule.

A ninth bias, called the **Substitution Effect**, can operate in some cases to influence the results of the experiment positively, that is, to overstate the amount of work reduction. According to Aaron, "the brief duration of the experiment is likely to lead . . . to estimates of the sensitivity of the labor supply to tax rates that are too high.''[53] The Substitution Effect refers to how the number of hours worked changes as a result of a change in a person's effective wage rate. The higher the marginal tax rate, as a result of benefit reductions for earned income, the lower the effective wage rate. The higher the marginal tax rate on earned income, the greater the expected reduction in work effort. However, in a temporary guaranteed income experiment, a person may reduce his work effort *more* under these circumstances than in a situation where the high tax rates on earned income are regarded as more permanent. In other words, he may be more amenable to reducing his work effort now if he expects his wage rate will increase in the future than if he perceives no wage increase later on.

It is generally assumed that husbands and female heads take a longer-term view of the labor market. For them the substitution bias in a short-term experiment is likely to be small. On the other hand, the substitution bias will probably be greater for wives and dependents. They probably view the time of the experiment as a period when leisure is relatively cheap, and may reduce their work effort more than they would under a permanent guaranteed income. In effect, they have a lifetime plan of working that includes more leisure than that of husbands and female heads, and they are apt to take a good chunk of this leisure during the experimental period when their loss of net income is low.

Now let us go back and review the actual results of the six major guaranteed income experiments—keeping in mind that, because of the many negative biases inherent in the experiments, their results seriously understate the predicted amount of work reduction that would occur under a national guaranteed income program. The average measured reduction in work effort for husbands with family responsibilities for all six guaranteed income experiments was 5 percent. The average measured reduction in work effort for wives was much larger, 22 percent. The changes in work effort for female-headed families was measured in only three of the experiments—Gary, Seattle, and Denver—and the average reported for these three was a reduction of about 8 percent.[54] One experiment, the Rural Income Maintenance Experiment, analyzed the effect of income guarantees on the work effort of dependents living with their families. During the experiment their work effort fell by 46 percent.[55]

The order of these results is what we might expect. Husbands, with family-support responsibilities, reduced their work effort the least (5 percent); female heads of families, in the same situation, reduced their work effort by only slightly more (8 percent); wives reduced it substantially more (22 percent); and dependents, with the least responsibility of all, reduced work effort the most (46 percent). While the relative order and degree of the reduction in work effort seem logical and consistent, the absolute magnitudes reported are obviously understated. Even if we discount all the other biases, the windfall nature of the guaranteed income experiments, by itself, introduces such a large bias that the expected work reduction inherent in a real guaranteed income may be understated by as much as four times for some categories of workers.

The ultimate purpose of the studies and experiments is to predict what would happen if a guaranteed income were established in the United States. Making such a prediction is fraught with difficulties and uncertainty. The studies and experiments cover different groups of people, under different circumstances, in different parts of the country, at different times. The specific nature of any guaranteed income can vary depending on the level of the basic income guarantee and the tax rate imposed on income earned by recipients of the basic guarantee. A precise prediction of what would happen if such a radical social scheme were tried is impossible. But while precise predictions are a will-o'-the-wisp, it is entirely feasible to construct an "order of magnitude" prediction that can give us a reasonably accurate idea of the direction and approximate extent of the social consequences that would flow from a guaranteed income.

As to the direction that these changes will take, the studies and experiments are all in agreement. Regardless of whether it is a study of an existing welfare program, or an economic and statistical analysis of survey data, or a controlled guaranteed income experiment; regardless of whether one considers the work response of husbands, or of wives, or of female heads—the results are consistent: a reasonable level of a guaranteed income causes low-income workers to *reduce* the number of hours they work, and the larger the amount of the guarantee relative to their income, the more they tend to stop working.[56] The high tax rates that would be a necessary part of any politically feasible guaranteed income plan would also cause low-income workers to reduce the number of hours they work, and the higher the marginal tax rate the more they would tend to stop working. As the report on the results of the Seattle and Denver experiments concludes, "The empirical results indicate that both disposable income and net wage changes induce husbands, wives, and female heads of families to *reduce* their labor supply. These results are statistically significant, are consistent with economic theory, and are relatively large, indicating that behavior is influenced by changes in incentives."[57]

What many people have suspected for some time is true. Poor people, like those with higher incomes, make rational economic decisions. If their income is little affected by working more, they will not work very much more. If their income is little affected by working less, then they will work less. This is not to say that the poor value idleness, but they do value leisure, just as much as the nonpoor. Whether they will spend that leisure time profitably or not we do not know. But it seems fair to say that bowling, fishing, working around the house, writing poetry, or, in some cases, just loafing for awhile, are clearly more attractive than many low-income jobs. The question is not will low-income people reduce their work effort if guaranteed an income with large implicit tax rates; the question is how much will they reduce it.

It is possible to calculate some reasonable estimates of the size of the work reduction inherent in a guaranteed income program. The studies of how female heads of families with children have reacted to existing welfare programs, for instance, estimate that these women will reduce their work effort by anywhere up to

40 percent. Considering that these welfare programs have a nominal work requirement and also carry a social stigma that a guaranteed income program probably would not have, Hausman's estimate of 40 percent does not seem out of line. A woman alone, with children to care for, would be strongly tempted to stop working outside the home if her income were guaranteed, especially if there were no requirement to work and the social stigma of being on welfare were removed.

The economic and statistical studies of survey data have focused on changes in the work effort of husbands with family responsibilities, and in some cases wives. With no nationwide guarantee, with the strong social pressure of the work ethic bearing on married men with families, and with a fairly strong work requirement, especially for men, the studies produced estimates of significant amounts of work reduction. Some of them were quite high. When the raw results of Greenberg and Koster's study were projected on a national basis, they showed that husbands could be expected to reduce their work effort by 29 percent. When the results of Kalachek and Raines's study were similarly projected, the estimate was 37 percent.

The six guaranteed income experiments were primarily devoted to measuring the work response of three major groups—husbands, wives, and female heads of families. The three most significant guaranteed income experiments in terms of measuring the national impact of a guaranteed income were the New Jersey and the Seattle and Denver experiments. The two rural experiments, in Iowa and North Carolina, and the Gary experiment do not provide as valid a base as the other three from which to project national results.

The measured results—unadjusted for biases—of the New Jersey and the Seattle and Denver experiments for husbands were similar: the measured reduction in the hours of work by white husbands in New Jersey was 6 percent; it was also 6 percent for both black husbands and white husbands in the Seattle and Denver experiments.[58] Even though the statistical results were similar, those of the Seattle and Denver experiments are probably more reliable. These experiments were larger and more comprehensive. They started later, incorporated more sophisticated analysis techniques, and in general had a number of advantages over the other four experiments. According to Michael Keeley of the Stanford Research Institute, "Perhaps the most important [advantages] are its much larger sample size (5,000 families are enrolled which exceeds the samples of all other income maintenance experiments combined) and more generous NIT [Negative Income Tax] plans which were designed to dominate the welfare system (including AFDC, AFDC-UP, and Food Stamps). In addition, sample income truncation is much less severe and there was no substantial change in the welfare system as occurred in the New Jersey case."[59]

Most important, the Seattle and Denver experimental results were adjusted to make them more valid when viewed in a national context. Because of the limited nature of any guaranteed income experiment, it is impossible to put together an experimental group of families from a small geographic area that will accurately reflect the characteristics of the entire population. To resolve this dilemma the analysts of the Seattle and Denver experiments constructed an economic model that allowed them to infer from their small experimental sample what would have happened if the experiment had been conducted on a national basis. As they carefully point out in their report, *"Mean responses* [experimental results] . . . *cannot be directly translated into national effects. . . .* To provide meaningful predictions of the effects of a particular national program, a labor supply response model . . . must be used."[60]

Using an income guarantee of $3,750 in 1974 and a marginal tax rate of 70 percent, their economic model predicted the following national effects of a guaranteed income program: husbands would reduce their work effort 11.2 percent, wives by 32.2 percent, and female heads of families by 9.4 percent.[61]

But these estimates, even though based on carefully controlled experiments and sophisticated economic analyses, seriously under-- state the extent of the work reduction that would take place in the real world with a real guaranteed income. As we have seen, the very nature of the experiments makes it necessary to conduct them in such a way that many powerful factors operate to bias the measured amount of work reduction downward. All of the biases except one—the Substitution Effect—tend to cause the experimen- tally measured amount of work reduction to be understated.

There is the Hawthorne Effect, the Small-Scale Effect, the Windfall Effect, the Welfare Effect, the Truncation Effect, the Non-random Effect, the Part-Time Job Effect, and the Early Retirement Effect. All of these factors cause the experimental results to be lower than they would be in a national program. When experimental results that are biased downward are fed into a national simulation computer model, the results of that national prediction are also biased downward.

Now some may assert that in the absence of hard experi- mental data you cannot infer any quantitative estimates of these biases, and that you should use only results that have been "mea- sured." This position is unreasonable for it says, in effect, that the quantitative magnitude of the biases is zero. And we know that is not true. It would seem to be preferable to postulate some quan- titative ranges of the size of the biases that we believe are likely to be of the right order of magnitude, based upon the evidence we now have from studies and experiments.

One way to approach this problem is to select a range of estimates for each bias that seems fairly reasonable, and then calculate the total effect of all the biases on the estimated amount of work reduction. Once such a model is established, the sensitiv- ity of the overall estimate to changes in the various bias param- eters can be tested. In Table 1 an illustrative range of three esti- mates has been postulated for the effect that each bias might have on each category of worker.

The first estimate is intended to be a "best case" estimate, one that assumes that the negative biases will be low, and the positive bias high. The second estimate is intended to be the "average or likely case," with the values chosen well within the range of feasibility. The third estimate is intended to be a "worst case" estimate, one that assumes that the negative biases will be high, and the positive bias low.

For example, the low estimate postulated for the Hawthorne Effect is one percentage point, and the high estimate of the range is five percentage points. The same is true for the Small-Scale Effect. The estimates for the Windfall Effect are larger. Theoretical studies, like the one by Fleisher, Parsons, and Porter, indicate that this factor could add as much as 35 percentage points to the results of guaranteed income experiments. In this category we have assumed a low estimate of five percentage points for husbands, 20 points for a medium estimate, and an upper bound of 30 points.

The same range is postulated for female heads, who have the responsibility of being the head of a household and are apt to react as husbands do in this regard. It is assumed that the effect on wives and dependents will be substantially less. The Welfare Effect applies primarily to female heads, although it can have some effect on husbands and wives. It is assumed to have no effect on dependents. Similar types of estimates have been made for the Truncation Effect, the Non-random Effect, the Part-Time Job Effect, and the Early Retirement Effect. The Substitution Effect biases the results in the other direction, and thus is subtracted. It is assumed that the effect of this bias will be higher for wives and dependents than for husbands and female heads.

Summing up the assumed estimates of the biases in Table 1 results in a fairly wide estimated range of the amount of work reduction that could occur if a guaranteed income were established in the United States. The amount of work reduction ranges from a low of 22 percent to a high of 69 percent for husbands, from 35 percent to 75 percent for wives, from 46 percent to 75 percent for dependents, and from 19 percent to 71 percent for female heads.

TABLE 1

CORRECTION FOR BIASES IN THE MEASUREMENT OF WORK REDUCTION
IN THE GUARANTEED INCOME EXPERIMENTS
(As Percent of Hours Worked by Controls)

	Category of Worker			
	Husbands	Wives	Dependents	Female Heads
Average measured reduction in work effort	6%[a]	15%[a]	46%[b]	14%[a]
Reduction in work effort projected to national base	12	32	46[c]	9

BIASES	Illustrative Range of Possible Corrections (In Percent: Best—Average—Worst)			
1) Hawthorne Effect	1—3—5%	1—3—5%	1—3—5%	1—3—5%
2) Small-Scale Effect	1—3—5	1—3—5	1—3—5	1—3—5
3) Windfall Effect	5–20–30	2–10–20	1–5–10	5–20–30
4) Welfare Effect	1—2—3	1—2—3	——	3—5–10
5) Truncation Effect	1—2—3	1—2—3	0—1—2	0—1—2
6) Non-random Effect	1—3—5	1—3—5	1—3—5	1—3—5
7) Part-Time Job Effect	1—2—3	1—2—3	1—2—3	0—1—2
8) Early Retirement Effect	1—2—3	——	——	1—2—3
9) Substitution Effect	(2—1—0)	(5—3—1)	(5—3—1)	(2—1—0)

| Range of measured work reduction, adjusted for biases | 22–48–69% | 35–54–75% | 46–60–75% | 19–46–71% |

[a] Measured results from Seattle and Denver Income Maintenance Experiments. Based on income guarantee of $3,750 and a marginal tax rate of 70 percent.

[b] Measured result from the Rural Income Maintenance Experiment in Iowa and North Carolina. Dependents were not included in any other experimental results.

[c] Assumes national projection would be the same as the measured experimental results.

Now it can be argued that these estimates are not precise (and they are not), and that the effects may not be neatly additive as there may be some interaction among them. But what seems to be inescapably clear is that even fairly modest adjustments for each of the bias effects substantially increase the amount of work reduction that is apt to occur. Even if we were to take the low estimate for each bias for each category of worker, we would still end up with estimated percentages of work reduction of 22 percent for husbands, 35 percent for wives, 46 percent for dependents, and 19 percent for female family heads.

It could be that 1 to 5 percent is not the correct estimated range for the Hawthorne Effect, or that 5 to 30 percent is not right for the Windfall Effect, or that 1 to 3 percent is not appropriate for the Non-random Effect. But the biases are there, and they do affect the results. We need a great deal more research in this area before we will be able to estimate these ranges with the kind of certainty we would like. But in the meantime, policy decisions will have to be made on the basis of the information available, and prudent estimates of these biases will lead to far more reliable estimates of the amount of work reduction that would take place under a nationwide guaranteed income than will an evasion of the reality of the biases.

To estimate the *total amount of work reduction* that would be brought about by a guaranteed income it is necessary to weight the results in Table 1 by the relative percentage that each of the four categories of workers comprises of the total low-income work force. According to Census Bureau statistics (regretfully, the only ones available), the breakdown of the low-income labor force—defined as families with incomes of less than $10,000 a year—is as follows: husbands (46 percent), wives (23 percent), dependents (18 percent), and female heads (13 percent).[62]

The results of weighting the range of estimates of work reduction for each of the worker categories by their respective percentage in the low-income labor force are shown in Table 2. If we use the "best case" estimate for each experimental bias, the

TABLE 2

Estimated Range of the Total Expected Work Reduction for the Low-Income Population under a Guaranteed Income

Category of Worker	Percent of Low-Income Labor Force*	Expected Amount of Work Reduction						
		Best Estimate	Weighted Best Estimate	Average Estimate	Weighted Average Estimate	Worst Estimate	Weighted Worst Estimate
Husbands	46%	22%	0.1012	48%	0.2208	69%	0.3174
Wives	23%	35%	0.0805	54%	0.1242	75%	0.1725
Dependents	18%	46%	0.0828	60%	0.1080	75%	0.1350
Female heads of families	13%	19%	0.0247	46%	0.0598	71%	0.0923
TOTAL WORK FORCE . .	100%	29%	0.2892	51%	0.5128	72%	0.7172

*Family income below $10,000 a year.

expected amount of work reduction for the entire low-income labor force is about 29 percent. If we use the "average case" estimate, the total amount of work reduction rises to just over 51 percent. If all the "worst case" estimates were to occur simultaneously, the amount of work reduction in this example would be almost 72 percent.

I am sure that there will be many who will disagree with the individual estimates of the experimental biases in Table 1. They *are* rough estimates. And, until more research is done and more refined data become available, the estimates will continue to be rough. But it is necessary to make *some* kind of estimate. I would urge anyone who is concerned about the accuracy of the estimates in the example to go through the exercise of reconstructing Table 1—bias by bias—using estimates they feel are more reasonable. And then calculate the expected total amount of work reduction for the low-income population that results from those estimates.

If it happened that all the bias estimates postulated in Table 1 were accurate, we could expect that the institution of a guaranteed income in the United States would cause—in round numbers —a minimum of a 30 percent reduction in the work effort of low-income workers. We could also expect that there would be a reasonably good chance the amount of work reduction could be as high as 50 percent. And there would be the remote possibility that it could exceed 70 percent.

The actual amount of work reduction that would occur as a consequence of a guaranteed income will never be known for sure unless we implement one and live with it for a decade or so. But based on the best evidence we now have—from studies of existing welfare programs, from economic and statistical analyses of survey data, and from six major guaranteed income experiments—we can be reasonably sure that the order of magnitude of the amount of work reduction that will occur will be substantial, substantial enough to make us think long and hard about the implications that a guaranteed income could have for our society.

CITATIONS—CHAPTER V

1 Arthur Burns, quoted in Jonathan Spivak, "Nixon Men Study Alternate Aids to Poor: National Minimums or Guaranteed Income," *The Wall Street Journal*, May 29, 1969, page 38.

2 Irwin Garfinkel, "Income Transfer Programs and Work Effort: A Review," in U.S., Congress, Joint Economic Committee, Subcommittee on Fiscal Policy, *How Income Supplements Can Affect Work Behavior*, Studies in Public Welfare, Paper No. 13 (Washington, D.C., February 18, 1974), page 1.

3 Ibid., page 4.

4 Erich Fromm, "The Psychological Aspects of the Guaranteed Income," in Robert Theobald (editor), *The Guaranteed Income: Next Step in Economic Evolution?* (Garden City, New York: Doubleday and Company, 1965), pages 177–179. (Italics added.)

5 Martin Anderson, *The Federal Bulldozer: A Critical Analysis of Urban Renewal, 1949–1962* (Cambridge, Massachusetts: The M.I.T. Press, 1964), pages 228–230.

6 Karl Polanyi, *The Great Transformation* (New York: Farrar and Rinehart, 1944), pages 78–82.

7 Leonard J. Hausman, "The Impact of Welfare on the Work Effort of AFDC Mothers," in the President's Commission on Income Maintenance Programs, *Technical Studies* (Washington, D.C., 1970), page 83.

8 Ibid., page 97.

9 Garfinkel, "Income Transfer Programs and Work Effort," page 26.

10 Ibid., page 25.

11 Ibid., page 26.

12 The studies are: "Estimating Labor-Supply Functions" by Orley Ashenfelter, professor of economics at Princeton University, and James Heckman, associate professor of economics at the University of Chicago; "The Economics of Labor Supply" by Michael J. Boskin, assistant professor of economics at Stanford University; "Asset Adjustments and Labor Supply of Older Workers" by Belton M. Fleisher, professor of economics at Ohio State University, Donald O. Parsons,

associate professor of economics at Ohio State University, and Richard D. Porter, economist at the Board of Governors, Federal Reserve System; "Income Guarantees and the Working Poor: The Effort of Income–Maintenance Programs on the Hours of Work of Male Family Heads" by David H. Greenberg, research economist at the Rand Corporation, and Marvin Kosters, assistant director for planning and analysis at the Cost of Living Council; "Waves, Income, and Hours of Work in the U.S. Labor Force" by Robert E. Hall, associate professor of economics at the Massachusetts Institute of Technology; "The Determinants of Labor Supply for the Working Urban Poor" by C. Russell Hill, assistant professor of economics at the University of Michigan. These six studies are in Glen G. Cain and Harold W. Watts (editors), *Income Maintenance and Labor Supply: Econometric Studies* (Chicago: Rand McNally and Company, 1973). The seventh study is "Labor Supply of Lower Income Workers" by Edward D. Kalachek and Frederick Q. Raines, both professors of economics at Washington University, in the President's Commission on Income Maintenance Programs, *Technical Studies*. The eighth study is "Labor Supply and Income Redistribution" by Sherwin Rosen, professor of economics at the University of California, Los Angeles, in *The Review of Economics and Statistics*, Volume LIII (August 1971).

13 Greenberg and Kosters, "Income Guarantees and the Working Poor," page 74.

14 Glen G. Cain and Harold W. Watts, "An Examination of Recent Cross-Sectional Evidence on Labor Force Response to Income Maintenance Legislation," in U.S., Congress, Joint Economic Committee, Subcommittee on Fiscal Policy, *How Income Supplements Can Affect Work Behavior*, page 74.

15 David Kershaw and Jerilyn Fair, *The New Jersey Income–Maintenance Experiment*, Volume 1: *Operations, Surveys, and Administration*, Institute for Research on Poverty Monograph Series (New York: Academic Press, 1976), page 13, Table 1.4, and page 18, Table 1.6.

16 Garfinkel, "Income Transfer Programs and Work Effort," page 7.

17 Kershaw and Fair, *New Jersey Income–Maintenance Experiment*, page 4. (Italics added.)

18 Ibid., page xix.

19 Henry J. Aaron, "Cautionary Notes on the Experiment," in Joseph A. Pechman and P. Michael Timpane (editors), *Work Incentives and*

Income Guarantees: The New Jersey Negative Income Tax Experiment (Washington, D.C.: The Brookings Institution, 1975), page 88.

20 Daniel P. Moynihan, *The Politics of a Guaranteed Income: The Nixon Administration and the Family Assistance Plan* (New York: Random House, 1973), pages 191–192. (Italics added.)

21 Ibid., pages 511n–512n.

22 Kershaw and Fair, *New Jersey Income–Maintenance Experiment*, page 4.

23 *Encyclopaedia Britannica*, 15th edition (1973), Volume 4, pages 961–962, and Volume 19, page 940. (Italics added.)

24 Kershaw and Fair, *New Jersey Income–Maintenance Experiment*, page 131.

25 Ibid., pages 149–162.

27 Ibid., pages 111–115.

27 Mordecai Kurz and Robert G. Spiegelman, "The Seattle Experiment: The Combined Effect of Income Maintenance and Manpower Investments," Papers and Proceedings of the 83rd Annual Meeting of the American Economic Association, *The American Economic Review*, Volume LXI (May 1971), page 27.

28 Kershaw and Fair, *New Jersey Income–Maintenance Experiment*, page 193.

29 Jacob Mincer, "Comments," in Pechman and Timpane, *Work Incentives and Income Guarantees*, page 155.

30 Aaron, "Cautionary Notes on the Experiment," page 108.

31 Michael Boskin, "Comments," in Pechman and Timpane, *Work Incentives and Income Guarantees*, page 112.

32 Garfinkel, "Income Transfer Programs and Work Effort," page 8.

33 Richard Nathan, "Comments," in Pechman and Timpane, *Work Incentives and Income Guarantees*, page 199.

34 Aaron, "Cautionary Notes on the Experiment," page 89.

35 "It is rather clear from the consumption data presented by Metcalf that the households were acutely aware of the transitoriness of the grants they were receiving. The marginal propensity to consume food out of the experimental payments was only one-half to one-third as large as the marginal propensity to consume out of normal income. The experimental payments were viewed the same way as transitory components of income, whereas public assistance subsidies were

treated as permanent. The same and perhaps an even stronger conclusion emerges from the data on purchases of appliances. Their timing was rather quick in response to the payments and more sensitive to the subsidies than to other variable components of income. This is to say that the windfall nature of the experimental payments was clearer than that of the other sources of income." Mincer, "Comments," page 154.

36 Ibid., page 152. (Italics added.)

37 Mordecai Kurz and Robert Spiegelman, *The Design of the Seattle and Denver Income Maintenance Experiments*, Research Memorandum 18 (Menlo Park, California: Center for the Study of Welfare Policy, Stanford Research Institute, 1972), pages 9–10. (Italics added.)

38 Aaron, "Cautionary Notes on the Experiment," page 89.

39 Boskin, "Comments," page 111. (Italics added.)

40 Fleisher, Parsons, and Porter, "Asset Adjustments and Labor Supply of Older Workers," pages 299–307.

41 Ibid., page 304.

42 Ibid., page 307.

43 Charles E. Metcalf, "Making Inferences from Controlled Income Maintenance Experiments," *The American Economic Review*, Volume LXIII (June 1973), pages 478–483.

44 U.S., Department of Health, Education and Welfare, *The Gary Income Maintenance Experiment: Summary of Initial Findings*, prepared by Kenneth C. Kehrer (Washington, D.C., March 1977), pages 11–12. (Italics added.)

45 Ibid., page 7, Table 1.

46 Garfinkel, "Income Transfer Programs and Work Effort," page 8. (Italics added.)

47 Aaron, "Cautionary Notes on the Experiment," page 96.

48 Ibid., page 96n.

49 Boskin, "Comments," page 110.

50 Aaron, "Cautionary Notes on the Experiment," pages 107–108. (Italics added.)

51 Boskin, "Comments," page 112. (Italics added.)

52 Ibid., page 111. (Italics added.)

53 Aaron, "Cautionary Notes on the Experiment," page 89.

54   U.S., Department of Health, Education and Welfare, *Gary Income Maintenance Experiment*, page 10, Table 2; and Michael C. Keeley, Philip K. Robins, Robert G. Spiegelman, and Richard K. West, *The Labor Supply Effects and Cost of Alternative Negative Income Tax Programs: Evidence from the Seattle and Denver Income Maintenance Experiments*, Part I: *The Labor Supply Response Function*, Research Memorandum 38 (Menlo Park, California: Center for the Study of Welfare Policy, Stanford Research Institute, 1977), page 25.

55   U.S., Department of Health, Education and Welfare, *Summary Report: Rural Income Maintenance Experiment*, prepared by Lee Bawden, Florence Setzer, William Harrar, and Stuart Kerachsky (Washington, D.C., November 1976), page x, Table 1.

56   Michael C. Keeley, Philip K. Robins, Robert G. Spiegelman, and Richard W. West, *The Estimation of Labor Supply Models Using Experimental Data: Evidence from the Seattle and Denver Income Maintenance Experiments*, Research Memorandum 29 (Menlo Park, California: Center for the Study of Welfare Policy, Stanford Research Institute, 1976), page 33, Table 5.

57   Keeley, Robins, Spiegelman, and West, *Labor Supply Effects and Cost of Alternative Negative Income Tax Programs*, Part I, page 26. (Italics added.)

58   Michael C. Keeley, Philip K. Robins, Robert G. Spiegelman, and Richard W. West, *Labor Supply Effects and Cost of Alternative Negative Income Tax Programs: Evidence from the Seattle and Denver Income Maintenance Experiments*, Part II: *National Predictions Using the Labor Supply Response Function*, Research Memorandum 39 (Menlo Park, California: Center for the Study of Welfare Policy, Stanford Research Institute, 1977), page 14, Table 4.

59   Michael C. Keeley, "The Economics of Labor Supply: A Critical Review" (unpublished manuscript, 1977), page 107.

60   Keeley, Robins, Spiegelman, and West, *Labor Supply Effects and Cost of Alternative Negative Income Tax Programs*, Part II, pages 14 and 16. (Italics added.)

61   Ibid., page 21, Table 6, and page 23, Table 8.

62   U.S., Bureau of the Census, *Money Income in 1974 of Families and Persons in the United States*, Series P-60, No. 101 (Washington, D.C., 1976), page 80, Table 38.

VI

THE IMPOSSIBILITY OF RADICAL WELFARE REFORM

> "Have some wine," the March Hare said in an encouraging tone.
>
> Alice looked all round the table, but there was nothing on it but tea. "I don't see any wine," she remarked.
>
> "There isn't any," said the March Hare.
>
> Lewis Carroll, 1865

Sixth Thesis: Radical welfare reform or any variety of a guaranteed income is politically impossible. No radical welfare reform plan can be devised that will simultaneously yield minimum levels of welfare benefits, financial incentives to work, and an overall cost to the taxpayers that are politically acceptable.

During the last fifteen years a number of economists and social science theorists have put forth plans for radically altering the welfare system of the United States from its current purpose of helping needy people to guaranteeing incomes for everyone. There has been a long string of specific proposals, including Milton Friedman's negative income tax (1962), Robert Theobald's guaranteed income (1965), James Tobin's guaranteed income plan (1965), R. J. Lampman's subsidy plan (1967), Edward Schwartz's guaranteed income (1967), the negative income tax plan of President Johnson's Income Maintenance Commission (1969),

President Nixon's Family Assistance Plan (1969), George Mc-Govern's $1,000-a-year plan (1972), Great Britain's credit income tax (1972), and HEW's Income Supplementation Plan (1974). The plans provided for minimum income guarantees ranging from $1,500 to $6,000 a year for a typical family of four. The effective marginal tax rates ranged from 50 percent to well over 100 percent. The costs of the plans ranged from several billions to over $50 billion a year. All would have added tens of millions of people to the welfare rolls.

A common thread running through each of these plans is the planner's dream of simplification. The welfare system we now have is difficult to understand and difficult to administer. It has multiple programs, varying payments, and regulations that vary from state to state. It is very complex. The radical reform plans would replace it with a single system that purportedly would be easy to understand and easy to administer, with the same payments and regulations applying to the entire country.

The current welfare system can be likened to a rugged terrain of hills, mountains, and valleys, a wonderfully complex array of programs, payment levels, and eligibility rules that change as one moves from city to city, from state to state. It can be argued that this is as it must be, a complex welfare system dealing with the very complex problem of the poor in America. This view is shared by a small, but influential group of welfare experts. One of them, Senior Fellow Richard Nathan of the Brookings Institution and formerly Deputy Undersecretary for Welfare of HEW, asserts flatly, "The existence of a 'welfare mess' tends to be overstated. Any system that provides aid to people in the lowest-income groups, who are highly mobile and often have limited job and literacy skills, is going to be difficult to administer."[1]

All of the radical welfare reform plans would like to level the hilly and mountainous terrain of the current welfare system, replacing it with broad, flat plains. One critical element in all these plans is the height of the plain that would replace the hills and mountains. If it is set lower than any of the hilltops and mountain peaks, welfare payments will be reduced for hundreds of thousands, perhaps millions, of Americans. If the new welfare plan is raised to the highest peaks and all the valleys are filled in, welfare payments will be sharply increased for millions of Americans and the costs will be extraordinarily high. There is no way out of this dilemma.

But the demography of low-income America has not hindered the quest for a guaranteed income plan that will work. Like medieval alchemists searching for the universal solvent, some modern social scientists continue to search for a feasible guaranteed income plan—a plan that will simultaneously provide a decent level of help to the poor, guarantee a basic income for all, have a reasonable cost, and be acceptable to the voting public. All would agree that such a plan is difficult to find; perhaps a more interesting question is whether or not such a plan is possible.

All radical welfare reform schemes have three basic parts that are politically sensitive to a high degree. The first is the basic benefit level provided, for example, to a family of four on welfare. The second is the degree to which the program affects the incentive of a person on welfare to find work or to earn more. The third is the additional cost to the taxpayers.

There are many other important aspects of welfare programs and the plans to reform them, but each of the above three is critical to the chance of any particular reform plan passing the Congress and being signed into law by the President. To become a political reality the plan must provide a decent level of support for those on welfare, it must contain strong incentives to work, and it must have a reasonable cost. *And it must do all three at the same time.* If any one of these parts is missing or deficient, the reform plan is nakedly vulnerable to anyone who wishes to attack and condemn it.

The typical welfare family of four in the United States now qualifies for about $6,000 in services and money every year. In higher-paying states, like New York, a number of welfare families receive annual benefits ranging from $7,000 to $12,000, and more.[2]

There is no way that the Congress, at least in the near future, is going to pass any kind of welfare reform that actually reduces payments for millions of welfare recipients. Even the most hardy welfare skeptics in the Congress will shy away from this possibility. The media response would be virtually unanimous—the "reform" would be denounced as cruel and mean-spirited. Countless documented case examples would soon drive the point home to everyone watching the evening television news. Even if the Congress were to pass a cut in welfare benefits for millions of Americans, no President could resist vetoing the bill.

Any radical welfare reform plan has to ensure that virtually no one now validly covered under any of our welfare programs would suffer any loss or reduction in benefits. This is especially true of programs for the blind, the aged, the disabled, and those on AFDC. The minimum level of support provided for a family of four by any reform plan must approach the level of payments in states like New York and California, where a large segment of the welfare population lives, a level that averages approximately $6,000 a year.

A second major consideration concerning the political feasibility of any radical welfare reform plan is the "welfare tax rate." All current welfare programs that are "income-tested" provide for a reduction in the amount of the welfare payment when the recipient of those payments begin either to earn money or to earn more money. And all of the proposed radical welfare plans incorporate some schedule of welfare payment reductions as a function of increasing income—the more you earn, the less you get from the taxpayers.

This welfare tax rate has the same effect on the financial incentive to work as normal taxes. The financial incentive for a welfare recipient to get a job, or to earn more money, is directly related to how much the person earns and how much welfare benefits are reduced because of those earnings. If a welfare recipient earns an additional $1,000 a year and his welfare check is reduced by, say, $200, the result is precisely the same as if he had to pay $200 in federal income taxes on $1,000 of income. In both cases the effective tax rate would be 20 percent. If welfare benefits are reduced $500 for every $1,000 increase in earnings, the tax rate would be 50 percent; if they are reduced $700 for every $1,000 increase in earnings, the tax rate would be 70 percent, and so on.

A person's desire for additional income is unquestionably diminished when he realizes that he can keep only half or one-fourth of it for himself. To make the financial incentive to work the main instrument for inducing potentially self-sufficient people to leave the welfare rolls and rise out of poverty, and then to impose on those people incentive-destroying rates of taxation far above that of the average worker, is unconscionable and clearly contrary to the expressed goals of welfare reform.

Any radical plan for the reform of welfare that does not ensure a strong financial incentive to work is vulnerable to the same charges that were leveled at President Nixon's Family Assistance Plan by the Senate Finance Committee with such devastating effect in 1969.

Exactly what constitutes a "strong" financial incentive to work is open to debate—a marginal tax rate that may discourage one person from working could easily have little or no effect on someone else. But in general terms we can say that low marginal tax rates, from zero to, say, 15 or 20 percent, seem to have a relatively minimal effect on work effort; that as tax rates move up into the region of 40, 50, or even 60 percent, an increasing number of people are adversely affected; and that as tax rates approach the confiscatory levels of 80, 90, or even 100 percent and more, the work disincentive becomes very powerful. The primary earner in a typical family of four does not begin to pay federal income taxes until his income exceeds $6,900 and the total effective marginal tax rate he then faces is just over 29 percent.*

---

* The introduction of the federal earned income credit has distorted the normal, even, upward flow of marginal tax rates. See Table B3 in Appendix B.

Practically speaking, a marginal tax rate that is low enough to provide welfare recipients with a strong financial incentive to work should probably be no more than it is for people who are first entering the labor force. This means a total marginal tax rate of 20 percent or lower. There is no way to know with certainty that this is the highest the marginal tax rate could go without seriously impairing the financial incentive to work. But we have had many years of experience with marginal tax rates of this order of magnitude for low-income workers with no apparent serious consequences. Looked at from a different perspective, one could ask why a person on welfare should be taxed more to enter the job market than a person who is not on welfare. A total marginal tax rate of approximately 20 percent is considered appropriate when one first begins to pay federal taxes, and if it is generally accepted that raising those tax rates introduces serious work disincentives for low-income workers. It therefore is difficult to understand the rationale behind the application of tax rates far in excess of 20 percent to welfare recipients, especially in view of the increasing reliance on financial incentives to induce people to leave the welfare rolls and become self-supporting.

Yet the nature of the radical welfare reform plans so far proposed is such that even the most timid plan involves marginal welfare tax rates of not 20 percent, but 50 percent and higher. The revised Family Assistance Plan, usually referred to by its bill number, H.R.1, which actually was passed by the House of Representatives in 1971, had marginal tax rates of well over 100 percent for the income range of $2,000 to $5,000.[3] Another plan, introduced by Senator Russell Long, had marginal tax rates that "averaged just under 100 percent on increments to earnings between $3,000 and $6,900 per year."[4] Neither plan managed to get past the Senate.

When one considers that the marginal welfare tax rates of existing welfare programs range well over 70 percent, it is understandable how people can propose welfare reform programs with marginal tax rates of 50 to 60 percent and consider them to be "low." While low in a relative sense, they are very high on an absolute scale, which is what affects the financial incentive to work. Any radical welfare reform plan that claims to have a strong financial incentive to work must obviously have tax rates that are reasonably close to 20 percent, and preferably much less.

Marginal welfare tax rates of 40 or 50 percent are a deterrent to working. Tax rates that approach 70 percent, and in some cases 100 percent or more, are confiscatory and virtually eliminate the financial incentive to work. As far as any new redical welfare reform plan goes, the marginal tax rate it establishes for welfare recipients should, if one is to continue to rely on financial incentives to induce people to get off welfare, at the very least not exceed the high rate now embedded in our current welfare programs. At least then the proponents of the plan could claim that they have not reduced the virtually nonexistent incentive to work even further. Of course, if we are serious about having a strong financial incentive to work, the marginal tax rate should probably be no higher than 30 percent, preferably 20 percent, or even lower.

When Milton Friedman was asked to testify before the House Ways and Means Committee on President Nixon's welfare reform plan, he emphasized the necessity of having strong financial work incentives, stating flatly, "In my opinion, the most important need in welfare reform is to provide a strong incentive for persons receiving governmental assistance to become self-supporting. . . . For the class of persons involved, 50 percent is a very high rate. Yet, given the present low exemptions under the positive income tax . . . it is hard to construct a feasible scheme with a much lower rate. In my own proposals for a negative income tax, I have reluctantly recommended a 50 percent rate, viewing it as the highest that would give families a strong enough incentive to work themselves off relief. . . . This Committee can enormously improve the present proposals by insisting that no combined marginal tax rate should exceed 50 percent."[5]

Plans containing truly effective financial work incentives would entail tax rates not exceeding 15 or 20 percent. Tax rates as high as 50 percent might be politically tolerable in today's context, but would not be effective in motivating people on welfare to work. Any radical welfare reform plan having tax rates that begin to stray up into the category of 70 and 80 percent and above has virtually no chance of gaining political acceptance. All some enterprising senator or congressman would have to do to demolish the plan would be to construct a few charts showing how welfare recipients' take-home benefits changed as they began to work and earn more money. It would quickly be proven that the financial incentive to work was almost nonexistent.

A third major consideration affecting the political feasibility of any radical welfare reform plan is the cost. The amount of money that any welfare reform plan can add to the federal budget and still be politically acceptable is a function of many factors and changes constantly. Among other things it is a function of whether people believe the amount now spent on welfare is sufficient or not, of how high welfare reform is on the public's list of spending priorities, and of the fiscal condition of the federal budget.

The current circumstances and the prospects for future change are not encouraging. A 1976 nationwide Harris poll cited earlier indicated that 58 percent of the public felt that spending on welfare could be *cut* by one-third without serious loss. The danger of double-digit inflation and high unemployment threatened by the huge budget deficits being incurred by the federal government is causing every new spending proposal to come under the strictest scrutiny. A major radical welfare reform plan could be financed only by increasing taxes, cutting expenditures on other federal programs, or borrowing money—or some combination of these.

The politically acceptable cost of welfare reform is difficult to estimate with precision. But given the public's attitude toward welfare spending in particular, and the widespread opposition to higher taxes in general, to spending cuts in other federal programs, and to increased federal budget deficits, there seems to be little hope of mobilizing the public support necessary for a substantial increase in welfare spending. In fact, any increase in federal spending for welfare reform may be out of the question in the near future.

For any radical welfare reform program to succeed politically—to be passed by the Congress and signed into law by the President—then, three necessary major conditions must be met: (1) total welfare benefits for a typical family of four cannot fall much below $6,000 a year; (2) the total effective marginal tax rate on welfare recipients' earnings should not exceed 50 percent, and cannot exceed 70 percent; and (3) there should be no substantial additional cost to the taxpayers.

The three basic elements involved in any radical welfare reform plan—the level of benefits, the marginal rate of taxation, and the overall cost to the taxpayers—are *inextricably linked to one another*. If the level of benefits is increased, and the tax rate is held constant, the overall cost must increase; if the overall cost is held constant, the tax rate must increase. If the tax rate is decreased, and the overall cost is held constant, the level of benefits must decrease; if the level of benefits is held constant, the overall cost must increase. If the overall cost is decreased, and the level of benefits is held constant, the tax rate must increase; if the tax rate is held constant, the level of benefits must decrease.

It is impossible to change any one of these three main variables without affecting the others. Setting the values for any two of them automatically determines the other one. There is a direct mathematical relationship among all three variables—minimum benefit levels, tax rate, and cost—that is fixed for any particular radical welfare reform plan, a relationship that cannot be broken.

When any two of the three basic elements of radical welfare reform are set at politically acceptable levels, the remaining element becomes unacceptable. For example, if both the minimum welfare benefit level and the tax rate are set so they will be acceptable in today's political context, the cost of radical welfare reform balloons into tens of billions of dollars, adding millions of Americans to the welfare rolls. On the other hand, if the welfare benefit level is set at a politically tolerable level, and the overall cost is held down, the result is a tax rate that approaches confiscatory levels and destroys the financial incentive to work. And, finally, if the cost is acceptable and the tax rate is low enough to create a strong financial incentive to work, the level of welfare benefits in the plan must be reduced to such a low level that the plan would have no chance whatsoever of being enacted. *There is no way to achieve all the politically necessary conditions for radical welfare reform at the same time.*

As long as Americans believe that poor people who cannot help themselves deserve a decent level of welfare support, that people's incentive to work should not be taken away from them, and that to increase their taxes to give money to someone who may not feel like working is unthinkable, the kind of radical welfare reform being discussed in some of today's best and brightest intellectual circles is going to remain an ideological fantasy, bereft of friends in the hard world of politics.

During the spring of 1969, as a member of the White House working group charged with putting together President Nixon's welfare reform package, I attended many staff meetings on welfare. As Nixon's welfare reform plan neared its final shape it became uncomfortably clear that there were serious problems. The meetings seemed to move in a circular pattern. At one meeting it would be pointed out that the financial work incentives in the plan were far too low, that we could not reasonably subject poor people to effective marginal tax rates of well over 70 percent. All would agree, heads would nod, and the plan would go back to the drawing boards at HEW. At the next meeting it would be noted with satisfaction that the marginal tax rate, while still very high at 50 percent, was a notable improvement and we could live with it. Then someone would point out that the revised plan now cost several billion dollars more than before, and was therefore unacceptable for budgetary reasons. All would agree, heads would nod, and the plan would go back to HEW.

The next time we got together, everything would seem fine—the marginal tax rate had stayed at 50 percent, the overall cost was within budget limitations. But then someone would complain that the annual payment to a family of four was far below what they were then receiving from current welfare programs. It was agreed that this was politically intolerable, heads would nod, and the plan would go back once again to HEW. At the next meeting the newly revised plan was examined more warily. The overall cost was within budget limitations and the minimum payment to a family of four seemed to be sufficient to live decently on. But then someone noticed that the effective marginal tax rate on earned income had gone back up to over 70 percent. All agreed this was unacceptable, heads nodded, and the welfare experts from HEW vowed to redraft it once again.

This game continued until the necessity of sending a bill to the Congress ended it. No one seemed to clearly comprehend that there was, in fact, no way out of the dilemma presented by the conflicting goals of reasonably high welfare payments, low tax rates, and low cost. To some it seemed that the plan was "such a good thing" that the possibility of it not being possible was never seriously considered. So Nixon sent the Family Assistance Plan, the version with the high marginal rates, to the Congress. The House of Representatives never did have the time to understand the complexities of the proposal and passed the bill (243 to 155). Subsequently, however, an understanding of the important and radical implications of Nixon's welfare reform plan began to spread, and by the time it reached the Senate Finance Committee enough members of that committee understood them well enough to ask the simple questions that destroyed it.

One of the most embarrassing exchanges during the Senate Finance Committee hearings, which took place in early 1970, occurred among Senator Russell Long of Louisiana, the committee chairman, Senator John Williams, the ranking Republican from Delaware, and Robert Patricelli, then Deputy Undersecretary for Policy of HEW who had had a major part in drafting the bill. Patricelli had also been a member of the White House working group and had pushed hard to send the bill to the Congress. As the hearings progressed, Senators Long and Williams quickly struck at the weakest link in the Family Assistance Plan:

> SENATOR WILLIAMS: . . . If they [welfare recipients] increase their earnings from $720 to $5,560 under this bill, they have a spendable income of $6,109, or $19 less than they would if they sit in a rocking chair earning only $720. Is that not correct?
>
> MR. PATRICELLI: That is correct, Senator. . . .
>
> SENATOR WILLIAMS: They are penalized $19 because they go out and earn $5,500. Is that correct?
>
> MR. PATRICELLI: That is correct.
>
> THE CHAIRMAN: How can anybody justify a situation where a fellow goes to work to help himself and his family and he makes $3,920; he gets up to where his total income is $6,986, and then if he makes $1,600 more, his total income drops to $6,109. Now, how can you justify the man having $800 less after he makes $1,600 more? How do you justify that? What possible logic is there to it?
>
> MR. PATRICELLI: There is none, Senator. . . .[6]

As Daniel Patrick Moynihan later admitted, "The hearings were a calamity."[7] The saddest aspect of this humiliating political defeat, from the viewpoint of the Republican Administration, was that it was totally unnecessary. Patricelli and other welfare experts from HEW were aware that the bill sent to the Congress contained defects that, if widely known, could cause its defeat. And they knew it when they sold the welfare reform plan to Nixon.

The lesson that comes from fifteen years of radical welfare reform plans—from massive computer simulations of every conceivable combination of welfare payment levels, tax rates, and cost, from hundreds of hours of congressional testimony, and from countless academic studies—is a gradually spreading awareness that radical welfare reform cannot be accomplished without incurring intolerable political costs. The Achilles' heel of all radical reform plans is that there is *no way* to combine the three elements of welfare payment levels, tax rates, and program cost that does not leave at least one of them too high or too low to be politically feasible.

During the last decade or so some of the most brilliant thinkers in economics, political science, and sociology have struggled to develop a welfare reform plan that would solve this dilemma of conflicting goals. None has succeeded. And now some of the experts in the field of welfare reform are reluctantly concluding that "it can't be done." For the most part the analyses and conclusions of these experts have been set forth in relatively obscure scholarly journals and government publications.

Perhaps the first person to point out clearly the irreconcilability of the three main features of a guaranteed income was Professor James Tobin of Yale University. In 1966 he wrote: "In the design of an integrated allowance and tax schedule a compromise must be struck among three objectives: (a) providing a high basic allowance for families with little or no earnings, (b) building in a strong incentive to earn more, and (c) limiting the budgetary cost of the scheme. . . . It is essential to keep in mind that some compromise is necessary, that *there are inexorable conflicts among the three listed objectives*."[8]

One of the nation's best-known experts on welfare reform today is Senior Fellow Henry Aaron of the Brookings Institution, who was chosen by President Carter to be Assistant Secretary of HEW in charge of developing his welfare reform proposals. Summing up his analysis of several radical welfare reform plans in 1973, Aaron wrote, "The reason Congress had found it difficult to find a plan that provides universal benefits at a level regarded as reasonable, that preserves work incentives, and that is not vastly more expensive than President Nixon's proposals is that *no such plan exists or can be devised: These objectives are mutually inconsistent.*"⁹

Leonard J. Hausman, associate professor of social research at the Graduate School for Advanced Studies in Social Welfare at Brandeis University, has similarly concluded, "When designing a cash transfer program, policymakers seek high guarantees, low tax rates, and low break-even income levels. But attaining any two of these objectives conflicts with the third. . . . *No system of transfers can escape the dilemmas of income maintenance programs.*"¹⁰

Samuel A. Rea, Jr., assistant professor of economics at the University of Toronto, conducted a comprehensive study of radical welfare reform plans in 1974 for the Joint Economic Committee as part of its overall examination of public welfare policies. In his conclusion he states: "Programs which minimize the reductions in work effort tend to be inefficient in their impact on poverty. Programs with ample benefits for those with low incomes tend to be extremely costly. A decrease in the marginal tax rate for a negative income tax increases the budget cost and gives more benefits to those above the poverty line. Conversely, reductions in benefits to those with higher income through an increased tax rate reduce the incentives to work and increase the real cost. . . . The central point of this paper is that *there is no way of simultaneously meeting all of these objectives for income maintenance programs.*"¹¹

Irene Lurie, assistant professor of economics at Union College and staff member of the Institute for Research on Poverty at the University of Wisconsin, organized a major conference on welfare reform policy in 1972. In her overview paper she concluded, "The dissatisfaction with each of the programs points to one of the major lessons of the conference: *All desired goals cannot be achieved simultaneously* and trade-offs among them must be made in designing a system of programs.*"¹²

Discussing President Carter's intention to reform welfare, Richard Nathan, senior fellow of the Brookings Institution, advised in early 1977, "Again there is talk of cleaning up the 'welfare mess' by instituting a brand new system which would end red tape and save the taxpayers' money. *My suggestion is that we abandon the search for a utopian solution to welfare problems* and instead build on the programs we have."[13]

In another recent major study of public welfare policy, two members of the staff of the Subcommittee on Fiscal Policy of the Joint Economic Committee, Vee Burke and Alair A. Townsend, summed up their research findings by stating, "Income maintenance programs can be judged for their progress toward several goals, especially poverty reduction, maintenance of work incentives, least budget cost, and enhanced equity. Unfortunately, these objectives are inherently at odds with each other.... *It is impossible to fulfill simultaneously all the desired objectives.*"[14]

In another major examination of our welfare system and the radical proposals to reform it, Edgar K. Browning, associate professor of economics at the University of Virginia, ruefully admitted that the negative income tax approach he favors has serious problems: "It appears advisable, then, to have a low breakeven income and a low tax rate, but a high income guarantee. *Unfortunately, it is impossible to achieve simultaneously all these aims*, because of the necessary relationship between the policy variables."[15]

Writing in the *Public Interest* in early 1977, Fred Doolittle, doctoral student in economics, Frank Levy, associate professor of public policy, and Michael Wiseman, assistant professor of economics, all at the University of California at Berkeley, assessed President Carter's promise of welfare reform and concluded, "It is the beginning of welfare wisdom to recognize that *such idealized systems cannot be achieved*, no matter how ambitious the legislation.... Any suggestion of 'total welfare reform' will expose every aspect of the existing system to new debate, guaranteeing political stalemate."[16]

The verdict is in. Whether it is the negative income tax, the Family Assistance Plan, McGovern's $1,000 Demogrant, H.R.1

(the revised Family Assistance Plan), or HEW's Income Supplementation Plan—they all have the same problem. At least one, and sometimes more, of the three necessary conditions for political acceptance are absent.

The political impossibility of radical welfare reform does not mean that such radical change is technically impossible. A program of radical welfare reform can be developed, as many already have been. The program can be passed into law, and it can be implemented. But if it is, there will be consequences—either lower welfare benefits or higher rates of taxation for the poor, or tens of billions of dollars of added federal, state, and local expenditures—that will politically be very painful for the elected officials who become identified with the support of that radical reform.

In addition to the three major determinants of political feasibility just discussed there are other factors that reduce the chances for political success of any radical welfare plan that attempts to guarantee incomes. First, any such plan would add millions of Americans to the welfare rolls. The lower the welfare tax rate, or the rate at which welfare benefits are reduced as earned income increases, the higher the annual income a person can have and still remain on welfare. Because of the existing distribution of income in the United States, even slight increases in the level of income a person can have and still remain on welfare will make millions of additional people eligible. As Leonard Hausman has pointed out, "It is impossible, under any scheme, to maintain low cumulative tax rates while extending substantial cash and in-kind transfers to the working poor without also extending the coverage of these programs to middle-income brackets."[17]

Second, any form of a guaranteed income will cause a substantial amount of work reduction among low-income workers in the United States. The reduction in work effort could easily run as high as 50 percent, and there is some chance it would be even higher. While scarcely appreciated now, this phenomenon could well turn out to be the most politically damaging aspect of a guaranteed income.

And finally, there are certain to be unanticipated social effects. For example, one striking result of the guaranteed income experiments was a sharp increase in the number of *broken marriages* for the low-income families who took part in the experiments. This unexpected phenomenon is ironic, as one important virtue often claimed for a guaranteed income is the strengthening of the family. Unfortunately, the measured results of the Seattle-Denver guaranteed income experiment revealed that the incidence of marriage breakup for whites, who had been given an income guarantee of $3,800 a year, increased 430 percent during the first six months of the experiment. Over the entire two-year period studied, family breakup—relative to the control group—increased 244 percent for whites, 169 percent for blacks, and 194 percent for Chicanas.[18]

Apparently many low-income women were dissatisfied with their marriages, but had remained with their families because they were unable to support themselves. When a guaranteed income gave them a sufficient degree of financial independence, even though only for a few years, they left.[19]

One could argue that these marriage breakups were a good thing—that the couples were unhappy together, and that the guaranteed income made it possible for them to separate or get divorced. On the other hand, there may be quite a few taxpayers who won't understand why their tax money should be used to subsidize the breakup of marriages, especially those that involve children.

If the insoluble conflict among the goals of adequate welfare benefit payments, low marginal tax rates, and low budget cost is ignored—as it can be—there still remains a delicate task for the politician who supports such radical welfare reform. In the next election, he is the one who will have to answer his opponent's charge that he voted for welfare "reform" that lowered welfare benefits for hundreds of thousands, or even millions, of poor people, or that subjected welfare recipients to higher tax rates approaching confiscatory levels, or that added billions of dollars to the welfare budget. He is the one who will have to explain why so many more Americans went on welfare, why so many of them stopped working, and, perhaps, why so many of their marriages broke up.

Politically, it's all very risky.

CITATIONS—CHAPTER VI

1   Richard P. Nathan, "Modernize the System, Don't Wholly Discard It," *The Los Angeles Times*, February 27, 1977, section VI, page 3.

2   David W. Lyon, Philip A. Armstrong, James R. Hosek, and John J. McCall, *Multiple Welfare Benefits in New York City* (Santa Monica, California: The Rand Corporation, 1976), page 51, Figure 4.1.

3   Henry J. Aaron, *Why Is Welfare So Hard to Reform?* (Washington, D.C.: The Brookings Institution, 1973), page 39, Figure 4–3.

4   Ibid., page 43.

5   U.S., Congress, House, Committee on Ways and Means, testimony of Milton Friedman on Family Assistance Program, *Social Security and Welfare Proposals, Hearings*, 91st Congress, 1st session, November 7, 1969, Part 6, pages 1945 and 1948.

6   U.S., Congress, Senate, Committee on Finance, *Family Assistance Act of 1970, Hearings on H.R. 16311*, 91st Congress, 2nd session, April 29 and 30 and May 1, 1970, Part 1, page 278.

7   Daniel P. Moynihan, *The Politics of a Guaranteed Income: The Nixon Administration and the Family Assistance Plan* (New York: Random House, 1973), page 469.

8   James Tobin, "The Case for an Income Guarantee," *The Public Interest*, Number 4 (Summer 1966), pages 37 and 39. (Italics added.)

9   Aaron, *Why Is Welfare So Hard to Reform?*, pages 68–69. (Italics added.)

10 Leonard J. Hausman, "Cumulative Tax Rates in Alternative Income Maintenance Systems," in Irene Lurie (editor), *Integrating Income Maintenance Programs* (New York: Academic Press, 1975), page 77. (Italics added.)

11   Samuel A. Rea, Jr., "Trade-offs between Alternative Income Mainte-
nance Programs," in U.S., Congress, Joint Economic Committee,
Subcommittee on Fiscal Policy, *How Income Supplements Can Affect
Work Behavior*, Studies in Public Welfare, Paper No. 13 (Washington,
D.C., February 18, 1974), pages 59–60. (Italics added.)

12   Lurie, *Integrating Income Maintenance Programs*, page 37. (Italics
added.)

13   Nathan, "Modernize the System," page 3. (Italics added.)

14   U.S., Congress, Joint Economic Committee, Subcommittee on Fiscal
Policy, *Public Welfare and Work Incentives: Theory and Practice*,
prepared by Vee Burke and Alair A. Townsend, Studies in Public
Welfare, Paper No. 14 (Washington, D.C., April 15, 1974), page 43.
(Italics added.)

15   Edgar K. Browning, *Redistribution and the Welfare System* (Washington, D.C.: American Enterprise Institute for Public Policy Research,
1975), page 67. (Italics added.)

16   Frederick Doolittle, Frank Levy, and Michael Wiseman, "The Mirage of Welfare Reform," *The Public Interest*, Number 47 (Spring
1977), page 63 and 77. (Italics added.)

17   Hausman, "Cumulative Tax Rates in Alternative Income Maintenance Systems," page 40.

18   Nancy Brandon Tuma, Michael T. Hannan, and Lyle P. Groeneveld,
*Variation over Time in the Impact of the Seattle and Denver Income
Maintenance Experiments on the Making and Breaking of Marriages*,
Research Memorandum 43 (Menlo Park, California: Center for the
Study of Welfare Policy, Stanford Research Institute, 1977), page 13,
Table 1.

19   Michael T. Hannan, Nancy Brandon Tuma, and Lyle P. Groeneveld,
*A Model of the Effect of Income Maintenance on Rates of Marital
Dissolution: Evidence from the Seattle and Denver Income Mainte-
nance Experiments*, Research Memorandum 44, Menlo Park, Cali-
fornia: Center for the Study of Welfare Policy, Stanford Research
Institute, 1977), page 3.

VII

PRINCIPLES OF WORKABLE WELFARE REFORM

I thank my God the sun and moon
  Are both stuck up so high,
That no presumptuous hand can stretch
  and pluck them from the sky.
If they were not, I do believe
  That some reforming ass
Would recommend to take them down
  And light the world by gas.
               Anonymous, c. 1832

Seventh Thesis: *Practical welfare reform demands that we build on what we have. It requires that we reaffirm our commitment to the philosophical approach of giving aid only to those who cannot help themselves, while abandoning any thoughts of radical welfare reform plans that will guarantee incomes. The American people want welfare reform that ensures adequate help to those who need it, eliminates fraud, minimizes cost to the tax-payers, and requires people to support themselves if they can do so.*

There are two ingredients necessary to a successful program of welfare reform. First, it must be built on a clear and accurate perception of the current nature of the welfare system in the United States; and, second, it must be guided by a deep appreciation for the attitudes of Americans toward caring for people who cannot care for themselves. A plan for radical welfare reform that assumes the current system is virtually a total failure and does not take into account the public's hostility toward any form of a guaranteed income will ultimately fail, if not in the halls of the Congress, then later during its implementation. But if the reform plan builds on the strengths of our current welfare system and embraces a philosophical approach that is familiar to and accepted by the American people, its chances of success are very high.

In spite of the rather dismal record of welfare reform over the past decade at the national level, there are a number of concrete examples of successful welfare reform at the state level. The most dramatic example of practical welfare reform is the program initiated in California by Governor Reagan in 1971. It is particularly important in that it demonstrates beyond doubt that relatively simple administrative and legislative changes can have a substantial effect. Unlike many radical welfare proposals that promise to accomplish certain goals, this series of reforms actually worked.

In matters of public policy, usually very little is accomplished until a problem reaches a crisis state. And this is where California found itself in 1970. By then approximately 2.3 million Californians were receiving welfare benefits, an almost fourfold increase in less than a decade. In 1970 alone the welfare caseload increased by 20 percent, and it was continuing to grow by about 40,000 additional recipients every month. The huge and increasing cost of welfare "portended either gigantic state and local tax increases or the continued diminution of other vitally needed public programs and projects."[1] Things were getting serious.

The reasons for this sharp increase in the welfare rolls, in California and elsewhere, have been speculated on and argued about time and again. But a new factor seemed to be operating in 1969 and 1970. There had been intensive, widespread publicity about the radical welfare reform proposal, the Family Assistance Plan, that President Nixon set forth in 1969. State and local welfare officials, apparently confident of the proposal's ultimate passage, seem to have relaxed their efforts to reform and control the growth of the welfare system. As one analysis has pointed out, "This new proposal [the Family Assistance Plan] was widely viewed as a panacea to the problems which had plagued the states and their counties. . . . Throughout the welfare system the President's message brought a sense of relief. . . . The result was the abandonment of many reform efforts pending the anticipated federal take-over."[2]

The reform approach that the California officials decided to use was relatively more sophisticated than those employed by other states seeking the same ends. Other states, faced with a mounting welfare crisis, had resorted to arbitrary methods that often hurt poor people who were in need of help. For example, some of the tactics employed included "a 20 percent across-the-board cut in grants in Kansas; a house-to-house search for non-supporting fathers in Nevada; and termination of grants to families with unemployed fathers in New Jersey."[3] California officials, on the other hand, chose the more humane and reasonable approach of "purifying" the welfare system. Using the "sharp scalpel" rather than the "meat-ax," they set out to trim from the welfare rolls those who had no business receiving welfare payments, and to prevent ineligible applicants from getting on the welfare rolls. Their "goal was to preclude or uproot those from the system who legally 'didn't belong there,' while making grants more equitable—even *increasing* them as warranted—to eligibles who did belong."[4] The major thrust of their reform actions was to reduce the welfare rolls, not by kicking people off but rather by tightening up the enforcement of eligibility rules and regulations to cut down the inflow.[5]

There were two phases involved in California's welfare reform program. At the same time that California officials were trying to get legislation passed that would change existing welfare laws, they moved to enforce more carefully the laws that were on the books. Much of this executive action took place during the nine-month period preceding the implementation of legislative changes in October 1971. The effect of the administrative changes alone was striking: "The welfare program consisted of both administrative and legislative changes. Administrative reform, under the leadership of newly appointed State Director of Social Welfare Robert B. Carleson, had already begun in January 1971. . . . The effectiveness of these administrative changes is shown by the fact that between March and October [of 1971] the welfare rolls decreased by 161,000 people."[6]

The results of the legislative changes, which went into effect in late 1971, were equally dramatic. By June 1973, there were 352,000 fewer people receiving welfare in California than there were in March 1971. Even by conservative estimates there were some 785,000 *fewer* persons on the welfare rolls than had been projected on the assumptions of no reforms. And while the overall cost of welfare did not decrease, it has been estimated that over $1 billion in additional costs were avoided.[7] The reason welfare costs did not drop as the size of the welfare rolls shrank was that the savings realized were directed toward increasing the amount of money paid to the truly needy. The size of the welfare grant to families with little or no income *increased by about 43 percent.*[8] Thus while other states, and the federal government, were struggling to hold down the rate of increase of the welfare rolls, the absolute size of the rolls in California dropped by over a third of a million and the size of the grants to the truly needy increased by over 40 percent.

All this was not accomplished without some difficulty. California's welfare reforms were opposed by "welfare rights organizations, social workers' unions, supporters of H.R.1 and political opponents of the Governor."[9] The reforms were bitterly opposed in the California legislature. But an avalanche of favorable public reaction overwhelmed the resistance of the legislators and the welfare reforms were enacted. After their enactment there were numerous lawsuits, thousands of complaints were filed, and the fair-hearing process was jammed with cases.[10]

But the furor gradually died down and the reforms held. Late in 1975, Jerry Brown, the liberal Democratic successor to Ronald Reagan, stated flatly in response to a reporter's question that the controversial welfare reform was "holding up." And then he added, "Considering the high unemployment, it is amazing that it has kept welfare down as much as it is.... The Reagan welfare reform did impose restrictions, and although there is a lot of paperwork, it has put the brakes on."[11]

Today, almost five years after the first administrative reforms were begun, it seems as if they never happened. Over a third of a million people were eliminated from the welfare rolls and perhaps hundreds of thousands more prevented from coming on, and it was done without major political consequences. The outcome of these state-initiated reforms—the sharp decrease in the size of the welfare rolls and the more than 40 percent increase in welfare payments to families with little or no income—has largely been forgotten, especially east of the Potomac. But what should not be forgotten is the reform approach that produced the results. "Purifying" the welfare rolls of those who were ripping off the welfare system (and keeping off those who might have done likewise) stabilized the overall costs of welfare. The resources flowing into the welfare system were simply redirected from those who neither needed them nor had a right to them to those who were truly unable to care for themselves.

From time to time attempts have been made to translate state experiences with welfare reform into national policy. The most recent attempt was the Welfare Reform Act of 1975. Co-sponsored by a bipartisan group of sixty-two congressmen and nineteen senators, and based largely on the California welfare reform experience, the legislation proposed a comprehensive plan of welfare reform based on the needy-only philosophical approach. It aimed at changing "a substantive body of law in the federal Social Security Act and accompanying Department of Health, Education and Welfare regulations that perpetuates the irrational allocation of public assistance funds and serves as a barrier to complete reform."[12] It set forth a long list of detailed welfare reforms, including the tightening of grant and eligibility requirements, the strengthening of child support regulations, the establishment of more effective fraud-control techniques, and the development of better work requirements. The approach was piecemeal and incremental, building on the strengths of the current system while closing loopholes that drained off public funds to those who were never intended to receive them.

The Welfare Reform Act of 1975 failed to pass, but it did demonstrate that it was possible to develop a comprehensive incremental welfare reform package and secure substantial, though insufficient, political support. There are a number of reasons why the kind of welfare reform that worked in a state like California has not yet succeeded nationally. Welfare reform worked in California in 1971 for three essential reasons: (1) the welfare problem was becoming extremely serious and was so perceived by the California voters; (2) the Governor's office was willing to take the lead in developing administrative and legislative reforms that reflected the sentiments of the vast majority of people in the state; and (3) the executive branch was willing and able to take the case for such welfare reform directly to the people, over the heads of the legislators and various welfare lobby groups, thus generating enough political pressure to overcome the powerful defense of the status quo. These three conditions have never been met at the national level.

The American people do view the welfare problem seriously. But their concern about what the federal government should do about it is small relative to their concern about other issues—such as inflation, unemployment, energy, and national defense—that they expect the federal government to deal with. And no President has yet proposed a comprehensive welfare reform package that is directly in tune with the basic philosophical beliefs of the American people, let alone fought for it. True, President Nixon did fight for his radical welfare reform plan, but it never had the basic latent public support necessary for such a policy offensive to work.

The experience of the last ten years clearly shows that the American public will accept changes in the welfare system if they move in the direction of reorienting the system toward the needy-only approach to welfare. A program of reform that increases benefits to the truly needy, controls costs to the taxpayers, eliminates fraud and abuse, and provides strong encouragement for people on welfare to become self-supporting is entirely feasible— socially, economically, and politically. The legislative details of such a plan would be numerous and complex, matching in size and complexity the array of welfare programs we now have. The welfare system is constantly changing in small ways as the regulations governing its implementation are adjusted by the welfare bureaucrats. Any reform specifics would depend on the current state of each of the programs.

There are, however, some relatively timeless principles that could guide the detailed development of any national welfare reform plan. If we begin with the premise that any serious plan for welfare reform must be politically, economically, and socially feasible, we are forced to operate within certain constraints: the plan must be consistent with what most Americans believe welfare should do, it must have a reasonable cost, and is must efficiently and effectively provide an acceptable level of welfare benefits to the truly needy.

There are are least seven guiding points for such a program:

Point One: Reaffirm the needy-only philosophical approach to welfare and state it as explicit national policy. A welfare program can succeed only if it is basically in line with what most people believe is right. In the short run it might be possible to pass legislation that would institute a guaranteed income for all or, at the other extreme, simply eliminate all government welfare programs over a period of time and allow private charitable efforts to take care of people in need. But neither of these approaches will work unless preceded or accompanied by massive changes in deeply held public beliefs. A major change in either direction is possible, but until such change begins to occur any move to reform welfare that is not based on the needy-only philosophical approach will be inherently unstable and destined to fail.

Further, it is important to have a clear statement of national welfare policy as a guide for those who formulate the specific laws and regulations governing the welfare system. With no clear, well-defined principles the criteria for judging specific changes in welfare programs are murky, leaving advocates, pressure groups, government officials, and politicians relatively free to support or oppose specific changes, guided only by their own personal philosophical views on what our welfare system should ultimately be. The mere promulgation of a national welfare policy would not eliminate this, but the presence of clear principles against which specific actions could be judged by outside observers would certainly attenuate such tendencies.

Point Two: Increase efforts to eliminate fraud. Perhaps the one single thing about our current welfare system that most infuriates the typical American is the flagrant and open fraud perpetrated by a sizeable percentage of welfare recipients.

The extent of fraud and dishonesty has been clearly and irrefutably documented numerous times in recent years. For example, there was the HEW study of New York City in 1973, corroborated by a parallel study conducted by the General Accounting Office, that showed that in the Aid for Dependent Children program alone, over 10 percent of the recipients were ineligible for any payment whatsoever, and 23 percent were being overpaid (8 percent were underpaid). A California study, conducted in 1972, showed that 41 percent of the state's welfare recipients were either ineligible or overpaid. Admittedly, some of these welfare irregularities were and are due to administrative error on the part of the welfare bureaucracy. But there is no question that hundreds of millions, probably billions, of dollars are taken from taxpayers every year and given to people who have no legal right to receive them.

Few Americans begrudge a truly needy person the money and services that our welfare programs provide, but most are enraged at the thought of someone who is fully able of caring for himself smugly cashing a government welfare check at the local supermarket. For many Americans welfare reform means only one thing—apprehend those who are defrauding the system and remove them from the welfare rolls.

Perhaps no other single issue has contributed more to the low status of welfare recipients than the public's conviction that a high percentage of those on welfare don't deserve it. Because there is no practical way to identify welfare cheats, a certain portion of the hostility generated by those who abuse the welfare system gets directed at all who receive welfare. As long as fraud is widespread, anyone on welfare is suspect to some degree in the minds of many people. A substantial reduction of welfare fraud would result in large cost savings and would greatly help restore confidence in and respect for the system. And it would wipe away the stigma of cheating from those who validly receive welfare.

Point Three: Establish and enforce a fair, clear work requirement. A welfare system based on the needy-only approach requires some means of ensuring that only those who truly cannot help themselves receive aid. During the last decade we have come to rely heavily on "financial incentives" to induce people on welfare to work if they are able to do so. Unfortunately, this has produced the dilemma described in Chapter II—the "poverty wall." There is no feasible way that the very high effective marginal tax rates imposed by our current welfare system on the poor can be reduced. The radical welfare reform plans proposed would only exacerbate the problem further. Any significant reduction in the welfare tax rates, significant enough to create an effective financial work incentive, would either be prohibitively expensive or result in a very low basic welfare payment.

We have gotten ourselves into the position of relying on a work incentive technique that is *unworkable*. Financial work incentives are fine in theory, but in the current welfare situation the constraints of cost and benefit levels have rendered them virtually useless. As a practical matter the financial work incentives produced by marginal tax rates of well over 70 percent are negligible—and there is no politically feasible way to decrease the rates enough to make them effective.

There is a way out of this dilemma, but it requires that we reexamine our commitment to using financial incentives to encourage people to remove themselves voluntarily from the welfare rolls and find work. The idea of trying to use financial incentives to induce people to get off the welfare rolls is faulty in principle. It attempts to *persuade* people to do something they should be *required* to do. If we assume that our welfare system is to provide help to the needy only, it then follows that either a person has a valid need for welfare payments and should be on the welfare rolls or that person does not have a valid need for welfare payments and should not be on the welfare rolls. If persons are capable of self-support, both for themselves and for their families, then there is no reason they should expect to receive any money from other members of the society who work and pay taxes. There is no reason people should be given financial incentives to do what they rightfully should be doing anyway.

The basic principle involved here is one of dependence versus independence. If a person is capable of taking care of himself, he is independent and should not qualify for any amount of welfare. To the extent that a person is dependent—that is, to the extent that he cannot care for himself—to that extent he qualifies for welfare. If he can earn part of what he needs, then he has an obligation to work to that extent.

The major difficulty with such a principle is its implementation. For someone must judge whether or not the welfare recipient is capable of work. But difficult as this may be, it can be done. As in all judicial-type decisions, there are things that reasonable persons can reach agreement on. It will, however, require a shift away from the growing trend toward a more automatic, check-mailing type of welfare operation to a more personalized, people-oriented kind of welfare administration that emphasizes both the authority and the responsibility of local government.

In sum, we must abandon the idea of depending on financial incentives to induce people to leave the welfare rolls. Instead, our welfare programs should be guided by the simple principle that a person gets welfare only if he or she qualifies for it by the fact of being incapable of self-support. If they don't qualify, they have no right to welfare. Rather than being encouraged to find work, they should be given reasonable notice and then removed from the welfare rolls.

Point Four: Remove inappropriate beneficiaries from the welfare rolls. There are certain categories of welfare recipients whose eligibility, while legal, is questionable. With the needy-only principle as a guideline the welfare rolls should be examined carefully and the regulations changed to exclude any groups who fail to qualify. Two prime candidates for disqualification would be workers who strike and then apply for welfare benefits claiming loss of income, and college students who queue up for food stamps.

Point Five: Enforce support of dependents by those who have the responsibility and are shirking it. Too often we fail to ask why people are on welfare. In many cases today, the answer is simple: a father deserts his family with the clear knowledge that because of the way the law works there is little chance that he will ever be called to account. Today a very high percentage of families receiving welfare payments have an absent parent who could contribute to their support. While increased efforts have been made in recent years to remedy this situation, it is time to strongly reassert the old idea that both the father and the mother have a responsibility to care for their children.

This kind of child support enforcement could substantially lower welfare costs. During 1976, the first year the federal government made any serious effort to track down runaway welfare fathers, the Department of HEW collected some $280 million. It is estimated that such collections could mount as high as $1 billion a year by 1980.

For every absent parent who can be required to contribute to the support of his or her spouse and children we could remove, on the average, three or four people from the welfare rolls. If only as a matter of justice, parents who desert their families should be tracked down—across state lines if necessary—and required to provide a reasonable level of support.

Point Six: Improve the efficiency and effectiveness of welfare administration. It seems that almost everyone agrees that the administration of the welfare system could be greatly improved—in effectiveness, efficiency, and responsiveness. The necessity for major improvements in countless areas of administration has been repeatedly documented. The reports and tales of gross mismanagement have become almost commonplace, and shocking revelations no longer seem capable of rousing a benumbed public. For example, in 1976 New York State's Welfare Inspector General estimated that "nearly $1 billion, or almost one-sixth" of welfare-related costs in New York, were "being dissipated through recipient and vendor fraud, administrative error or unnecessary and overbilled services."[13] A billion dollars a year being lost through bad management in one large state would have been a page one scandal not too many years ago. The *New York Times* carried the story on page 29.

Administration is perhaps the most unexciting, intractable area in which to initiate welfare reform. People's eyes glaze over at the first mention of reorganization, revised regulations, and improved personnel administration. But dull as the area may be to most, it is of critical importance to any effective welfare reform plan. Welfare reform cannot succeed until and unless administrative reform is made a matter of top national priority, unless clear standards of performance are set, and until those standards are rigorously enforced by rewarding those welfare managers who succeed and penalizing those who fail.

Point Seven: Shift more responsibility for welfare from the federal government to state and local governments and to private institutions. The question of which level of government—federal, state, or local—is best able to perform a particular function, or indeed whether the function should not be attended to by government at all but instead be left to private initiative, is one that has perplexed scholars and policymakers for a long time. When President Eisenhower took office in early 1953, one of his first acts was to establish a national commission of distinguished Americans (among them Oveta Culp Hobby, Clark Kerr, Hubert Humphrey, and Wayne Morse) to study this problem and recommend to him a set of specific actions. The commission worked intensively for almost two years and concluded, "Assuming efficient and responsible government at all levels—National, State and local—we should seek to divide our civic responsibilities so that we leave to private initiative all the functions that citizens can perform privately; use the level of government closest to the community for all public functions it can handle . . . [and] reserve National action for residual participation where State and local governments are not fully adequate, and for the continuing responsibilities that only the National Government can undertake."[14]

The public opinion polls now indicate strong support for such a shift. A 1976 nationwide Harris survey posed a number of propositions and asked whether the statement applied more to the federal government or to state government. The results revealed that the majority of the American people felt that state government was "closer to the people" (65% to 12%); state governments could "be trusted more" (39% to 15%); state governments "really care what happens to people" (36% to 14%); the federal government "is more out of touch with what people think" (56% to 12%); and the federal government "gives the taxpayer less value for the tax dollar" (44% to 23%).[15]

Another national Harris poll, designed expressly to determine how the American public feels about the role of state and local governments, produced results more directly relevant to the issue of welfare. When asked what level of government—state, local, or federal—should make key policy decisions in regard to welfare, the American public favored state and local governments over the federal government by a margin of 56 percent to 39 percent. Five percent were undecided.[16]

I can think of no more appropriate place to apply the progressive principles of decentralizing government than to our welfare system. It has been argued, and fairly so, that a good deal of the waste and inefficiency in our welfare programs, the growing impersonalization, and the strong desire to "automate" the whole thing, is directly linked to the increased federal role in welfare. As authority over welfare has become centralized in Washington, the policymakers have become increasingly remote and isolated from the welfare recipients. As government, at all levels, has taken a greater and greater role in welfare, people seem to have become more reluctant to contribute to private charitable institutions.

We can arrest this trend toward a centralized, impersonal welfare bureaucracy by moving on two fronts. First, we should encourage people to take a more active role in charitable endeavors by allowing people a tax credit for charitable contributions, perhaps with some limit as to the maximum credit that could be taken. If it is considered good to use a tax credit to finance political campaigns, wouldn't it be even better to use one to encourage the growth of private charitable endeavors? In addition, the current limit on the amount of charitable contributions that is deductible in computing taxable income should be raised significantly. If pursued properly, such a combined policy of deductions and credits for charitable contributions would gradually reduce government's role, while at the same time increasing the total resources available for welfare.

Second, for the continuing, large role in welfare that would remain for the government in the near future, an effort should be made to transfer both authority and responsibility for welfare programs, and the resources used to fund those programs, from the federal government to state and local governments. On balance, the closer the level of government is to the people, the more efficient and effective our social welfare programs are apt to be. As Dan Lufkin concluded, after serving for two years as Connecticut's first Commissioner of Environmental Protection, "The more the administration of policies and programs is brought down to the state and local level, the better the people will be able to judge who is fair, who is honest, who is creative, and who is productive and efficient."[17]

A comprehensive welfare reform plan that hewed to these seven basic principles could go far toward restoring equity and efficiency to our welfare system. Its cost would be minimal and, in fact, could even lead to reductions in welfare expenditures. The latent public support for such a plan is clearly there. What is missing is the strong national commitment for this kind of welfare reform that can come only from a White House initiative, followed by widespread public exposure. This exposure must be effective enough to generate the political pressure needed to overcome the resistance of advocates of a guaranteed income who, though small in number, now occupy strategic positions in government, the media, and academia.

CITATIONS—CHAPTER VII

1   Ronald A. Zumbrun, Raymond M. Momboisse, and John H. Findley, "Welfare Reform: California Meets the Challenge," *The Pacific Law Journal*, Volume IV (July 1973), pages 740–741.

2   Ibid., page 742.

3   Ibid., page 781.

4   Ibid., page 744. (Italics added.)

5   Interview with Robert B. Carleson, former Director of Social Welfare for the State of California and former U.S. Commissioner of Welfare, May 16, 1977.

6   Zumbrun, Momboisse, and Findley, "Welfare Reform," page 747. Figures cited are rounded to the nearest thousand.

7   Ibid., page 782.

8   Carleson interview.

9   Zumbrun, Momboisse, and Findley, "Welfare Reform," page 748.

10 Carleson interview.

11 Jerry Brown, quoted by Carl Ingram, UPI wire service (Sacramento, California), August 10, 1975.

12 Republican Study Committee, "The National Welfare Reform Act of 1975: A Proposal for Meaningful AFDC Reform," Background Paper for the 94th Congress, Number 3, mimeographed (March 1975), page II-89.

13 *The New York Times*, September 30, 1976, page 29.

14 Commission on Intergovernmental Relations, *Commission on Intergovernmental Relations: A Report to the President for Transmittal to the Congress* (Washington, D.C., June 1955), page 6.

15. *Current Opinion* (Roper Public Opinion Research Center), Volume IV (September 1976), page 89.

16 Dan W. Lufkin, *Many Sovereign States: A Case for Strengthening State Government—An Insider's Account* (New York: David McKay Company, 1975), page 225, Table 15.

17 Ibid., page 194.

VIII

POSTSCRIPT: PRESIDENT CARTER'S WELFARE REFORM PLAN

> The people often, deceived by an illusive good, desire their own ruin, and, unless they are made sensible of the evil of the one and the benefit of the other course by some one in whom they have confidence, they will expose the republic to infinite peril and damage. And if it happens that the people have no confidence in any one, as sometimes will be the case when they have been deceived before by events or men, then it will inevitably lead to the ruin of the state.
>
> Niccolo Machiavelli, c. 1516

Eighth Thesis: *President Carter's welfare reform proposal would add nearly 22 million more Americans to the welfare rolls. The federal cost of welfare would increase by about $20 billion a year, and most of that money would go to families with incomes above the poverty level. Effective marginal tax rates would remain very high and act as a serious financial disincentive to work. The proposed Program for Better Jobs and Income (PBJI) would be more complex, require more welfare workers, and be more difficult to administer than the current welfare system. The basic thrust of PBJI is to further the idea of a guaranteed income, expanding welfare into the heart of the middle class of America. It is a potential social revolution of great magnitude that could result in social tragedy.*

It is always somewhat risky to write books that deal with current public policy issues. A year or more can often pass between the completion of a manuscript and its publication as a finished work. During that time events may supersede what is discussed in the book. It is even more risky to make predictions about what might happen. For the future will provide the evidence by which those predictions can be judged.

The preceding chapters of this book were drafted before President Carter announced the details of his plan to reform our welfare system. Carter's plan is the latest in a long series of attempts to radically change our welfare system. Its appearance does not affect the analysis of the earlier chapters, but it does provide a clear test of that analysis. For Carter set out to do what our analysis has said cannot be done without grave political consequences. Has his Administration figured out how to untie the Gordian knot of welfare? Or, if not, has Carter decided to accept the heavy political costs of implementing a radical change in our welfare system by instituting the essentials of a guaranteed income? Or has he blundered, and failed to perceive the intractable obstacles that derailed all previous attempts?

Welfare reform was high on the domestic policy agenda of the Carter Administration right from the beginning. On January 26, 1977, less than a week after President Carter took the oath of office, Joseph A. Califano, Jr., the new Secretary of Health, Education and Welfare, proclaimed there would be "a major study of the U.S. welfare system to produce recommendations on how President Carter would carry out his campaign pledge to overhaul aid programs for the poor."[1] This study group was headed by Henry Aaron, the new Assistant Secretary of HEW for Planning and Evaluation and a former senior fellow at the Brookings Institution. Aaron was considered one of the top welfare experts in the country. At the same time it was announced that the recommendations of the study group were to be sent to President Carter on May 1, 1977. That gave the group ninety-five days to come up with a solution.

In general the announcement of Carter's plans to reform welfare were received quite favorably. Almost everyone knew of something that was wrong with the current system. Perhaps this plan would remedy it. The reaction of people who were familiar with our welfare system was more skeptical. They had heard all this many times before. Three of them, writing in the *Wall Street Journal* in April 1977, stated flatly: "The President will attempt to restructure the entire welfare system at once and in so doing will accomplish nothing at all."[2]

The first sign of trouble appeared on April 25, 1977, less than a week before the details of Carter's new plan were to be revealed. Daniel Patrick Moynihan, now the junior senator from New York, told the press that the White House would not send welfare legislation to the Congress until sometime in the fall. Instead, on the day the recommendations were due, the White House would issue a statement of principles rather than concrete legislative proposals.

Moynihan was indignant at the delay. His quest for a guaranteed income, which had begun under President Nixon, had never faltered. "This is HEW at it again," Moynihan said. "They produce wonderful books on how you cannot do it. . . . [A person] with a first-rate mind and three months' experience could draft legislation in a morning." And then he reminded everyone that welfare reform was a "fundamental pledge of the President and our party."[3]

Two days later the White House, perhaps a little embarrassed at the leak of its plans to delay welfare reform, boldly announced that the President would unveil "dramatic and fundamental" welfare reform recommendations shortly and that he "reaffirmed his commitment to welfare reform as a major policy of his administration."[4]

On May 2, 1977, President Carter, in spite of Moynihan's scolding, announced his goals of welfare reform, promising that the legislation would be drawn up later—by the first week in August. "The present welfare programs should be scrapped and a totally new system implemented," he stated. "This conclusion in no way is meant to disparage the great value of the separate and individual programs enacted by the Congress over the past decade and a half. . . . This conclusion is only to say that these many separate programs, taken together, still do not constitute a rational, coherent system that is adequate and fair for all the poor."[5]

And then the President laid out twelve goals for his welfare reform program. They were, in his words:

- No higher initial cost than the present systems.
- Under this system, every family with children and a member able to work should have access to a job.
- Incentives should always encourage full-time and part-time private sector employment.
- Public training and employment programs should be provided when private employment is unavailable.
- A family should have more income if it works than if it does not.
- Incentives should be designed to keep families together.
- Earned income tax credits should be continued to help the working poor.
- A decent income should be provided also for those who cannot work or earn adequate income, with Federal benefits consolidated into a simple cash payment, varying in amount only to accommodate differences in costs of living from one area to another.
- The programs should be simpler and easier to administer.
- There should be incentives to be honest and to eliminate fraud.
- The unpredictable and growing financial burden on state and local governments should be reduced as rapidly as Federal resources permit.
- Local administration of public job programs should be emphasized.[6]

President Carter was obviously sincere in his desire to overhaul our welfare system. But, like the two Presidents who preceded him, he had seriously underestimated the difficulty and complexity of doing so. At a briefing for reporters after his confident endorsement of comprehensive welfare reform, he admitted that "the complexity of the system is almost incomprehensible."

If his experience was anything like that of others who have come to Washington and peered into our welfare system, he must have been sorely tempted to back off from his campaign pledge until he had a better grasp of what was going on. In fact, he did seem to hedge somewhat when he announced that the details of his proposals would be delayed, and that his program, if enacted, would not go into effect for about four years. But when he laid down his "twelve commandments" of welfare reform he was irretrievably committed to coming up with a comprehensive plan, and soon.

It is unfortunate that new administrations rarely learn one lesson of governing any way but the hard way. The solutions to major problems that seem to cry out for answers have not been ignored on account of whim. Nor is it likely that the solutions have not been found for lack of intelligent, creative people in Washington. Almost always, the reason no solutions have been found is that there are profound, often conflicting, social, economic, and political problems that preclude simple answers. But few believe it until they experience it.

Within weeks some of President Carter's twelve fundamental goals of welfare reform were in serious trouble—especially his pledge of no additional cost to the taxpayers. Shortly after Carter announced his plans to the nation, two of his chief advisors on welfare reform, Secretary of Labor F. Ray Marshall and Secretary of HEW Joseph A. Califano, Jr., sent him a memorandum warning him that he could not live up to his pledges. The memorandum included the following points: "The politics of welfare reform are treacherous under any circumstances and they can be impossible at no higher initial cost, because it is likely that so many people who are now receiving benefits will be hurt. The states are our natural allies in welfare reform—most members of Congress would still prefer not to deal with the subject at all—and there is virtually no relief in this proposal for governors and mayors. In addition there will be problems in cutting benefits for the aged, the disabled, and the blind, and there will be disputes over our ability to put a significant number of the 3.4 million mothers on welfare to work."[7]

President Carter may have wondered why they didn't tell him all this before he made his May 2nd statement. It does place a President in a somewhat difficult position to tell him, after he has announced his plans for welfare reform to the nation, that those plans entail cutting welfare payments for the aged, the disabled, and the blind; that those plans involve forcing "significant" numbers of mothers with children to go to work; and that the mayors and governors probably won't support it anyway because there is no money in it for them.

The President had two choices: (1) he could break his pledge of no additional cost and allocate billions of dollars of federal money to redeeming his basic welfare reform package, or (2) he could watch the whole thing go down to a swift, humiliating defeat. Carter gave in and authorized "Califano and Marshall to develop a program along the outlines *they* set down."[8] So on May 25, 1977, Secretary Califano announced some of the details of Carter's welfare reform package, stressing that they were tentative proposals and that "no final decisions have been made on welfare reform."[9]

For the next two months, as the welfare professionals at HEW struggled to transform President Carter's principles into legislative specifics, the national discussion of welfare reform ebbed. Then, at a nationally televised news conference on July 28, 1977, the issue of welfare reform reemerged. As Carter responded to a question about how committed he was to holding welfare spending to its present level, it was obvious that he was still wrestling with the problem. "It's all very difficult," he complained. "I came over to my office this morning at 5:30 and I spent three hours working on the welfare question before my first appointment. And this afternoon I have two more hours of study and work with Cabinet members on the welfare question. . . . How to deal with these different questions and how to tie it in with a comprehensive tax reform is something that I'm spending a lot of time on." And then he reasserted his initial pledge of no additional cost, stating, "I'm trying to hold down the cost of the overall program and I think if you'll look at the careful wording of my goals, they said the initial costs would not exceed present expenditures. We're trying now to estimate also the ultimate cost of these programs—what they will cost in 1980 and 1985."[10]

During the early days of August 1977, Congressman Al Ullman, chairman of the House Ways and Means Committee, and others expressed dissatisfaction with major elements of the plan. Rumors that Carter might delay it once again surfaced in Washington. But on August 6, 1977—just two days short of eight years from the date President Nixon announced his Family Assistance Plan—President Carter unveiled the full details of his blueprint for comprehensive welfare reform from his hometown of Plains, Georgia.

It was called the **Program for Better Jobs and Income (PBJI)**. Fulfilling his campaign pledge, President Carter asked the Congress to "totally scrap our existing welfare system, and to replace it with a program for better jobs and income, which will provide job opportunities for those able to work, and a simplified uniform cash assistance program for those who are unable to work due to disability, age or family circumstances."[11]

The people of the United States clearly favored some kind of welfare reform. As welfare once again moved up front on the national policy agenda, a special Gallup poll was taken in May of 1977. Looking ahead to President Carter's welfare reform proposals, Gallup asked the following question: "Congress will soon begin many reforms in the way welfare is handled in the United States. What changes, if any, would you like to see made?" The kind of reform the American people wanted was clearly evident in their replies. To this open-ended question on welfare 52 percent answered that they would like *"better investigative/screening methods"* to eliminate cheaters. Another 28 percent said that *"those who can work should be taken off welfare."* More *"work programs"* were favored by 12 percent; 5 percent said there were general *"changes needed"*; 2 percent wanted *"costs reduced"*; and 2 percent thought that we should *"eliminate welfare"* altogether. Twenty-six percent said that there was *"not enough aid for the deserving,"* indicating a desire to increase welfare payments for the truly needy. Two percent said our welfare programs were *"fine as is, no changes needed."* And there were the usual minority—10 percent—who had no-opinion one way or the other.*

The pattern of the responses was consistent with what public opinion polls have shown over the past decade. The greatest concern most Americans have with our current welfare system is the widespread cheating they believe exists. At the same time, they overwhelmingly favor the continuation of welfare payments to those who cannot help themselves, with a significant number favoring an increase in welfare payments to the "deserving." Little, if any, sentiment is expressed for a guaranteed income, or for expanding welfare to those who are poor but able to work, or for a massive increase in government spending on welfare.

Before we can evaluate how well President Carter's proposal to reform our welfare system fulfills what the American public expects of welfare reform, it is necessary to determine what the plan would do. Who would it affect and how would they be affected? How much would it cost? Would it be simpler and easier to understand? Would it significantly reduce the number of people who receive welfare but shouldn't?

It would be nice if we could rely on what the Department of Health, Education and Welfare *says* about what a welfare reform plan will do, how much it will cost the taxpayers, how it will affect

---

*Total adds to more than 100 percent because of multiple responses.

both the poor and the nonpoor. Unfortunately, we cannot. This is not due to any incompetence or deception unique to the Carter Administration. Rather, it is the lesson we have learned the hard way during the past ten years or so. Radical welfare reform plans, such as Nixon's Family Assistance Plan (FAP) and the Income Supplementation Plan (ISP) submitted to Ford, have proven to be quite different from what they were claimed to be. Their costs were greatly underestimated. Their claims of simplicity, of reduced numbers of welfare workers, of greater financial incentives to work, and of improved aid to those unable to care for themselves were greatly exaggerated. And while little was said about a guaranteed income, the essence of one was an integral part of the proposed reforms.

In looking at President Carter's welfare reform plan we must differentiate—as was necessary for the welfare reform plans developed under President Nixon and President Ford—between what is claimed for the plan and what is. Presidential candidates and newly elected presidents enunciate policy principles and goals. They rarely, if ever, have the time and skilled staff to work out specific ways of implementing those principles and goals. They must rely, for the most part, on the advice and counsel of the experts who are a permanent part of the Washington bureaucracy. The consequence of this is that President Carter's proposed PBJI was drawn up by essentially the same folks who gave FAP to President Nixon and ISP to President Ford.

It is important not to forget that many of the welfare bureaucrats in HEW and other government agencies concerned with welfare programs are advocates. It is perhaps not unfair to say that most of the people intimately involved with the design and development of welfare reform proposals favor the expansion of welfare—more money, more services—to more people. Many of them favor a guaranteed income. They believe strongly in what they are trying to accomplish. They often stay in their jobs from administration to administration, and are quite adaptable to new presidents and their staffs. They know the current welfare system far better than those who have the authority to change policy—far better than they will ever know it.

When asked to develop specific proposals to reform the welfare system, the welfare professionals do not come up with a range of objectively analyzed alternatives. They will, of course, present a range of alternative proposals. But somehow, the alternative they personally favor usually—at least to the uninitiated—appears to be preferable to the others. When they present alternative proposals to a president, they, like other advocates, stress the good points and minimize the drawbacks. Sometimes they ignore the drawbacks. The president therefore will often be unaware of a number of major policy implications inherent in the alternatives set before him. This is particularly true of the negative political consequences of a course of action favored by the entrenched bureaucracy to whom he has turned for help.

However little a president and his top aides know about the full implications of any new policy they embrace, once they announce the details of that policy they become publicly committed to it on a grand scale. They want the proposed legislation to pass, to become law. For if it does not, they will suffer a certain amount of public embarrassment, which can often lead to political damage. If their political concerns become serious enough, they can easily become more interested in passing something—good or bad—than in admitting that their original proposal was flawed. In matters of this kind a president does not make "mistakes." What he sends to the Congress he usually fights for, regardless of future developments.

The Washington bureaucrats know this. If they can only get an administration publicly committed to a course of action, the chances are great that the administration will continue to follow that course, even though the going may get very rough.

Both the White House's selective presentation of new national policy initiatives and the manner in which the media communicate them to the public tend to contribute to locking an administration onto its initial course. Any public policy proposal as complex as comprehensive welfare reform is virtually impossible to digest and communicate to the public in the few hours reporters have to meet their deadlines. The White House knows that most of the material in its proposals, especially the numbers, will be seized on and used by the media. Later these numbers, and other points, may be refined and refuted by critical analyses. But the initial media thrust will faithfully reflect what the reporters have been given in official White House press releases. As a practical matter it has to be this way. Few, if any, White House reporters are welfare experts. And even if they were, time pressures would preclude any but the most cursory analysis.

The people who develop the details of a welfare reform proposal will be the same ones the White House calls on to draft the material it will hand out to the press. Thus, to a significant extent, what the American public first hears about a welfare reform proposal will be what the professional welfare reformers want them to know—no more, no less.

For example, most of the press reports of President Carter's welfare reform plan, PBJI, said it would cost $2.8 billion. Ignored was an additional $3.4 billion of lost tax revenues due to the planned expansion of the earned income tax credit. Why? Well, President Carter asserted in his briefing to the press that he "had established as a goal that the new reform system involve no higher initial cost than the present system," but that "after careful consultation with state and local leaders, members of Congress and many other interested persons throughout the country, we have now provided $2.8 billion in added benefits."[12] The more detailed press release from HEW did not mention costs until page 20 where, in a footnote, it specifically excluded the $3.4 billion cost of an expanded earned income tax credit, asserting simply that those tax reductions "are not considered a cost of the welfare program."[13] They are, of course, and more sophisticated news reports, such as those carried by the *New York Times*, correctly identified $6.2 billion as the claimed amount of additional spending.

In any event, the initial reactions to early reports on President

Carter's welfare reform plan were generally favorable. Headlines for the most part stressed exactly what the welfare bureaucrats and the White House wanted them to stress: CARTER ASKS NEW WELFARE SYSTEM WITH EMPHASIS ON REQUIRED WORK; NEW YORK COULD SAVE $527 MILLION (how could any New Yorker be against that?).... CARTER: SCRAP WELFARE SYSTEM.... SPENDING WOULD GO UP $2.8 BILLION.... WORK-WELFARE PLAN OFFERED BY PRESIDENT.... CARTER PROPOSES WORK-WELFARE PLAN IN PLACE OF "FRAUD-RIDDLED" SYSTEM.... REWARDS FOR WORK EFFORT. It was a press secretary's dream. The message being conveyed to the American people was exactly what the polls were showing the public wanted: a program to eliminate fraud, stress work effort, keep federal costs in line, and reduce costs to the states.

The people liked what they heard. A national Harris poll taken shortly after the media had explained President Carter's welfare reform plan to the nation revealed that an overwhelming majority of Americans, by a margin of 70 percent to 13 percent, supported the plan. They believed it would eliminate many of the abuses in the current system, be simpler in operation, and give people a strong incentive to work. Even Senator Moynihan thought that President Carter's PBJI was "magnificent and very well crafted."[14] This was not unimportant, for Senator Moynihan was now the chairman of the Senate subcommittee that would consider Carter's proposals.

In 1977 almost everyone liked what President Carter *said* his welfare reform plan would do. Initial media coverage was favorable and optimistic. But in 1969 the public, by a large margin, had also approved of what Nixon said he was going to do about welfare, and many governors and mayors had endorsed his plan. It wasn't until after many months of rigorous probing by congressional committees that the true nature of Nixon's Family Assistance Plan became known, and gradually, and then in increasing numbers, those who had initially endorsed it began to change their minds, and conclude that FAP was undesirable.

The question is whether or not PBJI is another FAP. Are the

claims for it reasonable? Are the cost estimates realistic? Are there any hidden consequences that were not spelled out in the original proposal? If President Carter's **PBJI** can do what is claimed, at the cost estimated, then it will probably be enacted into law. But before that happens **PBJI** must run a gauntlet of scrutiny by both the Congress and independent experts.

Some of the claims and estimates in Carter's **PBJI** proposal were received skeptically by many welfare experts in the Congress and outside of government. They had seen too many similar claims evaporate before. But they were hesitant to criticize the plan seriously until a careful analysis of the details had been made. And such an analysis was a difficult, time-consuming job. A new welfare plan of the scope and size of the one President Carter proposed can be analyzed only with the aid of a computer and enormous quantities of statistical data on the number of families involved and their income. The plan was put together at HEW, utilizing the department's powerful computers, a sophisticated and very complex computer program, and income data from the Bureau of the Census. In order to check HEW's estimates one must have access to an equally powerful computer, the same complex statistical data, a comprehensive computer program, many skilled analysts—and a large budget.

Until recently such a capability did not exist outside of HEW, and one was forced to either accept what HEW said on faith or, as was the case with Nixon's Family Assistance Plan, tediously work out specific case examples to illustrate what the plan would do. Congress was particularly vulnerable. It had to enact, amend, or reject the legislation sent to it by the executive branch, but had few resources with which to conduct an independent review of the claims and estimates in the proposals sent down by the White House. Welfare reform, though by no means the only issue over which Congress found itself in this dilemma, is an excellent example of why Congress needed an independent analysis unit.

To provide this kind of independent analysis capability the

Congressional Budget Office (CBO) was established in 1975. As soon as Carter's plan was announced, the CBO acquired HEW's computer program and, in cooperation with HEW, began its own analysis. It took the CBO about four months to penetrate Carter's welfare reform plan and to make its own estimates of the costs and the numbers of people involved. Many other analyses were begun, but the CBO analysis was the first major *independent* analysis of the PBJI proposal. In the following examination of Carter's plan we shall draw heavily on that work.

The details of any major welfare reform proposal, whether it be FAP or ISP or PBJI, are so numerous and complicated that it is literally impossible to conceptually grasp all of their elements. Plans for this kind of welfare reform involve tens of billions of dollars, tens of millions of people, tens of thousands of welfare workers, and hundreds of separate programs. To attempt to understand it all, unless you intend to make it your life work, is to ensure that you will miss its essence. It is all too easy to become so engrossed in the details that you miss the major thrusts of the proposed reforms.

However, there is one approach that can make it possible to get to the essence of any welfare reform proposal rapidly and easily. The bottom line in welfare reform is what happens to the people affected by the program—who gains, who loses, and who they are. Perhaps next to the bottom line is the cost to the taxpayers. To find out the essentials of what we need to know in order to evaluate a welfare reform proposal intelligently, all we must do is receive valid answers to a few specific questions. The questions we need answers to are the following:

- How many people are affected? How many new people are added to the welfare rolls? How many people lose welfare benefits? How many people get increased welfare payments? How many on welfare have their payments reduced? What is the income level of those people affected?
- How much extra does the new program cost? How is this cost estimate arrived at?

- What is the effective tax rate for typical families and individuals receiving welfare under the new plan? How does their net income change as a function of, say, $1,000 incremental increases in earnings? Are all effects on net income counted, such as social security taxes, state income taxes, city income taxes, state welfare supplements, public housing, and medicaid?

Dozens and dozens of other important questions can be asked about any major welfare reform plan. But having the answers to the above set of questions will enable us to see the core of the plan.

The cost of Carter's welfare plan

The estimated cost of any comprehensive welfare reform plan is very sensitive politically. The American public is simply not in the mood—and has not been for many years—to support massive increases in welfare spending. Moreover, any major spending increases by the federal government would widen the deficit, thereby lowering the chances for reducing both the rate of inflation and the rate of unemployment, key variables in any incumbent President's re-election plans. President Carter clearly understood the necessity for keeping the cost of his welfare reform proposal to a minimum. His initial order to HEW was to develop a reform plan that would cost nothing.

Carter obviously was sincere in his belief that this could be done. And this is perfectly understandable; many new presidents before him have believed similar things. But the policy undertow of Washington soon dragged him into substantial commitments of additional spending. When the President finally announced PBJI, he had been assured by HEW that the plan would cost some $2.8 billion (plus another $3.4 billion in the form of an expanded earned income tax credit). Although $6.2 billion was a very long way from zero cost, the dynamics of the welfare policymaking process had by then placed Carter in the position of accepting that amount of increase in the federal deficit or abandoning one of his domestic policy centerpieces.

But even as President Carter was retreating from his original conviction that welfare reform should cost nothing, and accepting this huge $6.2 billion increase, he was being seriously misled. The actual costs would be much, much higher.

After Carter's plan was announced there was a good deal of skepticism about the cost estimates among people familiar with welfare reform. Earlier in the year, HEW had estimated that the cost of a plan similar to the one President Carter embraced would be somewhere between $11 billion and $16 billion a year.[15] The Heritage Foundation, a research foundation in Washington, D.C., reviewed the cost estimates of PBJI and revised them upward to $17.8 billion. In October 1977, one of the country's leading experts on welfare reform, Richard Nathan* of the Brookings Institution, testified on President Carter's plan before the House Welfare Reform Subcommittee. The following exchange took place between Nathan and the ranking minority member of the committee:

CONGRESSMAN VANDER JAGT: Have you had an opportunity to cost out the administration's program? Have you had a chance to address that?

DR. NATHAN: I worked on that when I was in the government. I have recently attended a lot of meetings where people have been asking penetrating questions about the costing of the administration's plan, and the answers don't convince me. There are some things included that one should be skeptical about. And there are some far-reaching assump-

*Nathan was quite knowledgeable about the costs of welfare reform, having served as the Assistant Director of the Office of Management and Budget for Human Resources and as Deputy to the Secretary of HEW for Welfare Reform during the time the Nixon Administration was trying to enact the Family Assistance Plan.

tions that are not up front enough, that unemployment assumption, for example.

So I think their plan is very much bigger by a magnitude of *two or more in cost* than they have said. But there are other people—

CONGRESSMAN VANDER JAGT: Two or more times?

DR. NATHAN: Two or more times what they have said. But there are other people who are much more expert in detail than I am on the kinds of problems I have cited as problems that would lead me to say that they are *quite far off*. When I was in government I had to defend the cost estimates we made of the impact of the Family Assistance Plan. There are some things about the administration's cost estimates that frankly I don't think we would have done.[16]

The suspicions and doubts about the cost estimates of Carter's welfare reform plan were confirmed in early December 1977, when the Congressional Budget Office completed its computer runs and issued its own analysis of PBJI. The CBO estimated that President Carter's welfare reform program would cost the federal government *$42 billion a year* by the time it went into full operation in fiscal 1982. This is over $23 billion *more* than the federal government now spends on the welfare programs that PBJI would replace.

There are a number of other factors that should be considered when using these cost estimates. Many assumptions go into a cost estimate of a program of this magnitude and scope—some decreasing the cost, others increasing it. For example, the CBO also estimated that the welfare programs that PBJI would replace —AFDC, SSI, food stamps, the earned income tax credit, and the work incentive program—would increase in cost from their current $18.8 billion a year to $22.8 billion by fiscal 1982. If that estimate of a $4 billion increase in the cost of the current programs is correct, then Carter's plan would cost the federal government only $19 billion more, by comparison, in fiscal 1982.

Other social welfare programs might be affected by PBJI, including child nutrition, housing assistance, unemployment insurance, and medicaid. Some of their costs could increase, others could decrease. The CBO estimated that the cost of these programs would decrease by $1.2 billion if PBJI were enacted. This would lower the overall cost of PBJI further to $17.8 billion.

On the other hand, there are some aspects of the cost analysis done by the CBO that can lead to an understatement of the cost of PBJI. In calculating the cost of PBJI it was assumed that the unemployment rate in fiscal 1982 would be 4.5 percent. This is a very optimistic and perhaps unrealistic assumption. If it turns out to be incorrect and unemployment is substantially higher, PBJI could easily cost billions more.

A second major factor not accounted for in CBO's cost estimate is the possibility of a large expansion in the number of people eligible for medicaid. As the Assistant Director of the Congressional Budget Office, Robert D. Reischauer, cautioned in his testimony before the House Committee on the Budget in October 1977: "The proposal [PBJI] does not address the most rapidly growing welfare cost of these governments, namely, the medicaid program. . . . Any fiscal relief gained by the states from welfare reform could quickly be dissipated if they felt the need or were required to provide medicaid coverage to significant numbers of persons covered under the expanded cash assistance and jobs programs."[17] A major expansion of medicaid because of PBJI could add several billions more to the cost.

Still another area which may understate CBO's estimate of the costs of PBJI is the earned income tax credit. The CBO estimates that it will cost $2.6 billion in fiscal 1982. But in testimony before the Welfare Reform Subcommittee on September 20, 1977, Laurence Woodworth, Assistant Secretary of the Treasury for Tax Policy, indicated that the earned income tax credit under PBJI could cost about $1 billion a year more than the CBO estimated.

According to the CBO, part of the increase in the federal cost of welfare would be caused by a shift of some welfare costs from state and local governments to the federal government. The amount of this shift is estimated to be about $4.2 billion. The CBO also speculated that federal and state income tax collections might increase by $3.1 billion because of the additional employment that it is claimed PBJI would produce, and that social security tax collections would go up by $0.9 billion.[18]

Even the best cost estimates of programs of social change that are as large and complex as President Carter's PBJI are uncertain, requiring numerous assumptions. But it seems reasonable to conclude that the order of magnitude of the costs associated with Carter's welfare reform plan is far, far greater than the $2.8 billion initially claimed for it. The gross federal budget costs of PBJI, according to the CBO analysis, would be over $23 billion more than the current costs of the programs it would replace. Even allowing for a 20 percent increase in the cost of our current welfare programs by fiscal 1982, the CBO estimates that "*net direct federal budget costs would increase by $19.2 billion*" by fiscal 1982 if PBJI were enacted into law.[19]

On the basis of our past experience with the estimated costs of major welfare reform plans, the judgment of independent welfare experts, and the CBO's extensive computer analysis completed in late 1977, it seems reasonable to conclude that PBJI would cost the federal government about $20 billion a year more than our current welfare programs—to begin with. The long-range costs have yet to be estimated.

Who gets the welfare?

The most important aspect of any welfare reform proposal is how it affects the people involved. How many people qualify for the welfare benefits? Who are they? How much income do they have before welfare? When PBJI was announced, this aspect of President Carter's welfare reform plan was scarcely mentioned. In Carter's briefing to the national press corps on August 6, 1977, he alluded to it once in his opening statement when he declared that

PBJI "will significantly *reduce* the number of people who rely on welfare payments."[20] The President then patiently answered seventeen questions about his welfare reform proposals. No one asked him how many people would be affected by it.

That same day President Carter sent a twelve-page message to the Congress explaining his welfare reform proposal. No mention was made of the number of people involved. HEW issued a forty-eight-page analysis of the President's welfare reform program at the same time. It never once mentioned the number of people who would be affected. HEW did, however, make available twenty-six copies of its large briefing charts. The nineteenth chart, headed "Impact on Welfare Rolls," stated that some 32 million people would receive welfare benefits under PBJI compared with 30 million people who received them under the current welfare system. Unfortunately, not very many reporters managed to dig into that chart handout, and none of the major news stories contained any reference to the number of people who would be affected.

But the core of any valid welfare reform is the number of people affected and how they are affected. One of the first items the CBO tackled when it began its analysis of PBJI was what it called the program's "distributive impact." Among the questions the CBO sought answers to were (1) how the program would affect "the distribution of [welfare] recipients and benefits by income level," and (2) "the number and types of families that would gain or lose benefits relative to the current welfare system."[21]

The preliminary results were astonishing. According to the estimates of the CBO, approximately 44 million people in the United States currently receive some form of welfare aid from such programs as Aid to Families with Dependent Children, Supplemental Security Income, state general assistance, the earned income tax credit, and food stamps. Carter's welfare reform proposal would increase by almost *22 million* the number of Americans receiving some form of welfare.[22] Once President Carter's PBJI was in full operation some 66 million Americans would be receiving welfare. That is just about one-third of the nation.

What emerges from the careful estimates of the Congressional Budget Office that we have reviewed so far is a picture of massive welfare expansion, not welfare reform. Some $20 billion more is to be spent on welfare by the federal government every year, and about 22 million more Americans will be getting some of it. And that raises some serious questions. As shown in Chapter I, the massive increase in welfare spending during the past decade has dramatically reduced poverty in the United States. So much so that there are few poor people left. Will Carter's plan substantially increase welfare payments to the poor? Who are those 22 million Americans who will be receiving their first welfare benefit? Are they the major beneficiaries of Carter's welfare reform?

Perhaps the most important criterion by which to judge any welfare reform plan is the incidence of its benefits. How efficient is the plan in directing welfare aid to those who need it the most? In this respect the welfare changes proposed by President Carter have an unexpected effect. The vast majority of the people who would receive welfare checks for the first time come from the middle-income group. A few come from the upper-income group. Table 3 divides people receiving welfare benefits under the current system and under Carter's welfare program into five income classes. We can see that the number of people from families with pre-welfare incomes of less than $5,000 a year increases only slightly (5 percent) under the proposed reform. As we move up into the higher-income classes, however, Carter's welfare reform begins to have a greater impact. The number of people in families earning between $5,000 and $10,000 a year increases by 36 percent.

But the greatest impact occurs in the income brackets between $10,000 and $25,000. Carter's plan would give welfare benefits, including earned income tax "credits," to 11.6 million more Americans who come from families earning between $10,000 and $15,000 a year, an increase of 322 percent. And 4 million Americans who now receive no welfare and come from families with incomes between $15,000 and $25,000 a year would also benefit—a 154 percent increase.

The CBO's analysis of how the distribution of welfare benefits would change under Carter's proposed welfare reform clearly and dramatically shows that most of the new beneficiaries under PBJI would come from America's middle-income class. There is a minimal effect on people in poverty. Of the almost 22 million

TABLE 3

DISTRIBUTION OF WELFARE RECIPIENTS BY PRE-WELFARE
FAMILY INCOME CLASSES UNDER CURRENT WELFARE POLICY
AND UNDER PRESIDENT CARTER'S WELFARE REFORM PLAN (PBJI)

Family Income Class	Number of People Receiving Benefits under Current Welfare Policy[a]	Number of People Receiving Benefits under Carter's Reform Plan	Number of People Added by Carter's Reform Plan	Percent Increase
Less than $5,000	25,600,000[b]	26,900,000	1,300,000	5%
$5,000 to $9,999	12,000,000	16,300,000	4,300,000	36
$10,000 to $14,999	3,600,000	15,200,000	11,600,000	322
$15,000 to $24,999	2,600,000	6,600,000	4,000,000	154
More than $25,000	600,000	1,000,000	400,000	67
TOTAL	44,400,000	66,000,000	21,600,000	49%

SOURCE: Robert D. Reischauer, Assistant Director for Human Resources and Community Development, Congressional Budget Office, statement to Task Force on Distributive Impacts of Budget and Economic Policy, Committee on the Budget, "Preliminary Analysis of the Distributional Impacts of the Administration's Welfare Reform Proposal," October 13, 1977, page 13, Table 2(a). Preliminary estimates as of October 12, 1977. Based on earlier CBO studies, an average family size of 2.824 was used to convert numbers of families to people.

[a] Includes Aid to Families with Dependent Children, Supplemental Security Income, state general assistance, food stamps, and the earned income tax credit.

[b] Number of people rounded to nearest 100,000.

additional people who would receive welfare under Carter's plan, 74 percent would come from families having incomes of over $10,000 a year. And more than 94 percent of them would be from families with incomes that exceed $5,000 a year. Carter's welfare plan, in its broad thrust, focuses on aiding people not now receiving any welfare.

Gainers and losers

The welfare changes recommended by President Carter do not benefit everyone who is currently on welfare. Some will gain, but some will lose. The Congressional Budget Office concluded that PBJI would have its greatest impact on those families below the poverty level: "Only 30 percent of these families would be unaffected by the reform. *Twenty-seven percent of all poor families would be losers*, while 43 percent would be gainers."[23] Many states, perhaps all of them, would simply not allow this to happen if Carter's plan were passed. They would undoubtedly "grandfather" the benefit with a special state welfare payment that would ensure that no truly poor person lost benefits. But if the states did not act, the proposed reforms would reduce welfare payments for millions of Americans. Five million people with incomes below the poverty level would have their welfare benefits reduced by more than $100 a year. Over 2 million of these would experience a cut of more than $500 a year.[24]

On the other hand, there are quite a few "gainers" under Carter's plan. Over 8 million people in families with incomes below the poverty level would see their welfare checks increased by over $100 a year. Some 4.5 million would get an increase of over $500 a year. But the largest group of gainers under PBJI would be those families whose incomes are *above* the poverty line. Well over 40 million people who are not poor will gain welfare benefits of $100 a year or more. And some 21 million Americans who are not poor will receive over $500 a year in added benefits.[25]

Let's take a closer look at the expected changes in the overall level of welfare benefits for certain categories of individuals and families. If the states did not choose to supplement the federal payment under PBJI and did not "grandfather" those whose benefits dropped even with the state supplement, some strange things would occur.

People who are blind, aged, or disabled—both single persons and married couples—would have their welfare checks *reduced* by an average of 5 percent by PBJI.

The largest potential reductions in welfare benefits would fall on AFDC mothers and their children. The average female-headed family with one, two, or three small children could have its welfare check *cut* by more than 30 percent.[26]

The losers in Carter's program would be the aged, the blind, the disabled, and mothers with small children.

The gainers would be single people, childless couples, and married couples with children. The average welfare check received by a single person would increase by over 70 percent. A childless married couple would see their welfare check increase by almost 90 percent. And a married couple with children could count on a 100 percent increase in their welfare check.[27]

In addition, many single persons, childless married couples, and married couples with children who do not now qualify for any welfare payments would qualify under Carter's plan.

Cut to its essence, Carter's welfare reform proposal involves a massive shift in this nation's welfare priorities. Welfare benefits would be lowered for the blind, the aged, the disabled, and for mothers with small children. Billions, probably tens of billions, of dollars would be added to our current level of welfare spending. And the main beneficiaries would be single people, childless couples, and couples with children. *What is being proposed is not a "reform" of the current welfare system. What is being proposed is a radical, fundamental change in our entire approach to welfare.*

The American people have believed that those who cannot support themselves—particularly the blind, the disabled, the aged, and mothers with small children—should receive welfare. Our welfare programs have been designed to provide help for such people. But Americans, in general, have never felt that healthy single individuals, childless couples, and families with both parents present deserve much welfare. There seems to be little barrier to employment for those with no childrearing responsibilities. As for families in which both the husband and the wife are present, it is generally assumed that at least one spouse can manage to work at a full-time job to provide for the family (assuming, of course, that they are not blind, disabled, or aged).

President Carter's welfare reform plan radically challenges this basic philosophical view of welfare. Under the guise of reforming the current welfare system, the real purpose of **PBJI** is to sharply expand it, bringing onto the welfare rolls massive numbers of single people, childless couples, and families with both parents present. The thrust of **PBJI** is to guarantee incomes for all, even at the risk of making some of the truly needy worse off.

The states would, of course, not allow benefits to be cut for the blind, aged, disabled, and mothers with small children. Most, probably all, states would establish state welfare programs to supplement the federal payments under **PBJI**. And they would "grandfather" people in addition so that no one needing help would have his or her welfare benefits cut off or significantly reduced. So there would be little change in the welfare payments received by the aged, the blind, the disabled, or mothers with small children. Their federal welfare payment under **PBJI** would be lower, but political pressures would force the states to make up the difference through some combination of local welfare programs.

Carter's plan would guarantee a basic level of welfare support for most of those now on welfare *and* for millions more. For many current welfare recipients the level of support would be lower than what it is now. Nevertheless, for them **PBJI** would not make a great deal of difference, because the states would make it up. But for millions of people who are not eligible for welfare now, **PBJI** would make a significant difference. Under our current welfare system, they receive nothing. Under **PBJI** they would receive welfare—either in the form of government checks or as special tax "credits."

The key to understanding Carter's welfare reform proposal lies in the changing mix of welfare recipients. Those who society now considers poor would experience little change. PBJI represents essentially a massive expansion of welfare into the middle class of America. It is the latest vehicle of those who want a guaranteed income for the United States. PBJI would achieve what the proponents of FAP and ISP failed to do. It would provide cash welfare payments to three main groups heretofore generally considered ineligible for welfare—single persons, childless couples, and married couples with children.

The basic plan

The welfare reform plan proposed by President Carter has three basic parts. The first and most important part is the direct cash payment program administered by the federal government. Under PBJI the following welfare programs would be eliminated: Aid to Families with Dependent Children (AFDC), federal food stamps, Supplemental Security Income (SSI), and certain types of state general assistance. In their place PBJI would establish a comprehensive cash assistance program. The minimum payment would be the same throughout the country, regardless of where the recipient lived. Carter's welfare reform plan "expands cash assistance coverage for the first time in this country to *all* families, single individuals and childless couples."[28]

Welfare recipients would be divided into two categories: those who are not expected to work and those who are. The welfare payment for a family of four that had no one in it who was expected to work would be $4,200 a year. The actual payment would depend on family size, being smaller for families with less than four members and larger for families with more than four members. If someone in the family worked, the federal PBJI payment would be reduced by 50 cents for every dollar of additional earnings.

On the other hand, if someone in the family could work and was expected to work, the family would still qualify for welfare payments but at a lower benefit level. The amount of the payment would vary according to family size. For a four-person family the basic welfare grant would be $2,300 a year.

The earnings of those who are expected to work would be treated differently from the earnings of those not expected to work. The additional earnings of someone not expected to work would cause a substantial reduction in welfare payments from the very first dollar of earnings. But the additional earnings of someone expected to work would have no effect whatsoever on the amount of the welfare payment until earnings exceeded $3,800 a year. Thus, if someone from a family where no one was expected to work got a job and earned $3,800 a year, the family's welfare payment would be reduced by $1,900—from $4,200 down to $2,300. The family's net income would then be composed of $2,300 in welfare payments and $3,800 in earnings—a total of $6,100. In the case of a four-person family where someone is expected to work, earnings of $3,800 a year would not affect the welfare payment. And the family's net income would be $6,100 ($2,300 in welfare and $3,800 in earnings).

The federal cash payment part of PBJI is a direct descendant of Richard Nixon's FAP. The numbers differ slightly. But the concept of a basic income guarantee—a certain amount of earnings "disregarded," and a 50 percent reduction in welfare after a certain point for additional earnings—is exactly the same in PBJI as it was in FAP.

The second part of PBJI uses the federal income tax system to make welfare payments to people with earnings. It does this through both a *tax reimbursement* scheme and an earned income tax "credit." Because of the way the direct federal cash assistance part of PBJI works, a family could still be receiving welfare when it had to begin paying federal income taxes. When a family began to pay federal taxes, it would receive a "reimbursement" of 20 cents on each dollar earned above this level of income up to a higher level of income where the federal welfare payments stop. Thereafter the "reimbursement" would be phased *down* by 20 cents on each dollar earned above this level of income until the amount of tax "reimbursement" became zero. For example, a family of four would receive a basic **PBJI** payment of $4,200. This payment would be reduced by 50 cents of each additional dollar earned. Thus the family would continue to receive welfare up to the point where its earnings were $8,400 a year. At $7,200 it would begin to pay federal income taxes. For earnings between $7,200 and $8,400 it would receive a special federal tax "credit" of 20 percent on all earnings over $7,200. The maximum "reimbursement" would be $240 at $8,400 of income. Between $8,400 and $9,600 of earnings the "reimbursement" would be reduced by 20 percent of earnings over $8,400, and would phase out completely at $9,600 of earnings. Depending on the size of the family, some amount of tax "reimbursement" could be available for earnings as high as $16,800 a year.

PBJI would also expand and make permanent the temporary *earned income tax credit* (EITC) on the federal income tax. Under the proposed revision the EITC would equal 10 percent of additional earned income up to a maximum amount based on the size of the family. Beyond that maximum the EITC would be reduced by 10 percent of earnings until the "credit" became zero. For example, for a family of four the EITC would increase up to a maximum of $655 for earnings of $9,100 a year. It would then be reduced at the rate of 10 percent of additional earnings and phase out completely when the family's earnings rose to $15,650 a year. For a seven-person family the maximum credit would be $850 and not phase out until earnings reached $21,500. The EITC would be available only to families with a child or disabled dependent adults.

The use of the federal income tax system to provide welfare payments through tax "credits" and tax "reimbursements" would expand the impact of **PBJI** well up into the middle-income group and account for a large number of the new people receiving some form of welfare payment. Any such tax "credit" system must be phased out gradually as income increases; otherwise the marginal rate of taxation over certain ranges of incremental income would be so high that financial work incentives would be destroyed. In fact, they could, at times, go over 100 percent. But when the "credits" and "reimbursements" are phased out slowly, this automatically extends the range of income over which people are eligible for welfare payments. The amount of welfare these higher-income families would receive would be generally much lower than the payments received by the poor. In the end, though, they would in principle be on welfare as surely as the poor.

In summary, under just the *federal* cash assistance part of the "simplified" welfare reform plan, a family of four would have to deal with two separate taxes, a welfare payment, a tax "credit," and a tax "reimbursement." These would be the welfare payment received from **PBJI**, the expanded earned income tax credit, the federal income tax, the federal income tax reimbursement, and the social security tax. If a four-person family, for example, earned $8,000 a year, the federal government would:

- give them $200 in **PBJI** welfare payments,
- take from them $120 in federal income taxes,
- give them $600 as an earned income tax "credit" on their federal income taxes,
- give them $160 more as a federal income tax "reimbursement," and
- take from them $484 in social security taxes.

The family would net $356 from the federal government.

The third major part of **PBJI** is an expanded employment opportunities program. It has two basic components—the Job Search Assistance (JSA) program and the Public Service Employment (PSE) program. The Job Search Assistance program is designed to help people find jobs. Existing state employment agencies and their local employment service offices would operate the main part of this program. In addition, other prime sponsors operating under the existing CETA (Comprehensive Employment and Training Act) program could also assist in the job search.[29] Once someone entered the job search program an eight-week search period would begin. A person "must accept a bona fide job offer *unless* the pay in the job is less than the minimum wage, the job involves impractical hours for a single parent with any child between the ages of 7 and 13, or the conditions of work are unreasonable given such factors as hours of work, health or safety conditions or geographic location."[30] If someone refused a job, except for these reasons, he or she would become ineligible for welfare under PBJI. If, after five weeks of searching, a private or public job could not be found, an attempt would be made to find the principal wage earner in the family a special Public Service Employment job. This second part of PBJI's employment opportunity program would attempt to create 1,400,000 government jobs in such fields as building and repairing recreational facilities, clean-up and pest/insect control, public safety, child care, home services for the elderly and the ill, and cultural arts activities.

A good deal of skepticism has been expressed about the ability of the federal government to create this many useful jobs, especially when it intends to pay only the minimum wage. Some of the practical kinds of problems the government would face are these: Carter's PBJI assumes that 150,000 new jobs as teaching aides will be created. During 1975 approximately 450,000 people were employed as teachers' aides in the United States. To create 150,000 new jobs as teaching aides would require "nearly a 33 percent increase in an occupation where the industry has recently faced declining school enrollments and teacher layoffs."[31] PBJI proposes to create 150,000 jobs in the field of public safety. This would imply an "increase of about 25 percent over the 594,000 persons employed as guards in 1975."[32] A total of 375,000 construction jobs—building and repairing recreational facilities, creating facilities for the handicapped, improving school facilities, and weatherizing—would be created. For most of these jobs, unfortunately, you would have to be a skilled construction worker. And if you were a skilled construction worker, you probably would not be in this program. There will be some very real difficulties in creating PSE jobs under PBJI. And if our experience with past federal job programs is any guide to the future, it is highly unlikely that the jobs will be available.

If, after eight weeks of job searching, neither a regular private or public job nor a special PSE job can be found that is suitable, then the person becomes eligible for full welfare benefits of, say, $4,200 for a family of four.

The administrative complexity of PBJI

So far we have dealt only with the high points of the federal portion of Carter's welfare reform plan. However, the states play a major and central role. When their part is included, the whole thing gets even more complicated.

Eventually, probably all the states would choose to supplement the federal welfare payment made under PBJI. In an effort to limit the increase in welfare costs that would occur, the federally guaranteed minimum welfare payment in PBJI was set quite low. Most people on welfare now receive more than the federal portion of PBJI would pay them. This is especially true in the high-population states where the bulk of welfare population lives. To accomplish the state supplementation of the federal PBJI payment, it would be necessary to maintain or establish a state administrative unit capable of coordinating this activity with the federal welfare bureaucracy in Washington. And that could mean up to fifty separate state welfare programs supplementing the welfare income of the poor.

Each state would also maintain its current program for providing *social services* to the poor on welfare. Under PBJI, perhaps as many as 50 percent more people would be eligible for some kind of benefits. It is unlikely that they would require the same degree of services now provided for the poor. However, it is clear that the PBJI group would be a much larger and more diverse group than is now on the welfare rolls. There would almost surely be some expansion of social services. And that expansion would require the hiring of more welfare workers. After the implementation of PBJI there would still be fifty separate welfare agencies providing social services to the poor.

There is also a special state *emergency assistance* component of PBJI. The comprehensive federal part of PBJI apparently cannot cope with the complexity of the needs of the nation's poor. In addition to the welfare payment supplementation program that will be necessary in almost every state, PBJI provides $600 million a year to establish an emergency assistance program in every state. The purpose of this program is to meet any unmet income needs on a "discretionary" basis. This aspect of PBJI seems to go counter to one of its main goals: to increase uniformity across the country by making the administration of welfare less discretionary at the local level. As a recent study by the Urban Institute in Washington, D.C., concluded: "Emergency Assistance would be totally discretionary. The program is under Title XX; it would probably be controlled by the *same social workers* who run Title XX social services and prefer a discretionary approach to welfare benefits. The result could be a recrudescence of just the kind of welfare administration which PBJI is intended to eliminate."[33] State emergency assistance would mean fifty more separate welfare programs.

If Carter's welfare reform plan were implemented, we could easily have as many as 150 separate state welfare programs providing supplemental payments to the basic federal PBJI payment, social services, and "emergency services" such as welfare payments for unmet needs. The simplicity sought by comprehensive reform seems to slip away as the reality of welfare is confronted.

Now let us look at some other features that compound the

administrative complexity of PBJI. There are two ways the federal cash payment part of PBJI can be administered. Under the first option, called the *federal option*, the administration of welfare—including the determination of who is and who is not eligible—would be run from Washington, probably through some agency like the Social Security Administration. This in itself could cause administrative problems. Moreover, the experience that we had when the Social Security Administration took over the Supplemental Security Income welfare program "suggests that the SSA may not be any better than state welfare departments at running a program like PBJI."[34]

Under the second option, called the *state option*, the states may elect to administer much of the program. The states would receive applications for welfare, develop eligibility and payment information, and forward it to Washington. If a number of states did decide to run much of it themselves (and we have no reason to believe that many of them would not), the administration of the program would be greatly complicated. For example, you could have a situation in which, say, thirty-five states, randomly scattered across the country, would elect to administer welfare in their states. In the other fifteen states the federal government would be running things, except, of course, for the state supplementation programs, the social services programs, and the emergency assistance welfare programs.

Further complicating matters are two other aspects of PBJI. The first is the *maintenance-of-effort* requirement. Under this provision of PBJI, "states must maintain set percentages of their present spending for income maintenance programs for the first three years of PBJI. An alternative requirement would allow some high-spending states to qualify at somewhat lower percentages."[35] The second is the *hold-harmless* provision. This is a sort of federal catch-all payment to the states to enable them to take care of unforeseen problems that would surely spring up if radical welfare reform were tried. Under the hold-harmless provision the "federal government will pay specific state expenditures above the maintenance-of-effort level, to ensure that all states obtain at least 10 percent fiscal relief from these costs."[36]

One almost certain consequence of the enactment of PBJI would be a significant increase in the number of welfare administrators and case workers. Carter's proposal claims that PBJI would reduce the number of federal and state welfare personnel from 143,000 to between 100,000 and 120,000. Commenting on this claim, the Urban Institute in Washington, D.C., cautioned in a recent study that "the basis of this estimate is *unknown*. . . . The new program would be assembled substantially out of pieces of old ones—state welfare administrations, prime sponsors, and SESA's [state employment security agencies]. The personnel and overhead costs of these operations would remain largely as now. They would, in fact, *probably increase* because of an increased caseload over existing programs."[37]

PBJI is not a simple program. It is an extraordinarily complex, convoluted, complicated program. If enacted, it could be decades before its full implications are known. Even the most intelligent, most knowledgeable welfare experts in the country have had a difficult time fully understanding it. As Richard Nathan recently commented when testifying before the House Subcommittee on Welfare Reform, "The Carter Administration's 163-page welfare reform bill represents an intricate compromise of different goals and programs. It is, in fact, so intricate that *few understand it* and fewer still (among organizations and experts) have endorsed it with enthusiasm and without reservation. The plan raises fundamental questions of cost, concept, and workability."[38]

There have been a lot of plans developed over the past decade whose purpose was to transform our welfare system into a guaranteed income. But Carter's PBJI proposal has got to be the "Rube Goldberg" of all the radical welfare reform plans. It is part income guarantee, part incremental reform, part tax reduction, and part federally created jobs.

It is simply not a simple plan.

Financial incentives to work

A key aspect of all radical welfare reforms in the past has been their attempt to increase the welfare recipient's financial incentive to work. To do this the effective marginal income tax rate—determined both by the rate of welfare reduction and by the rate of increase in taxes as earnings increase—must be kept low. President Carter recognized the importance of this factor. In his opening statement to the national press corps on August 6, 1977, he stated flatly that his welfare reform proposal contained "strong work incentives."[39]

How "strong" are these incentives? Numerous factors in PBJI combine to make it extremely difficult to lower the effective marginal tax rate. The marginal tax rate of just the federal cash payment part of PBJI is 50 percent. Social security taxes are approximately 6 percent. At slightly higher ranges of income the federal income tax rate starts at 14 percent. Many states now have income tax rates of their own in the range of 4 to 5 percent for the levels of income we are concerned with here. And some cities (New York, for example) have their own income tax that could add another 4 or 5 percentage points. The state supplementation program could add another 20 percent. Thus, without even considering the effects of medicaid and public housing, we are talking about effective tax rates that could range as high as 98 to 100 percent.

In an attempt to avoid these incredibly high rates, PBJI employs both the earned income tax credit and a tax "reimbursement" scheme. These would effectively lower the marginal tax rate to about 70 percent for the range of earned income between $5,000 and $8,000 a year.[40] An unfortunate consequence of lowering the marginal income tax rate over this range of income is an *increase* in the marginal rate over higher ranges of income. Even disregarding the tax effects of state supplementation, medicaid, and public housing entirely, the marginal tax rate under PBJI would run well over 40 percent for earned income between $8,000 and $10,000 a year for a family of four. And it would remain over 35 percent for earned income between $10,000 and $16,000 a year. The addition of state supplementation, medicaid, and public housing could increase these rates to 55 percent, 60 percent, and more over these higher ranges of income.

As a study of Carter's welfare proposal, prepared for the use of the Joint Economic Committee by three staff members of the University of Wisconsin's Institute for Research on Poverty, has pointed out: "While the cumulative marginal benefit reduction rate in the proposed plan is frequently less than in current practice—thus, increasing work incentives—it may still be substantial (*up to 80–90 percent after State supplementation*) for some recipients. Moreover, there are undesirable notch problems with some existing programs, notably Medicaid and in the asset test."[41] Furthermore, the social security tax will increase sharply in the near future. This increase in social security taxes, which would apply to the earned income of people in the lower-income brackets, will further weaken the financial incentive to work.

The effective marginal tax rate on earned income under PBJI is of the same order of magnitude that it is under the current welfare system. As has been demonstrated again and again—in theory and in practice—there is *no* way to devise a radical welfare reform plan that has a strong financial incentive to work unless we are prepared either to spend tens and tens of billions of dollars or to live with an extremely low welfare benefit level.

The work incentive in Carter's welfare reform plan is very, very weak. This is true even before considering the effect of medicaid, public housing, and other welfare programs. If housing and health care programs were taken into account, the marginal tax rate could approach 100 percent—and there would be no financial incentive to work.

The missing links

Although PBJI purports to be a comprehensive welfare reform plan, it fails to deal with a number of major elements in our current welfare system. The medicaid program, which provides billions of dollars of health care services to millions of poor Americans, is blithely ignored. It is assumed that a national health insurance program will be enacted in 1978 or sometime thereafter and that the medicaid problem will be dealt with then. Ignoring medicaid will not make it go away. The presence of medicaid raises serious problems of cost, work incentives, and administrative complexity. As an Urban Institute study of PBJI has recently pointed out: "[Carter's] proposal makes no attempt to reconcile the eligibility provisions of PBJI with those of Medicaid, a major part of the existing welfare system.... In fact, enactment of NHI [national health insurance] is probably a good deal more remote than welfare reform. . . . If Medicaid still exists at the time PBJI comes into operation, and if eligibility for Medicaid is not made part of PBJI benefits, virtually the entire existing system of state–local welfare eligibility determination would have to remain in operation alongside the new system. . . . The distinction between Medicaid and PBJI eligibility could also generate unexpected pressures to expand Medicaid eligibility and, hence, Medicaid spending."[42] Many more people would be receiving welfare benefits under PBJI and there would be great pressure to expand medicaid eligibility to them.

The existence of medicaid also weakens the work incentives of Carter's welfare reform proposal. Medicaid health benefits, like other welfare benefits, are a function of the amount of income a family earns. When a family's income increases beyond a certain point these health benefits are lost. This loss sharply increases the effective marginal rate of taxation on added income. Often referred to as the "notch" problem, it exists now and would continue to be a problem under the proposed reform.

Other major welfare programs that pose problems similar to those posed by medicaid are housing assistance and day care. Both, like medicaid, would continue to be add-ons if PBJI were enacted. And both would raise new problems of cost, work incentives, and administrative complexity.

As Richard Nathan stated cogently in testimony before the House Subcommittee on Welfare Reform: "You cannot enact a welfare bill until you have a health bill because you have a difficult problem of people going into their job program and losing Medicaid benefits. Until the administration tells you what they are going to do with Medicaid, you cannot seriously consider their welfare bill."[43] That could also be said for the day care program and the housing assistance program.

Conclusion

The welfare reform that President Carter proposed in 1977 would probably cost somewhere in the neighborhood of $20 billion a year more than our current welfare system. Nearly 22 million more Americans would receive some form of welfare. Effective marginal tax rates would continue to remain very high and act as a serious disincentive to work. The administrative complexity of welfare would be compounded and more welfare workers would probably be needed to handle the increased caseload.

The problems caused by the separate existence of medicaid, day care, and housing assistance programs are ignored. An examination of the gainers and losers under PBJI shows clearly that those who need welfare the least would gain in the greatest numbers. Those who cannot truly care for themselves and are on welfare now would benefit little. The thrust of Carter's plan is to further the idea of a guaranteed income, expanding welfare into the heart of the middle class of America. This is not welfare reform. This is a potential social revolution of great magnitude, a revolution that, if it should come to pass, could result in social tragedy.

And so, President Carter has begun the next chapter of radical welfare reform. As this book is being written, the outcome is still in doubt. If the evidence from past efforts at radical welfare reform is a faithful guide to the future, President Carter's plan will fail like the rest. If that happens, one can confidently predict that a new plan will spring, phoenix-like, from the intellectual ashes of the old ones. On the other hand, Congress may be so weary of denying the welfare professionals that it might finally decide to try radical welfare reform to see if it works. It could be a costly experiment.

CITATIONS—CHAPTER VIII

1 "Huge Study Planned of Welfare System," *San Francisco Chronicle*, January 27, 1977, page 7.

2 Fred Doolittle, Frank Levey, and Michael Wiseman, "Reforming Welfare: Neat, Efficient System Is Mirage," *The Wall Street Journal*, April 13, 1977, page 26.

3 "The Welfare Reform Plan Is Delayed," *San Francisco Chronicle*, April 26, 1977, page 22.

4 "Carter to Unveil Dramatic Welfare Reform Plan," *Palo Alto Times*, April 27, 1977, page 1.

5 "Text of Carter Welfare Remarks" (statement of May 2, 1977), *The New York Times*, May 3, 1977, page 34.

6 Ibid.

7 Austin Scott, "Carter Endorses Tentative Plan on Welfare Reform," *The Washington Post*, May 26, 1977, pages 1 and 16.

8 Ibid., page 1. (Italics added.)

9 "Statement of Secretary Joseph A. Califano, Jr., on Welfare Reform," *HEW News*, May 25, 1977, page 2.

10 "Transcript of the President's News Conference [July 28, 1977] on Foreign and Domestic Matters," *The New York Times*, July 29, 1977, page 8.

11 "Transcript of President's News Conference [August 6, 1977] on His Proposals to Overhaul Welfare," *The New York Times*, August 7, 1977, page 41.

12 Ibid.

13 "Welfare Reform," *HEW News*, August 6, 1977, page 20.

14 Myra MacPherson, "President's Proposal Draws Praise, Denunciation," *The Washington Post*, August 7, 1977, page 1.

15   Kathryn Waters Gest, "Welfare Reform: Carter Studying Options," *Congressional Quarterly Weekly Report*, Volume XXXV, Number 33 (April 30, 1977), page 796.

16   Richard P. Nathan, Senior Fellow, Brookings Institution, statement before the House Welfare Reform Subcommittee of the Committees on Agriculture, Education and Labor, and Ways and Means, October 12, 1977, pages 1314–1315 (manuscript of testimony). (Italics added.)

17   Robert D. Reischauer, Assistant Director for Human Resources and Community Development, Congressional Budget Office, statement to Task Force on State and Local Government, Committee on the Budget, House, "The Fiscal Impact of the Administration's Welfare Reform Proposal on State and Local Governments," October 27, 1977, page 14.

18   Alice Rivlin, Director, Congressional Budget Office, letter to Congressman Guy Vander Jagt, ranking minority member, House Welfare Reform Subcommittee, November 25, 1977, Tables 1 and 2.

19   Ibid., page 2. (Italics added.)

20   "Transcript of President's News Conference [August 6, 1977] on His Proposals to Overhaul Welfare," *The New York Times*, August 7, 1977, page 41. (Italics added.)

21   Robert D. Reischauer, Assistant Director for Human Resources and Community Development, Congressional Budget Office, statement to Task Force on Distributive Impacts of Budget and Economic Policy, Committee on the Budget, "Preliminary Analysis of the Distributional Impacts of the Administration's Welfare Reform Proposal," October 13, 1977, page 11.

22   Ibid., page 13, Table 2(a). The Congressional Budget Office estimated the number of families involved. Based on earlier CBO studies an average family size of 2.824 was used to convert numbers of families to numbers of people.

23   Ibid., page 21. (Italics added.)

24   Ibid., page 22, Table 5(a).

25   Ibid.

26   U.S., Congressional Budget Office, "Program for Better Jobs and Income" (working paper), page 13.

27   Ibid.

28   Ibid., page 7. (Italics added.)

29   Ibid., page 30.

30   Ibid., page 31. (Italics added.)

31   U.S., Congressional Budget Office, "Major Issues Related to the Jobs Program" (working paper), pages 15 and 16.

32   Ibid., page 16.

33   The Urban Institute, "The Welfare Reform Proposal: Implementation Issues," Working Paper 5102-01 (Washington, D.C., October 1977), page 23. (Italics added.)

34   Ibid., page 5.

35   Ibid., page 19.

36   Ibid.

37   Ibid., page 48. (Italics added.)

38   Nathan, statement before the House Welfare Reform Subcommittee, October 12, 1977, page 1280. (Italics added.)

39   "Transcript of President's News Conference [August 6, 1977] on His Proposals to Overhaul Welfare," *The New York Times*, August 7, 1977, page 41.

40   U.S., Congressional Budget Office, "Program for Better Jobs and Income," table (between pages 34 and 35).

41   U.S., Congress, Joint Economic Committee, *The Program for Better Jobs and Income—A Guide and a Critique*, prepared by Sheldon Danziger, Robert Haveman, and Eugene Smolensky (Washington, D.C., October 17, 1977), page 24. (Italics added.)

42   The Urban Institute, *Welfare Reform Proposal*, pages 17 and 18.

43   Nathan, statement before the House Welfare Reform Subcommittee, October 12, 1977, pages 1291–1292.

APPENDIX A

SOCIAL WELFARE PROGRAMS

The number and variety of social welfare programs have pro-liferated sharply during the last few decades to the point where it is difficult to even comprehend their scope, let alone under-stand clearly how they work and to whom they provide help. In 1974 the Subcommittee on Fiscal Policy of the Joint Economic Committee published, as part of its wide-ranging studies in public welfare, a comprehensive list of these programs. While the array of social welfare programs is ever-changing, this listing does provide some perspective and feel for the nature of the overall social welfare effort of the United States.

The following text and list of social welfare programs is taken directly from a publication of the Joint Economic Committee.*

Federal programs for income security can be grouped according to their eligibility rules about current income: (1) No income rules; (2) limit on wages; (3) limit on wages and on some public benefits; and (4) limit on wages, some public benefits, and on unearned private income. The last group of programs is for the needy only, and it is several times larger than the others.

---

*U.S., Congress, Joint Economic Committee, Subcommittee on Fiscal Policy, *Public Welfare and Work Incentives: Theory and Practice*, pre-pared by Vee Burke and Alair A. Townsend, Studies in Public Welfare, Paper No. 14 (Washington, D.C., April 15, 1974), pages 45–54.

Federal programs are listed below, arranged by these group-
ings.

NO LIMIT ON INCOME

These non-income-tested programs can be viewed as providing
income security of two varieties: (1) Deferred compensation for
past service (examples are civil service and military retirement
and veterans' educational benefits); and (2) income transfers
from taxpayer to recipient (examples are meals for the elderly
and special social security benefits for those over 72).

[1] **Medicare (hospital and doctor services).** —21 million aged
persons and 1.7 million disabled persons had medicare insurance in July 1973. During fiscal 1973 medicare provided
hospital services to 4.7 million persons and doctor services
to 10.5 million.

[2] **Compensation to veterans for service-connected disability.**
—3 million veterans and dependents, June 1973.

[3] **Dependency and indemnity compensation to veterans' dependents for service-connected death.** —200,000 widows and
118,000 surviving children, January 1974.

[4] **Veterans' housing loans.** —305,000 home loans guaranteed or
insured by the Veterans' Administration during 1973. Face
value of average loan, $25,000. Cumulative total (1944–73),
8.6 million home loans with face value of $101.7 billion.

[5] **Veterans' hospital, domiciliary, and medical care (service-
connected disability).** —Fiscal 1974 beneficiaries of free hospital care, 300,000 veterans (estimate).

[6] **Veterans' educational assistance.** —A stipend per academic
month ($220 for single veterans). Maximum period of help,
36 months, given for 18 months' military service; 1.5 million
civilian beneficiaries in November 1973 (plus others in military service). Additional cash for tutorial help ($50 monthly)
and for dependents ($41 for one dependent, $78 for two).

[7] **Vocational rehabilitation for veterans.** —For those with at least a 30 percent disability, a subsistence allowance ($170 monthly if single) plus free tuition, books, and supplies. In December 1973, 13,000 veterans attended college, and 3,000 attended other schools under this program.

[8] **War orphans' and widows' educational assistance.** —For survivors of veterans and for dependents of disabled veterans, a stipend ($220 per academic month of full-time study). In fiscal 1973, 58,000 children and 11,000 wives and widows received benefits (averaging $1,516 per child and $1,185 per widow and wife).

[9] **Federal civil service retirement.** —1.1 million retirees and survivors, September 1973.

[10] **Military retirement (benefits affected by disability payments.)** —950,000 beneficiaries in fiscal year 1973.

[11] **Social security—Special benefits for persons aged 72 and over.** —For those without social security earnings records (funded by Treasury); 362,000 beneficiaries, November 1973. Benefits cannot go to recipients of supplemental security income or any government pension, but are permitted to recipients of workmen's compensation or veterans' compensation.

[12] **Federal employees' compensation.** —Compensation for job-related illnesses or injuries to federal workers, their dependents and survivors. In fiscal 1973 direct beneficiaries (workers and survivors) averaged 41,615 per month. Payments to injured workers with families include dependent's allowances. (The federal government also administers workmen's compensation for longshoremen and for workers in the District of Columbia; states operate their own workmen's compensation programs.)

[13] **Meals for the elderly.** —Where available, this new service offers five hot meals per week for those over 60 years old (and their spouses) who are unable to afford proper meals or without ability or desire to prepare them. Regulations prohibit

any test of need. In mid-January meals averaged 65,000 daily (expected to rise to 200,000).

WAGE-TESTED

Social security's trio of cash benefits places a limit on earned income for beneficiaries under 72 years of age. September 1973 beneficiaries:

[14] **Old-age insurance.** −18.9 [*sic*] retired workers and dependents.

[15] **Survivors' insurance.** −7 million survivors (4.2 million surviving spouses, 2.8 million children, and 25,000 parents). To be eligible, widowers and parents must have received at least one-half of their support from the deceased worker, but this is not required of widows.

[16] **Disability insurance.** −3.4 million workers and dependents.

WAGE- AND BENEFIT-TESTED

Remaining social insurance programs count not only wages but some other public benefits (typically social security and workmen's compensation and, sometimes, unemployment insurance).

[17] **Railroad retirement, disability, and survivor benefits.** −One million beneficiaries, September 1973.

[18] **Federal-state unemployment insurance.** −1.3 million recipients, July 1973.

[19] **Railroad unemployment insurance.** −9,000 recipients. September 1973.

[20] **Trade readjustment allowances (for workers displaced by imports).** −11,500 beneficiaries in calendar 1973.

[21] **Black lung disability and survivors' benefits.** −423,000 miners, dependents, widows, and surviving children, December 1973.

TESTED FOR ALL (OR MOST) CURRENT INCOME
(WAGES, BENEFITS¹ AND OTHER UNEARNED INCOME)

Programs for the needy offer aid in the form of cash, food benefits, health services, subsidized housing, education aids, jobs and training, social services, and business subsidies.

[22] **Aid to families with dependent children.** — 3.1 million needy families with 7.8 million children, September 1973. States determine payment level and eligibility. Median state guarantee to a family of four was $235 per month ($2,820 per year).

[23] **Supplemental security income.** — 3.4 million needy aged, blind, and disabled persons at start of program, January 1974 (fiscal year 1974 estimate, 5.3 million). SSI federal guarantee, $140 monthly per person, $210 per couple, rising to $146 and $219 on July 1, 1974 (these amounts are supplemented by many states).

[24] **Emergency assistance.** — 17,882 needy families, August 1973, Benefits sometimes take the form of vouchers for various consumption items.

[25] **Assistance to Cuban refugees.** — 75,500 beneficiaries, November 1973 (but more than half were transferred to SSI in January 1974). Administration plans to phase out program, July 1974–77.

[26] **General assistance to Indians.** — 63,118 average monthly number aided, 1973.

[27] **Pensions for veterans (non-service-connected disability).** — 1.9 million needy veterans and dependents, June 1973.

[28] **Pensions for survivors of veterans (non-service-connected death).** — 1.9 million needy widows and children, June 1973.

[29] **Death compensation for survivors of veterans (service-connected death).** — 200,000 needy parents, January 1974. (Total

---

¹ Federal law forbids treating food stamp benefits as income for tax or welfare purposes.

includes recipients of dependency and indemnity compensation.)

[30] **Black lung survivors' benefits.** —Surviving relatives (parent, brother under 18, sister) who were totally dependent on coal miner who died without a wife or child; 1,100 beneficiaries, December 1973.

FOOD BENEFITS

[31] **Food stamps.** —12.5 million recipients, November 1973 (expected to average 15 million in fiscal 1975). Gross income limit, family of four, $6,800 (higher in case of extraordinary rent or medical expense). In January 1974, program guaranteed a minimum monthly income, in the form of food stamps, of $42 to a single person, $78 to a couple, $142 to a family of four.

[32] **Food commodities** (obtained by the government in surplus removal and price support operations). —2 million needy members of families; 9 million needy children in schools, 1.3 million needy persons in institutions, November 1973. (Although program rules require institutions to keep records showing how they determine eligibility, a government survey in 1972 disclosed that 11 percent did not know how the number of "needy" was determined. Between 20–25 percent of the institutions were receiving food for more persons than their number of residents.) Commodity distribution to families is to cease on July 1, 1974, when food stamps are to be available in all counties.

[33] **School lunches and school breakfasts.** —8.6 million free school lunches and 1.1 million free school breakfasts to needy children, 472,000 "reduced price" lunches and 36,000 "reduced price" breakfasts to near-poor children (plus almost 16 million lunches and 70,000 breakfasts subsidized at a lesser rate, and served to children without regard to income); food service (meals) to 190,000 children in day care centers, settle-

ment houses, and similar institutions, November 1973 daily averages. For children to receive free school meals, pretax income limits in January 1974 were $4,250 (family of four); for reduced price meals, $7,440.

[34] **School milk.** —Free milk to children in especially needy schools (111,000 half pints, daily average, fiscal 1973). In other schools 13.5 million cartons were sold daily at reduced prices without regard to income of the children. This milk is separate from that included in school lunches and breakfasts. (The new school lunch act requires that the income rules for free and subsidized lunches apply also to school milk. Hence, all children who qualify for a free school lunch will also receive extra free milk as well, provided the school participates in both programs.) In 1973 almost 3 percent of the total nonfarm consumption of fluid milk occurred in school programs.

[35] **Special supplemental feeding.** —Foods donated by federal government for pregnant and lactating women (and infants up to 13 months old) who receive free or substantially free medical care. In November 1973, 151,000 beneficiaries.

[36] **Special supplemental feeding for women, infants, and children (WIC).** —A specific package of foods (financed by cash grants to state departments of health) for pregnant and lactating women and children up to 4 years old who receive free or subsidized health care. In fiscal 1974, first year of program, 216,000 beneficiaries were expected.

HEALTH BENEFITS

[37] **Medicaid.** —For those on cash welfare, plus in about half the states, the "near-poor" among categories covered by welfare. May 1973, beneficiaries, 7.8 million. During fiscal 1973 medicaid served a total of 23.5 million persons.

[38] **Veterans' hospital, domiciliary, and medical care (non-service-connected disability).** —Fiscal 1974 beneficiaries of

free hospital care, 700,000 needy veterans (estimate).

[39] **Comprehensive health services.** —For areas with high concentration of poverty and marked inadequacy of health services for the poor. Comprehensive health centers (about two-thirds of which were originated by the Office of Economic Opportunity), totaled 157 in January 1974, as follows: neighborhood health centers, 64; family health centers, 39; and community health networks, 54.

Family health centers have income cutoff of $5,000 for a family of four, but some of the former OEO centers extend eligibility to $8,400, charging fees as income rises. About 1.2 million persons used the centers in January 1974, their bills paid by: federal grants, 53 percent; medicaid, 41 percent; medicare, 3 percent; private insurance, public assistance, and private help, 3 percent.

[40] **Dental health of children.** —Dental care, especially in low-income areas, for children who otherwise would lack care. Projects operated by local health departments. Fiscal 1973 beneficiaries, 10,000 children (expected to double in 1974).

[41] **Health care of children and youth.** —Comprehensive health care for children in low-income areas who otherwise would lack care. Fiscal 1973 beneficiaries 504,000 (estimate).

[42] **Intensive infant care project.** —First-year health care to very high risk infants who otherwise would lack care. Eight projects in fiscal 1973. (Four of these projects aided more than 7,000 babies in 1972, reducing infant mortality rates, in some cases, by 12 to 20 percent.)

[43] **Maternity and infant care projects.** —Prenatal and postnatal care, including dental services, for mothers who otherwise would lack care; intensive care for high risk infants. Fiscal year 1973 beneficiaries, 142,000 mothers and 48,000 babies.

[44] **Crippled children's services.** —Diagnostic and medical care for crippled children. States determine what crippling conditions to treat and how much, if anything, to charge parents with varying resources. The states bill medicaid for qualify-

ing services to eligible children. Federal rules require free diagnosis for all. In fiscal 1972, 513,000 children received physicians' services and 81,000 received hospital services.

HOUSING (GENERAL)

[45] **Low-rent public housing.** —933,772 units occupied, June 1972. New construction applications suspended in January 1973 (leased housing component of public housing reactivated in September 1973). Local housing authorities set income limits. A government survey of 25 cities in 1973 found that the income cutoff for admission ranged from $4,700 to $7,800 (family of four), with $5,600 the median.

[46] **Homeownership for tenants of public housing** (including programs that permit tenants, by performing maintenance labor, to build up "sweat equity" in the unit).—42,000 units, June 1972.

[47] **Homeownership loans** (sec. 235).—A total of 400,710 units, August 1973 (new applications suspended, January 1973). Insured mortgages and interest subsidy payments for low- and moderate-income families. In general, "adjusted" family income (which is total income less 5 percent, less $300 for each family member under 21 years old) cannot exceed 135 percent of the income limit established for the same size family by local public housing. Median family income, 1972, $6,500. Of families, 13 percent had income below $5,000.

[48] **Rent supplements.** —A total of 38,751 units, June 1972 (new applications suspended, January 1973). Family pays 25 percent of adjusted family income for rent, and the federal government pays the remainder of rent (at fair market value). In general, income limits are the same as for local public housing. Median family income, 1972, $2,400. Of families, 93 percent had income below $5,000.

[49] **Interest subsidies for rental housing** (sec. 236). —A total of 60,006 units, June 1972 (new applications suspended, Janu-

ary 1973). Income limits the same as for homeownership loans. Median family income, 1972, $5,300.

[50] **Mortgage insurance for low- and moderate-income families** (sec. 221(d)(2)).—Loans for purchase of proposed or existing low-cost housing for one to four families or for rehabilitation of such housing. Calendar 1973 total, 47,552 units.

[51] **Mortgage insurance for low- to moderate-income families** (sec. 234). —Insured loans for purchase of condominium homes. Calendar 1973 total, 3,318 units.

[52] **Mortgage insurance for families who are special credit risks.** —Approximately 70,000 families received loans in 1973.

HOUSING (RURAL OR FOR SPECIAL GROUPS)

[53] **Rural housing loans** (sec. 502). —For low- to moderate-income families. Loans to buy, build, improve homes and farm service buildings. Insured loans and, for low-income families, interest subsidy payments. In general, for interest subsidies, adjusted family income limit is $5,000; but exceptions may be allowed to $7,000, and with approval of national office, higher. In fiscal 1973, 109,183 families received loans. From 1950–73 a total of 688,000 families received loans (including some sec. 504 repair loans).

[54] **Low-income housing repair loans** (sec. 504). —Direct loans for essential minor repairs for low-income rural homeowners who cannot obtain insured loans. In fiscal 1973, 2,596 families received loans.

[55] **Rural rental housing insured loans** (sec. 515).—For construction, purchase, improvement of multifamily rural housing to be rented to low- and moderate-income persons (except that a building erected for profit may admit a senior citizen without regard to income). In fiscal 1973, loans were made for 8,544 units. Cumulative total (1963–73) 23,633 units.

[56] **Farm labor housing** (sec. 514 and 516). —Insured loans and grants for housing farm labor (chiefly migrants). In fiscal

1973 program financed housing for 639 families and (in dormitory style) 97 individuals. Cumulative total, 1962–73, housing for 6,965 families and 3,599 individuals.

[57] **Rural self-help housing technical assistance** (sec. 523). — Grants for nonprofit organizations to hire persons who will train low-income families to build their own homes in rural areas.

[58] **Rural housing site loans** (sec. 523 and 524). —Direct, guaranteed, and insured loans for purchase of building sites on which families may build their own homes. During fiscal 1972, 552 sites were provided.

[59] **Indian housing improvement program.** —Grants to needy Indians for housing repair and construction. From 1963–73 a total of 19,653 houses were repaired and 2,787 houses built.

[60] **Indian housing technical assistance.** —Assistance to enable Indian tribes to develop public housing. Total units, 1963–73, 5,574 for renters, and 9,899 for homeowners.

[61] **Appalachian housing program.** —"Seed" money (planning loans), site development, and technical assistance for construction of housing for low- and moderate-income persons in Appalachia. Total units built, 1968–73, approximately 3,440. At the start of 1974, 4,160 other units were under construction or in final stages of processing.

EDUCATION (COLLEGE AND OTHER POSTSECONDARY)

[62] **Basic educational opportunity grants.** —For needy college students and for students in vocational and technical schools. In 1973–74, first year of program, two-thirds of the 250,000 recipients were from families with total annual income below $9,000 (and general income cutoff for family of four was $11,000). Maximum grant was $452; average, $285. Maximum grant expected to exceed $800 in 1974–75 due to increased funding. Federal government certifies eligibility.

[63] **Supplemental educational opportunity grants.**—For students

of exceptional need. In 1969–70, 73 percent of grants went to students whose family income was below $6,000. Grants totaled 304,000 in 1973–74, averaging $670 per student. Schools determine eligibility. The Nixon administration plans to end this program, replacing it with basic grants.

[64] **College work-study.** —Jobs for needy students in colleges and approved postsecondary schools (wages paid by federal government). In 1969–70, 83 percent of students aided had family income below $9,000. Average earnings of 545,000 students aided in 1973–74 were $580.

[65] **National direct student loans.** —Three percent loans for students from needy families. (U.S. government provides capital for the loans, administered by colleges; interest reverts to loan fund.) In 1969–70, 74 percent of loans went to students whose family income was below $9,000. Loans totaled 673,000 in 1973–74, averaging $690 per student. Schools determine eligibility.

[66] **Interest-free guaranteed loans** (interest paid by federal government).—For college students from needy families. Before March 1973, families with "adjusted" income below $15,000 (equivalent to gross income of about $20,000) generally were deemed needy, but new law requires detailed needs analysis of each family. Under the old guidelines, 1.1 million loans were made in fiscal year 1973, averaging about $1,100 per student. In fiscal 1972, one-third of loans went to families with gross income greater than $12,000. Schools determine eligibility.

[67] **Nursing education.** —Low-interest loans for students in need and outright grants for those in "exceptional" need. In 1973–74, 26,250 nursing students received loans averaging $1,000. Schools decide students' need.

[68] **Medical education.** —Low-interest loans for students in need and outright grants for those in "exceptional" need. For students at schools of medicine, osteopathy, dentistry, optometry, podiatry, pharmacy, or veterinary medicine. In fiscal

1972, 31,200 students received loans averaging about $1,000, and 21,600 received grants averaging $700. Schools decide students' need but funds made available to them take into account the proportion of their students from "low-income" families, as defined by special guidelines higher than those of OEO.

EDUCATION (PRIMARY AND SECONDARY)

[69] **Head start for preschoolers from needy families** —Educational, nutritional, and social services for needy children (10 percent may be from nonneedy families, using poverty guidelines of OEO). During fiscal 1973, a total of 379,000 children were enrolled.

[70] **Follow through.** —Research and demonstration projects seeking to sustain gains from head start through educational, medical, and social services, for children (kindergarten through third grade) from low-income families (OEO poverty guidelines). Low-income children numbering 81,000 were enrolled in January 1974, plus 15,000 who received instruction but not the auxiliary services given to the poor. Program to be phased out, 1974–77.

[71] **Upward bound.** —Special preparation for college for young people from low-income families (OEO poverty guidelines). Students aided in fiscal year 1973, 28,000 (estimate).

[72] **Talent search.** —Program to identify talented youths who are needy (OEO poverty guidelines) or culturally disadvantaged, and to encourage them to continue their education. A total of 125,000 students aided in fiscal year 1973 (estimate).

[73] **Special services for low-income and physically handicapped students in postsecondary schools** (20 percent may be nonneedy).—A total of 74,000 students aided in fiscal year 1973 (estimate).

[74] **Vocational education work study.** —Part-time jobs for vocational education students who need earnings to stay in school. A total of 130,000 students aided in fiscal 1973 (estimate).

JOBS AND TRAINING

[75] **Neighborhood Youth Corps.** —Federally funded jobs and training for students from poor families; 1,189,500 students aided in fiscal year 1973. Eliminated as a national program by the Comprehensive Employment and Training Act (CETA), signed into law in late December 1973.

[76] **Operation mainstream.** —Federally financed jobs for adults with poverty-level income who are chronically unemployed (40 percent must be more than 55 years old); 59,400 aided in fiscal year 1973. (Eliminated as a national program by CETA.)

[77] **Senior community service employment.** —Jobs for low-income persons 55 or older with poor job prospects. New program. Jobs are to pay at least the federal minimum wage ($1.60 per hour) and a maximum (about $2.90 per hour) is anticipated.

[78] **Job Corps.** —Job training, counseling, health care in 65 residential centers. For low-income young men and women, 16–21; 66,100 persons enrolled in fiscal 1973.

[79] **Work incentive projects.** —On-the-job training and work experience for welfare recipients; 171,400 enrolled on June 30, 1973.

[80] **Public service careers.** —On-the-job training for low-income and disadvantaged.persons. In fiscal 1972, 20,000 jobs. (Eliminated as a national program by CETA.)

[81] **Concentrated employment program.** —Outreach program that offered to the poor in their neighborhoods one-stop job and training referral service. In fiscal 1972, 130,000 persons aided. (Eliminated as a national program by CETA.)

[82] **Manpower development and training.** —Classroom vocational skill training for the jobless and underemployed. In fiscal 1972, 150,000 trainees (half with income below the poverty line). (Eliminated as a national program by CETA.)

[83] **Job opportunities in the business sector (JOBS).** —Subsidized jobs and training for poor persons who are school dropouts;

APPENDIX B

MARGINAL TAX RATES ON EARNED INCOME

The marginal tax rate paid by a worker in the United States is generally assumed to begin at about 14 percent and then move smoothly upward until it peaks at 50 percent. The shape of the actual marginal income tax rate schedule is markedly different. Because of the multiplicity of income taxes paid, and the deductions, exemptions, and special tax credits involved, the course of marginal income tax rates is anything but smooth.

There are a great many possible tax situations, depending on the size and composition of the tax-paying unit, the kind of income earned, and the size of that income. For the purposes of this analysis let us assume that (1) the typical working household in the United States is a family of four—a husband, a wife, and two children; (2) they file a joint return; (3) they take the standard deductions rather than itemizing; (4) their income comes solely from wages and salaries; (5) they pay three major taxes on income—social security tax, federal income tax, and state income tax; and (6) the family lives in California and pays California's income tax.

Social security tax

The social security tax rate in 1976 was 5.85 percent, and was paid on all wage and salary income up to $16,500 a year. The marginal tax rate of 5.85 percent is constant over the entire range of income from zero to $16,500.

TABLE B1

FEDERAL INCOME TAX–1976:
Joint Return for Family of Four (Two Children)

Adjusted Gross Income (1)	Exemptions and Deductions (2)	Tax before Credits (3)	General Tax Credit (4)	Earned Income Tax Credit (5)	Tax Paid/ (Refund) (6)	Marginal Tax Rate (7)
$ 1,000	$ 5,100	——	$ 140	$ 100	$ (100)	—10.0%
2,000	5,100	——	140	200	(200)	—10.0
3,000	5,100	——	140	300	(300)	—10.0
4,000	5,100	——	140	400	(400)	—10.0
5,000	5,100	——	140	300	(300)	10.0
6,000	5,100	$ 124	140	200	(200)	10.0
7,000	5,100	273	140	100	33	23.3
8,000	5,100	432	140	——	292	25.9
9,000	5,100	599	140	——	459	16.7
10,000	5,100	786	140	——	646	18.7
11,000	5,100	976	140	——	836	19.0
12,000	5,100	1,166	140	——	1,026	19.0
13,000	5,100	1,356	158	——	1,198	17.2
14,000	5,240	1,551	175	——	1,376	17.8
15,000	5,400	1,727	180	——	1,547	17.1
16,000	5,560	1,914	180	——	1,734	18.7
17,000	5,720	2,101	180	——	1,921	18.7
18,000	5,800	2,304	180	——	2,124	20.3
19,000	5,800	2,554	180	——	2,374	25.0
20,000	5,800	2,804	180	——	2,624	25.0

under 22 years old or over 44; handicapped; needy Vietnam veterans; or subject to special employment barriers. In fiscal 1973, 77,800 beneficiaries. (Program sharply modified by CETA.)

[84] **Senior companions.** —Part-time jobs for low-income persons, 60 or over, to provide supportive services to persons (other than children) with exceptional needs. OEO poverty guidelines for eligibility, with allowance for higher income in high-cost areas. New program. Jobs are to pay the federal minimum wage. Stipends are tax free and cannot be counted as income by any benefit program.

[85] **Foster grandparents.** —Part-time jobs for low-income persons, 60 or over, to provide services to children. Participants receive the federal minimum wage, transportation expenses, and, sometimes, lunch. Stipends are tax free and cannot be counted as income by any benefit program; 10,258 persons enrolled in September 1973.

[86] **Career opportunities program.** —Jobs for low-income community residents and Vietnam veterans as teacher helpers and other paraprofessionals in schools (in areas with highest concentration of low-income families). Approximately 13,500 participants in January 1974.

[87] **Vocational rehabilitation services.** —Vocational training, medical and physical restoration, counseling, and job placement for mentally and physically handicapped persons. States determine eligibility and how much, if anything, to charge for services. In fiscal 1974, 1,290,000 were aided (of whom 375,000 were "rehabilitated" to useful or remunerative work). One of five beneficiaries was a recipient also of cash welfare.

SOCIAL SERVICES

[88] **Services to needy families on welfare (and to former and potential welfare families.** —Services include counseling (money and home management, child development, family

planning), day care, homemaker services, health care. In fiscal 1974, 5,040,000 families with 14,600,000 children are expected to receive one or more services.

[89] **Services to needy aged, blind, or disabled.** —Homemaker service, chore services, assistance in getting medical care, and similar aid. Current, former, and potential recipients of SSI (and state welfare) are eligible. Fiscal 1974 beneficiaries expected to total 2.1 million.

[90] **Legal services for the poor.** —Local communities set income rules. In the District of Columbia, for example, a family of four was eligible in January 1974 if take-home pay were less than $120 per week ($6,240 per year)—higher with extraordinary expenses. For a single person the limit was $70 per week. In early 1974, 1.2 million persons were being helped.

BUSINESS AID

[91] **Economic opportunity loans.** —Direct or guaranteed loans and advisory services to enable persons of low income to establish, preserve, and strengthen small businesses. In fiscal 1973, a total of 7,662 loans were made. Cumulative total (1964–73), 41,895 loans with face value of $595 million.

21,000	5,800	3,054	—	180	2,874	25.0
22,000	5,800	3,309	—	180	3,129	25.5
23,000	5,800	3,589	—	180	3,409	28.0
24,000	5,800	3,869	—	180	3,689	28.0
25,000	5,800	4,149	—	180	3,969	28.0
26,000	5,800	4,444	—	180	4,264	29.5
27,000	5,800	4,764	—	180	4,584	32.0
28,000	5,800	5,084	—	180	4,904	32.0
29,000	5,800	5,404	—	180	5,224	32.0
30,000	5,800	5,732	—	180	5,552	32.8
31,000	5,800	6,092	—	180	5,912	36.0
32,000	5,800	6,452	—	180	6,272	36.0
33,000	5,800	6,812	—	180	6,632	36.0
34,000	5,800	7,178	—	180	6,998	36.6
35,000	5,800	7,568	—	180	7,388	39.0
36,000	5,800	7,958	—	180	7,778	39.0
37,000	5,800	8,348	—	180	8,168	39.0
38,000	5,800	8,744	—	180	8,564	39.6
39,000	5,800	9,164	—	180	8,984	42.0
40,000	5,800	9,584	—	180	9,404	42.0
41,000	5,800	10,004	—	180	9,824	42.0
42,000	5,800	10,430	—	180	10,250	42.6
43,000	5,800	10,880	—	180	10,700	45.0
44,000	5,800	11,330	—	180	11,150	45.0
45,000	5,800	11,780	—	180	11,600	45.0
46,000	5,800	12,236	—	180	12,056	45.6
47,000	5,800	12,716	—	180	12,536	48.0
48,000	5,800	13,196	—	180	13,016	48.0
49,000	5,800	13,676	—	180	13,496	48.0
50,000	5,800	14,160	—	180	13,980	48.4
51,000	5,800	14,660	—	180	14,480	50.0

Federal income tax

The federal income tax rate on earned income varies from 14 percent to 50 percent. The amount of taxable income is affected by deductions, exemptions, and credits. In 1976 the *standard deduction* for a joint return was $2,100. *Exemptions* were $750 per person, or in our case example of a family of four, $3,000, making a total of $5,100 in deductions and exemptions. The *general tax credit* was $35 per person, or $140 for a family of of four. The net result of these deductions, exemptions, and credits is that a family of four incurs no federal income tax *liability* until its income exceeds $6,100 a year. (See Table B1.)

It should be noted that the standard deduction is constant at $2,100 until one reaches the income level of $13,125. It then rises gradually to a maximum of $2,800 at $17,500 of income. The general tax credit changes in a similar fashion. It is constant at $140 for all income up to $12,100. It then increases, reaching a maximum of $180 at $14,286 of income.

In 1975 an *earned income credit* was temporarily added to the federal tax code. Though called a tax credit, it is actually a form of welfare payment to low-income families who file tax returns. The earned income "credit" is 10 percent of earnings up ot $4,000 a year. A family with no earnings receives no "credit." If it earns $1,000 it gets a "credit" of $100. At that level of income there are no taxes owed to the federal government to which the "credit" can be applied. So the federal government mails the family a check for $100. This "credit" increases to a maximum of $400 for earnings of $4,000. Then it begins to decline. For earnings of $5,000 the "credit" is reduced to $300. At $6,000 it is $200. At $7,000 it is $100. And when earnings reach $8,000 a year the earned income "credit" is phased out completely.

The earned income "credit" is really a negative income tax. The federal government now pays low-income workers a bonus on all earnings up to $4,000 a year. Beyond $4,000 the federal bonus become a decreasingly smaller percentage of earnings until it disappears at $8,000. (See Table B1, column 5.)

When the federal earned income credit is included, the typical working family of four receives from the federal government an indirect welfare payment, varying in amount, until earned income exceeds $6,900 a year, after which the family begins to pay taxes to the federal government. (See Table B1, column 6.) The net effect of the earned income credit on the effective marginal federal income tax rate is a dual one: it *decreases* the marginal tax rate by 10 percent for all earnings between zero and $4,000 a year; and it *increases* it by 10 percent for all earnings between $4,000 and $8,000 a year. (See Table B1, column 7.)

State income tax

Forty-two states and the District of Columbia now have an income tax. The tax varies from state to state and for this analysis it will be assumed that the California state income tax is a representative one. (In 1976 eight states had no tax on income, and eleven states had marginal income tax rates that exceeded or equalled California's.) In 1976 the standard deduction for a joint return in California was $2,000. An exemption credit of $25 for each parent and $8 for each child was allowed, making the total exemption credit for a family of four $66. In addition there was a special low-income credit of $80 for family incomes up to $10,000 a year; this credit was phased out over the next $160 of annual income. As a result the typical family of four living in California paid no state income tax until its income exceeded $10,000 a year. (See Table B2.)

Total income tax

Thus, a family of four living in California in 1976 paid social security taxes of 5.85 percent on all income up to $16,500, and began paying federal income taxes at $6,900 and state income taxes at $10,000.

The total marginal tax rate is the sum of the three marginal tax rates of social security taxes, federal income taxes, and state income taxes. The marginal tax rates applicable to a family of four are listed in Table B3. Earned family income is graduated in $1,000 increments, and the marginal tax rate is calculated for each increment. Earned income from zero to $51,000 a year is shown in column 1. The marginal social security tax rate is shown in column 2. The marginal federal income tax rate, taking into

TABLE B2

CALIFORNIA STATE INCOME TAX–1976:

Joint Return for Family of Four (Two Children)

Adjusted Gross Income (1)	Tax before Credits (2)	Low-Income Credit (3)	Exemption Credit (4)	Tax Paid (5)	Marginal Tax Rate (6)
$10,000[a]	$ 130	$80	$66	—	—
11,000	160	—	66	$ 94	9.4%
12,000	190	—	66	124	3.0
13,000	230	—	66	164	4.0
14,000	270	—	66	204	4.0
15,000	309	—	66	243	3.9
16,000	360	—	66	294	5.1
17,000	410	—	66	344	5.0
18,000	460	—	66	394	5.0
19,000	520	—	66	454	6.0
20,000	580	—	66	514	6.0
21,000	640	—	66	574	6.0
22,000	710	—	66	644	7.0
23,000	780	—	66	714	7.0
24,000	850	—	66	784	7.0
25,000	930	—	66	864	8.0
26,000	1,010	—	66	944	8.0
27,000	1,090	—	66	1,024	8.0
28,000	1,180	—	66	1,114	9.0
28,000	1,270	—	66	1,204	9.0
30,000	1,360	—	66	1,294	9.0
31,000	1,460	—	66	1,394	10.0
32,000	1,560	—	66	1,494	10.0
33,000	1,660	—	66	1,594	10.0
34,000	1,770	—	66	1,704	11.0

[a] No taxes on earned income less than $10,000.

TABLE B3

MARGINAL INCOME TAX RATES FOR A TYPICAL FAMILY OF FOUR
IN THE UNITED STATES—1976

Annual Earned Income (1)	Social Security Tax (2)	Federal Income Tax[a] (3)	State Income Tax (4)	Total Income Tax[b] (5)
$ 1,000	5.85%	—10.0%	——	—4.2%
2,000	5.85	—10.0	——	—4.2
3,000	5.85	—10.0	——	—4.2
4,000	5.85	—10.0	——	—4.2
6,000	5.85	10.0	——	15.9
7,000	5.85	23.3	——	29.2
8,000	5.85	25.9	——	31.8
9,000	5.85	16.7	——	22.6
10,000	5.85	18.7	——	24.6
11,000	5.85	19.0	9.4%	34.3
12,000	5.85	19.0	3.0	27.9
13,000	5.85	17.2	4.0	27.1
14,000	5.85	17.8	4.0	27.7
15,000	5.85	17.1	3.9	26.9
16,000	5.85	18.7	5.1	29.7
17,000	2.93	18.7	5.0	26.6
18,000	——	20.3	5.0	25.3
19,000	——	25.0	6.0	31.0
20,000	——	25.0	6.0	31.0
21,000	——	25.0	6.0	31.0
22,000	——	25.5	7.0	32.5
23,000	——	28.0	7.0	35.0
24,000	——	28.0	7.0	35.0
25,000	——	28.0	8.0	36.0
26,000	——	29.5	8.0	37.5
27,000	——	32.0	8.0	40.0
28,000	——	32.0	9.0	41.0
29,000	——	32.0	9.0	41.0
30,000	——	32.8	9.0	41.8
31,000	——	36.0	10.0	46.0
32,000	——	36.0	10.0	46.0
33,000	——	36.0	10.0	46.0
34,000	——	36.6	11.0	47.6
35,000	——	39.0	11.0	50.0
36,000	——	39.0	11.0	50.0
37,000	——	39.0	11.0	50.0
38,000	——	39.6	11.0	50.6
39,000	——	42.0	11.0	53.0

TABLE B3—*Continued*

Annual Earned Income (1)	Social Security Tax (2)	Federal Income Tax[a] (3)	State Income Tax (4)	Total Income Tax[b] (5)
40,000	——	42.0	11.0	53.0
41,000	——	42.0	11.0	53.0
42,000	——	42.6	11.0	53.6
43,000	——	45.0	11.0	56.0
44,000	——	45.0	11.0	56.0
45,000	——	45.0	11.0	56.0
46,000	——	45.6	11.0	56.6
47,000	——	48.0	11.0	59.0
48,000	——	48.0	11.0	59.0
49,000	——	48.0	11.0	59.0
50,000	——	48.4	11.0	59.4
51,000	——	50.0	11.0	61.0

NOTE: The typical American family is represented here as a husband, wife, and two children living in California; earnings include wage and salary income only; standard deductions are taken.

[a] Includes earned income credit.

[b] Rounded to the nearest tenth of 1 percent.

account the earned income "credit," is shown in column 3. (It is unclear whether or not the Congress will make the earned income credit a permanent feature of our tax laws.) The marginal state income tax rate is shown in column 4. Column 5 shows the full effect of our current tax laws, with the earned income credit operative, on the total marginal income tax rate paid by a typical family of four.

As shown in column 5 of the table, the total marginal tax rate is a *negative* 4.2 percent for the first $4,000 of income. The federal government pays a net 4.2 percent "bonus" on anything you earn up to $4,000. But after hooking you on working, the situation changes dramatically when earned income exceeds $4,000. The marginal tax rate then becomes *positive* and rises steeply over the next few thousand dollars of income, reaching almost 32 percent for earnings between $7,000 and $8,000.

Then an odd thing happens. Because of the interaction of the three income taxes, the total marginal tax rate does not move smoothly upward as one would expect. For income between $8,000 and $9,000 the marginal rate drops sharply to 22.6 percent, then turns around and climbs back up to 34.3 percent for income between $10,000 and $11,000. Then, like a roller coaster, the marginal income tax rate drops back to 27.1 percent for income between $12,000 and $13,000. It rises slightly for the next $1,000 of income to 27.7 percent, drops off to 26.9 percent for the next $1,000, jumps up to 29.7 percent for the next $1,000, slides back down again to 26.6 percent and 25.3 percent for the next two $1,000 increments of income, and then leaps on up to a full 31 percent for income between $18,000 and $19,000. The total marginal tax rate then moves smoothly upward. It hits its maximum rate of 61 percent at $49,800 and remains at that level for all further increases in earned income.

The three major downward breaks in the total marginal income tax rate occur at earned income levels of $8,000, $11,000, and $16,000. The first break, at $8,000, occurs when the 10 percent marginal tax rate, caused by the reduction of the earned income credit, is phased out. The second break, at $11,000, is due to an anomaly resulting from a special low-income tax credit in California. While this special tax credit totally eliminates any state taxes on earned incomes less than $10,000 a year, it does impose a relatively high marginal tax rate of 9.4 percent on income between $10,000 and $11,000. For the next $1,000 of income earned, the state marginal tax rate drops sharply down to 3.0 percent, and this causes the overall total marginal rate to decline.

The third major downward break in the marginal tax rate schedule occurs when the social security tax stops at $16,500. The effect of the cessation of social security taxes, combined with the changes in the federal and state income tax rates, is a decrease in the total marginal income tax rate from 29.7 percent to 26.6 percent and then to 25.3 percent. This decrease in marginal tax rates due to the cessation of social security taxes at $16,500 affects taxpayers across the entire country, whereas the bulge in the total marginal tax rate for a family living in California, when its income increases from $10,000 to $11,000, is an anomaly peculiar to that state.

These three income taxes, two at the federal level and one at the state level, interact to produce a final pattern of marginal income tax rates that is bewildering and illogical.

The marginal income tax rate for $1,000 increments of income reverses itself *eight* times over the relatively narrow, but critically important range of income between $8,000 and $19,000. This range embraces the bulk of middle-income taxpayers. Few of them, if any, are likely to know precisely how their marginal income tax rates jump around. But the wild variation in marginal income tax rates may account for some of the vague, uneasy feeling a growing number of people have about the fairness of our entire tax system.

How does one go about explaining that a person currently earning $18,000 pays an income tax of 25 percent on an additional $1,000 of income, whereas someone earning only $7,000 a year pays 32 percent on the same amount of additional earnings?

The jigsaw pattern of the marginal tax rate seriously distorts the financial incentives of the income tax system. It is understandable how the social security tax distortion came about, and one can appreciate the difficulties of trying to develop an overall tax system that is fair and systematic when all fifty states are free to impose whatever income tax structure they find appropriate, including no income tax at all. But what is difficult to understand, let alone appreciate, is how the U.S. Treasury Department could implement an earned income "credit" that grossly distorts the tax rate structure of the federal income tax. As it now stands it is a tax curio.

Perhaps the intent of the earned income "credit" was to redistribute income from the middle- and upper-income taxpayers to low-income workers. This it does, but it violates a clear principle of welfare when, in the income range from zero to $4,000 a year, the amount of money received from the government is *inversely* proportional to the need. Here, the more you earn, the more welfare you receive.

Perhaps its intent was to encourage low-income people to work. This it does, at least for those contemplating work for $4,000 a year or less. On everything earned up to $4,000 one gets a 10 percent federal welfare bonus. But in order to make that welfare bonus possible, and to phase back into the rest of the tax rate structure, it was necessary to impose an additional 10 percent tax on all income between $4,000 and $8,000—a far more critical range insofar as financial incentives are concerned.

Perhaps its intent was to institute the principle of a negative income tax. This it does to some extent, but it is such a strange and twisted version of the negative income tax—with its rising and falling subsidy—that it really contributes little to our understanding of the workings and consequences of a negative income tax.

One thing the earned income "credit" does do, which is clearly not intended, is to provide a tidy subsidy to employers who pay low wages. Employers in low-wage industries know that any employee earning $4,000 over the course of a year will also receive a federal bonus check of $400. To some extent, this will be taken into consideration in the determination of the employees' pay.

For a typical family of four, the total marginal tax starts off at a constant and slightly "negative" rate for the first $4,000 of income. It then jumps abruptly by 20 points to about 16 percent for the next $2,000 of income. And then—from $6,000 to $19,000 —the level of the marginal tax rate rises by another 15 percentage points. Over the entire range of income from $6,000 to $19,000 the marginal tax rate, while fluctuating, averages a surprisingly high 28 percent. After $19,000 the marginal tax rate begins its normal, steady, upward climb.

The net effect of recent efforts to use the tax system to accomplish certain social goals, such as giving more income to poor people and increasing the incentive to work for low-income workers, has had some serious and largely unforeseen side effects. The marginal income tax rate structure has been so distorted that a graph of the marginal tax rates looks more like a side view of a roller coaster than a professional chart.

If the marginal tax rate structure that results from the interaction of all the deductions, exemptions, and special credits were spelled out as one comprehensive reform plan, it would be dismissed as self-evident nonsense. But the nonsense is masked by the variety and complexity of the taxes, and it is not self-evident. We now have an embarrassing marginal federal income tax rate structure that should be corrected as soon as possible before the distorting effects become permanently enmeshed in our economy. The way it now works is unconscionable.

INDEX

INDEX

About the Author

MARTIN ANDERSON was a member of the small White House working group that developed Nixon's Family Assistance Plan, the only member who concluded the plan was unsound and recommended that it not be submitted to the Congress.

Since early 1968 he has been deeply involved in the analysis and formulation of national welfare policy—as director of research for Richard Nixon's 1968 presidential campaign, as Special Assistant and Special Consultant to the President from 1969 to 1971, as the head writer for the 1972 Republican party platform, as chairman of the White House task force on welfare reform that reviewed HEW's Income Supplementation Plan for President Ford in 1974, and as Ronald Reagan's issue advisor in the 1976 presidential campaign.

A summa cum laude graduate of Dartmouth, Anderson received his Ph.D. from M.I.T. and taught economics and corporate finance at the Graduate School of Business at Columbia University for six years before becoming involved in national politics. In early 1971 he resigned his position at the White House to become a Senior Fellow at the Hoover Institution, Stanford University.

He has been a member of Nelson Rockefeller's Commission on Critical Choices for Americans, the Defense Manpower Commission, and the Council on Trends and Perspective of the U.S. Chamber of Commerce. He is a member of the Committee on the Present Danger and on the board of directors of the Federal Home Loan Bank of San Francisco.